I0826599

WALDPORT PRESS

Rhetorical Rape

Daniel Broudy is Associate Professor of Rhetoric & Applied Linguistics in the Graduate School of Intercultural Communication at Okinawa Christian University. He serves on the editorial board for *Synaesthesia Journal* and is author of *Clearing a Vygotskyan Path*. As a veteran of combat operations, he researches the intersections of power and discourse in the generation of meaning.

Barry Pollick is Professor of Communication at University of Maryland University College. He has worked as a journalist for newspapers in Cleveland, Ohio and has authored and co-authored several scholarly papers on public speech and the mass media. He coordinates a Japanese-English linguistic exchange program in Okinawa and researches cross-cultural approaches to negotiating truth claims.

Rhetorical Rape:

The Verbal Violations of the Punditocracy

Daniel Broudy and Barry Pollick

Rhetorical Rape:

The Verbal Violations of the Punditocracy

Library of Congress Cataloguing-in-Publication Data

Broudy, Daniel, 1964 –, Pollick, Barry, 1961 –

Rhetorical Rape: The Verbal Violations of the Punditocracy

p. cm.
Includes bibliographical references and index.
ISBN 13: 978-0-9820534-2-3 (pbk.: alk. paper)
ISBN 10: 0-9820-5342-8

1. political pundit 2. corporate—media 3. framing—rhetoric
4. propaganda—model 5. critical—discourse—analysis

Printed and bound in the United States.
Set in Eurostile

The publisher's policy is to use permanent paper from mills that operate sustainable forestry policy, and which has been manufactured from pulp processed using acid free and elementary chlorine-free practices. The publisher ensures that text paper and cover board used have met acceptable environmental accreditation standards

Waldport Press
3151 Shadowbrook Ln.
Oak Harbor, WA 98277 USA

For further information on Waldport Press, visit our website:
www.waldportpress.com

DEDICATION

To our exceedingly patient spouses, Yuna and Setsuko

CONTENTS

Acknowledgements

This work is the result of exceptionally enriching academic environments in Okinawa, Japan, stretched across two diverse university cultures and countless talks with linguists, political scientists, sociologists and theorists, economists, historians and mathematicians. We feel fortunate as researchers to have been able to observe our subjects at a reasonable distance from the source in order to gain at least a modest level of objectivity. Even so, we freely acknowledge that sometimes, when the subject would warrant, we would forgo efforts in achieving a balanced tone of rational objectivity and offer analysis that is, in the words of Slavoj Žižek, "engaged and extremely 'partial', — for truth is partial, accessible only when one takes sides, and is no less universal for this reason" (2009). For their critical comments, suggested revisions, and valuable contributions to the current body of literature, we offer sincere thanks to professors and researchers in the social sciences and humanities, Peter Wodarz, Jeffery Klaehn, John Whalen-Bridge, Jacqueline Jenkins, Christopher Valvona, Eugene Caruso, Randolph Thrasher, David Ulvog, Jay Hurwitz, Dennis Shah, Ken Levitt, Kevin Murphy, Christopher Melley, Charlotte V. T. Murakami, Andrew J. Madigan, Hitoshi Hamagawa, Daniel Hart and Peter Simpson.

Thanks

We express our sincere appreciation to Brian Laurich, a massively gifted artist, whose politics in no way reflect his cover art contributions nor the content of this book. Displays of his work can be found and commissioned at www.vintagesigns.com

Preface

Bothered by the possible imprecision of our own title, we agonized also over its emotional import, solicited perspectives from well-respected academics, and were stunned to see a perfect split in opinions regarding the perceived fairness in our use of the term "rape." As this word tends to imply, almost exclusively and at once, some violent sexual assault, we apologize first to anyone offended or who sees our use of "rape" in the title as an irresponsible appropriation of the term. We reference, in the title, one denotation that from time to time also appears in the public discourse. Rape is also an act of plunder, a violent seizure, or abuse, a despoliation or violation. It is, according to the *Oxford English Dictionary*, taking action to acquire anything by force (1989, p. 186).

The "force" we allude to in the title refers to the relative power that corporate media personalities arrogate for themselves in the public discussion and the rhetorical methods they employ to impose their will and perspectives on an audience. The "anything" that these personalities mean to "acquire" is the public's uncritical consent. True, no one is forcing listeners to go on engaging as audience members, but news consumers do, initially, place some level of trust in hosts even as they betray that trust and use their position to attempt to gain control over the emotions and ultimately the political sensibilities of their audience. We liken this process to the snake who slips his date the ideological equivalent of a Rohypnol, putting her into a propagandistic stupor while he penetrates her political sensibilities. And this is what passes today for fairness and balance. Given that some commentators present themselves as "fair and balanced," as modeling "excellence in broadcasting," or as offering a "no-spin zone," the practically free and incredibly lucrative access to the airwaves they enjoy must be exchanged for, at least, a modest civic obligation to use them more responsibly. That is, to practice the excellence they pretend to embody.

The perpetual pursuit of higher ratings and the filthy lucre those ratings ensure have virtually guaranteed, it seems, irresponsible usage of the airwaves. Talk show hosts may nowadays compare presidents or their policies to extremely offensive historical figures or extremist ideologies, and those comments, in turn, serve as fodder for commentary on a dozen other shows in the echo chamber of the news media — thereby boosting the notoriety of the political pot stirrers.[1] We concur with Neal Gabler that central to the problem with extremism

---

[1] As Edward Guthmann points out, "in the publishing world, 2003 is likely to be remembered as the year of the political pot-stirrer — a year when Liberals and Conservatives unleashed their invective, wrestled in the mud and caught our attention with a rude and rancorous Punch and Judy show" (p. D-1).

> as an attention-grabber isn't that we don't know what to do about it. The real problem is that it works. By knocking down the Twin Towers and announcing a constant stream of threats, the Islamic radicals got and continue to get publicity out of proportion to their numbers — just as the Tea Partiers have been dominating the national airwaves even though their ranks, according to survey data, constitute no more than 13 percent of the American public. Similarly, Glenn Beck and Rush Limbaugh are very well remunerated for their high-decibel hate. In other words, we may say we hate fanaticism, but we pay attention to it and may even reward it. (Gabler, 2010)

As you will see, the imperative to keep people listening to talk radio for three hours or staying tuned to a particular cable show (as opposed to a dozen others) motivates the host to stir the pot of hatred that has been simmering in American society arguably since the Emancipation Proclamation.[2]

For years, Rush Limbaugh, for example, has branded the Democrats and their government solutions to problems as socialistic — warning that government intervention or regulation (in healthcare or banking, etc.) is the first step toward a Canadian or Social-Democratic, Euro-styled system of government. But in the wake of the recent economic crises, mostly

---

[2] Paul Krugman (2007) elaborates on this point in his book, *The Conscience of a Liberal*. Krugman argues that even though white farmers in the South shared many of the same of the economic interests as black farmers, whites couldn't join forces because of their lingering bitterness over the loss of the antebellum South and their former privileges.

due to a lack of government regulations, Limbaugh's usual fear-mongering no longer gains as much traction (e.g., 72% of the public supports a public health insurance option according to a recent poll[3]).

So, he has shrewdly upped the ante: comparing Obama not to Canadian-style "Socialists" but to Hitler. Specifically, Limbaugh has exploited the myth that Obama wants "Death Panels" to decide the fate of the elderly in order to draw a (far-fetched) parallel between the Hitler death camps and Obama's "death panels," aka end-of-life counseling option — ironically something that George W. Bush and Sarah Palin had themselves endorsed.

To understand how spurious the so-called "Death Panel" claims are, consider Paul Krugman's recent de- construction of this red herring:

> Right now, the charge that's gaining the most traction is the claim that health care reform will create 'death panels' (in Sarah Palin's words) that will shuffle the elderly and others off to an early

---

[3] The February (2010) Kaiser Health Tracking Poll finds the public still split on health care reform legislation, with 43 percent in favor and 43 percent opposed. However, the poll also finds that majorities of Americans of all political leanings support several provisions in the health reform proposals in Congress and most attribute delays in passing the legislation to political gamesmanship rather than policy disagreements. Furthermore, another poll Thomson Reuters Corp. finds that Just under 60 percent of those surveyed said they would like a public option as part of any final healthcare reform legislation..." http://www.reuters.com/article/idUSTRE5B20OL20091203

> grave. It's a complete fabrication, of course. The provision requiring that Medicare pay for voluntary end-of-life counseling was introduced by Senator Johnny Isakson, Republican — yes, Republican — of Georgia, who says that it's 'nuts' to claim that it has anything to do with euthanasia.
>
> And not long ago, some of the most enthusiastic peddlers of the euthanasia smear, including Newt Gingrich, the former speaker of the House, and Mrs. Palin herself, were all for 'advance directives' for medical care in the event that you are incapacitated or comatose. That's exactly what was being proposed — and has now, in the face of all the hysteria, been dropped from the bill. (2009)

In response to these sorts of bizarre claims in corporate media, we are not suggesting that audience members are simply passive participants helpless to turn the channel and ignore the virulent cant and obfuscation. Rather, we are suggesting that the inbuilt power of commentators, by dint of their practically free access to the airwaves, should oblige them to uphold higher ethical standards in serving up so-called facts for public consumption.[4]

Like all other spectators, readers, and listeners who absorb with a critical eye and ear the narratives emanating from corporate media, we

---

[4] While Limbaugh, for example, insists that he is an entertainer foremost, we argue that since he unceasingly opines on political issues and appears to have so much political influence, he should exercise that power more conscientiously.

assert that we often come away from certain media assaults on our sensibilities feeling violated, insulted, abused, and forced to continually test the suspicious claims about the reality of the world and the lives of people outside the influences of corporate cultures. Yet even more insidious than the effect on critical listeners/viewers, who after all can tune out at their leisure, is the effect on the *un*critical audience member, whose trust is being subtly exploited. Sean Hannity's fairly recent violation of that trust, for example, appears in his November 2009 commentary when actual footage of a modestly attended Michelle Bachman rally was "inadvertently" replaced by footage from a widely attended "Tea Party" rally from several months earlier. Hannity then stressed the significance of the "multitudes" gathered for Bachman's rally.[5]

The words we use to describe this feeling of betrayal, too, are not mere hyperbole meant to exaggerate the physical effects of increased heart rates and warm pulses of blood shooting up the sides of our faces when lies pretending to be gospel truths penetrate our psyche. Instead, we feel that we must protect our powers of reason from various forms of propaganda offered in today's marketplace of ideas. In contemporary usage, a "rape" of the Amazon rainforest, of Nanking, of Appalachia, Gaza, or of emergency medicine all draw, in legitimate ways, on

---

[5] Only after Jon Stewart publicly exposed this deception did Hannity acknowledge the "mistake."

the same figurative and literal uses of language. We thus wish to reclaim some of the logic and reason lost in the fight against these fallacious appeals to emotion. The term "rape" in the title is useful only insofar as it suggests that words, when used to seize from people their autonomous power of reason, can do further injury to the Democracy we all wish to protect and continue participating in.

This book began as a retort to pundits who asserted what seemed then to be highly questionable claims about certain candidates during the American general election of 2008. Our discussion of pundits' schemes in attempting to seize control of the national conversation in recent years continues into the present.

FOREWORD

The 'propaganda model' of media operations advanced by Edward Herman and Noam Chomsky in their classic work, *Manufacturing Consent* (1988, 2002), hypothesizes that structural, political-economic elements influence overall patterns of media performance, encouraging a systematic and pervasive right-wing bias within media discourses that is consistent with the interests of power. The model suggests that ideological power and material power intersect and reinforce one another. Herman and Chomsky maintain that careful analysis of media discourses (and the social, political and economic contexts in which they are produced) can enable insights into the dialectic between ideology and power. Given the globalizing economy and ever-increasing (global) power, reach and influence of transnational corporations and financial institutions — in the face of growing poverty and powerlessness amongst the vast majority of the world's population — Herman and Chomsky's propaganda model is arguably more relevant today than when it was initially advanced.

The propaganda model assumes that elites are motivated to exercise power in a multiplicity of ways according to self-interest. The model also assumes that economic power enables social, political and ideological power. Contemporary media exist within this context, functioning under corporate rather than state control, thus their behavior is shaped by what is, in effect, a 'guided market system' underpinned by five filters — the operative principles of the propaganda model. Media, according to this framework, need not be controlled, nor must their behavior be covertly monitored. Self-censorship becomes a matter of routine. Media themselves are fully integrated into the institutional framework of society and act in unison with other dominant ideological sectors in establishing, enforcing, reinforcing and policing corporate hegemony. The propaganda model's first-order prediction logically follows: media will tend to 'manufacture consent' for elite preferences, both in terms of domestic and foreign policy issues, in ways that are both hegemonic and paradigmatic.

Within democratic societies the major mass media play important roles in making the electorate aware of important issues, events and viewpoints. Given that new media are now being colonized by traditional, corporate-dominated media, it is vitally important for students and scholars and those outside academia alike to analytically and conceptually engage with the intersection between communicative power and cultural politics. This is precisely the task taken up herein.

In this interdisciplinary and important new book, Daniel Broudy and Barry Pollick assess ways in which power meets meaning within media discourses. The authors deploy Critical Discourse Analysis to bolster the propaganda model and enrich its overall analytical capability as they explore media and communicative power in relation to cultural politics and public pedagogy. They ask a question which strikes to the heart of the democratic process: how is it that we come to see and understand the world around us?

Jeffery Klaehn
Kitchener, Ontario, Canada
May 1, 2010

Notes on Organization & Usage

We have organized the major sections of this book into three categories of discussion: (a) current theory; (b) influential personalities and their approaches to the public discourse; and (c) major filters and some of the ways they are used to help sell the 'right' ideas and opinions.

Some readers may infer that we have imbued our discussions with some avant-garde blend of genres throughout the book. To this, we would say that we have, indeed, whenever we felt the topic called for such adjustments. Wherever it was appropriate or useful to the clarification of our points, we code switched our tone, moving at times from an academic register to a more casual one, from descriptive to narrative, from critical to ironic.

Since we make numerous claims and bring together a wide range of topics from rather diverging disciplines to back those claims, we also decided upon footnotes instead of endnotes, largely for convenience. Though somewhat unsightly and cumbersome, the footnotes are meant to serve readers who seek quick cross-references to sources and a better understanding of the wider historical contexts we are drawing upon to defend our critiques.

Readers may notice a profusion of uppercase letters not only for proper nouns but also certain proper adjectives that refer to particular ideologies and schools of thought and which contrast with references to general concepts and actions. What Facebook, Twitter, text-messaging, and other mediated forms of communication have helped do for the demise of the uppercase letter, we wish to reverse.

Left or right, for example, does not necessarily refer to a direction, a past action, state of correctness, nor reference to seating arrangements in the French Senate or National Assembly. In North America, the Left and Right refer to particular strains of politics. Just the same, for the sake of precision, we raise the initial letter in all of the other references to political parties and ideologies even when those references act as modifiers.

METHODOLOGICAL OBJECTIONS TO THE STUDY

One objection to our study is that it examines only male hosts, perhaps undermining our call for more democratic, participatory programs. It's a fair criticism. Note, however, that over a year and half ago when we began our study, Rachel Maddow (apparently the first female to host a TV talk show) did not yet have her own MSNBC show. Furthermore, we wanted to choose the best known Conservative and Liberal talk shows. However, we do plan to undertake a study of the role that powerful female voices play in the discourse.

Why did we choose one TV show and two radio shows per ideology? Because there are significantly more political *radio* shows than TV shows. What's more, a year and a half ago — before Ed Schultz had his on MSNBC — precious few Liberal shows existed.

A further objection that can be leveled is that we ignored Glenn Beck, who is now explosively popular, garnering almost as many viewers as Bill O'Reilly. Unfortunately, at the time we began this study, Beck did not have a TV show on Fox, and his radio show was not as popular as Limbaugh's or Hannity's. Finally, even with Beck's growing popularity, O'Reilly still attracts slightly more viewers (although at a more viewer-friendly time (8 p.m.) to Beck's (6 p.m.)).

Critics of our efforts may also object that our study does not employ the scientific rigor that many scholarly content analyses do. Indeed, ironically, we are about as opinionated as those we are examining. It is true that we could have examined a month of each host's programs, systematically counting the number of, say, *ad hominem* attacks and sweeping generalizations, but (a) is there really any doubt that Rush Limbaugh or Keith Olbermann (who was recently castigated by Jon Stewart for using too many *ad hominems*) flood the airwaves with polemics? (b) such a study would likely sedate our readers; and (c) we wish to slip away from the cult of objectivity that seems to pervade the social sciences. To borrow the words of preeminent historian Howard Zinn from his autobiography, *You Can't Be Neutral on a Moving Train*.

> From the start, my teaching was infused with my own history. I would try to be fair to other points of view, but I wanted more than 'objectivity'; I wanted students to leave my classes not just better informed, but more prepared to speak up, to act against injustice wherever they saw it. This, of course, was a recipe for trouble. (1994)

Though our aim is hardly to teach, we do think it is best to identify our theoretical assumptions and let our readers weigh for themselves the worth of our reasoning and discoveries. We began this study with the following suppositions: (a) Given the imperatives of commercial television and radio, hosts must attract and maintain massive audiences. Witness Glenn Beck's dramatic declarations that President Obama is deeply racist or Keith Olbermann's rant against Scott

Brown, calling the Senator-elect "an irresponsible, homophobic, racist, reactionary, ex-nude model, tea-bagging supporter of violence against women and against politicians with whom he disagrees" (2010). (Olbermann, to his credit, ultimately apologized for his words after giving an insincere *mea culpa* and being prodded by Jon Stewart to be more sincere.) A corollary assumption is that colorful attacks are more likely to gain viewers than careful reasoning and muted dialogue; therefore, hosts will tend to oversimplify complex issues and employ various *ad hominem* attacks with little evidence to support them, thus coarsening the national dialogue and perhaps reinforcing rampant political polarization in society.

And this is the crucial point: Because these hosts do not exist in the ether of outer space, their words and actions have consequences for public discourse that reach far beyond their individual programs. Indeed, is it any coincidence that the increasing popularity of ideologically polarizing talk radio and TV shows seems to correlate with the increasing use, or threatened use, of the filibuster by opposition parties in the Senate? This relationship may partly explain the increasingly zealous partisanship in our national politics, which has resulted in the extinction of the "Republican Moderate" and the inability of Congress to pass significant bills as the Republican Party uniformly opposes Obama's policy initiatives and nineteen Senators of the Democratic

Party, so far, have recently signed a petition calling on Majority Leader Harry Reid and President Obama to bypass the necessary 60-vote majority and seek to pass healthcare reform through reconciliation. [6] Partisans rule the day.

Because this pervasive political polarization has created a stalemate at precisely the time when America most needs to resolve daunting healthcare-related, economic, environmental, and security problems, we wanted to discover which of the hosts we are examining most reliably resists the temptation to polarize and demonize. Even more importantly, we were hoping to find and extol the virtues of hosts who foster constructive, solution-oriented dialogues that give voice to as many of what Richard Nixon called 'the silent majority'.[7]

---

[6] Under reconciliation, Obama and Reid only need 51 votes instead of the usual 60) to pass a bill, in this case healthcare reform. However, reconciliation can only be used for bills that involve government budget, such as the so-called public option, but not for, say, the elimination of pre-existing health conditions.

[7] We define 'silent majority' in striking contrast to Nixon's denotation. Whereas Nixon was referring to law and order, pro-Vietnam War Conservatives, we are referring to the many Americans who voted for change in 2008 because they want Government to solve problems and regulate industry and banking. For example, although the public option was passionately opposed by the loudest voices—amplified by Fox News (a key sponsor of the Tea Parties movement)—polls consistently show that a clear majority of Americans support the proposal.

Part I.
Theoretical Frames

"We are America, ... we do not f*cking torture!"

—*Shepard Smith (2009)*

PROPAGANDA & THE PUNDITOCRACY

Folly and fibbing abound in the work of politicians. So goes the conventional wisdom. But, what about the work of political pundits? As observers of the political circus, don't we often assume that while the pundits we *oppose* tend to lie, or at least bend the truth and exhibit bias, *our* pundit is "fair and balanced"? Yet, are they not filled with as much falsehood as the politicians they both glorify in one breath and crucify in another? These questions come not from a barely-conscious attempt at stale understatement, but a premise whose soundness we hope our readers come to agree with.

When did the efforts put forward herein begin to take shape for us? A serendipitous appearance of real events unfolded just as our return to various theories of modern mass communication commenced, fortifying, for us, the now-apparent connection between mere fanciful hypotheses and concrete practices.

This book represents an effort to expose the rank hypocrisy at work in the political talk arena, to disentangle Neo-conservative and Liberal ideologues from their claims of truth so as to uncover in the great clutter of discourses a more reasoned perception of reality stripped of its socio-political baggage. Another struggle in baring the lovely naked truth.

In this age when loose nukes or lethal carbons, for example, pose existential threats, pundits with national reach need to cease fueling the very polarization that paralyzes our ability to both understand and address these grave threats and, instead, strive to stake out common ground and find mutually beneficial solutions. For example, instead of consistently demonizing a billion or so Muslims, who had not been previously hostile toward Americans, commentators could focus more on what beneficial qualities the three major religions have in common, such as the long history of service to society's oppressed. This is the essence of Utilitarian Democracy: the greatest good for the greatest number.

From David Barsamian's earlier interviews with Noam Chomsky, collected and published in the spring of 2001, we were fascinated to rediscover, though, that contrary to the idealistic pabulum we are fed as grade-school students — namely that American Democracy guarantees an equal voice for all citizens and that our leaders are chosen by the people — Democracy, American style, means a system in which elites set the rules and choose the leaders and have utter contempt for the "unwashed masses."[1] In accord with the logic of the

[1] In 2001, Dick Cheney convened an energy task force apparently attended by corporate players in the energy industry. It appears that

corporate and political establishment, rather than being some romantic ideal of how to organize society, Democracy is a political philosophy just too potent for the people to apply to their lives and to expect their highest leaders to observe in any tangible way. It is an idea whose boundaries are to be set by those who run the country, the elite. The early masters of handling, indeed shaping, public opinion then suggested as much in the early 1920s, during the infancy of modern political science, the public relations industry, and mass media.[2] These new arts of Democracy were to be used to fashion society's important ideas and habits. Such perspectives were, and still are, thought to be the predominant views of the establishment.

But beginning in the 1960s, with the advent of the student movement, the consumer rights movement, women's liberation, and later the environmental and gay rights movements, America grew bottom-up, driven by grass-roots efforts to transform the establishment's policies on institutionalized racism, the Vietnam War, industrial pollution, and a host of

---

the purpose of this meeting was to discuss which companies would be granted what oil assets, presumably after the Iraq invasion. When Judicial Watch, a Conservative public interest group, demanded that Cheney reveal the minutes of the meeting, arguing that it was in the public's interest, Cheney refused to reveal the details, arguing that it was his Executive Privilege to maintain the secrecy of the meeting. Judicial Watch sued and eventually won the right to examine at least some of the documents discussed at the meeting. This is but one of many examples in which the Bush Administration had used a fig leaf of Executive Privilege to conceal its machinations.

[2] Chomsky recalled the words of Edward Bernays who had observed in the 1920s that we can regiment " ... the public mind every bit as much as an army regiments the bodies of its soldiers." Chomsky went on to extend Bernays' suggestion by observing that "we should do it, because we're the good guys and smart guys and they [the masses] are stupid and dumb, and therefore we have to control them for their own good. And, we can do it because we have these marvelous new techniques of propaganda" (2001, p. 151).

other issues. These challenges led to constructive Democratic reforms, became institutionalized in the form of the Consumer Safety Commission, the Environmental Protection Agency and in the form of such sunshine laws as the Freedom of Information Act, which allowed greater public access to government meetings, documents and actions. Democracy appeared to be working to serve the masses.

But then came September 11, 2001. Everything seemed to change as so many citizens wondered why they [the 'terrorists' and whomever they represent] 'hate us so much.' We were told that to protect freedom and Democracy that we had to defend these cherished ideals, indeed, defend by essentially offending another nation whose people didn't hold these same beliefs as ours. Naturally skeptical of theories that pin the blame for society's dysfunction on any single particular social, political, ethnic or religious group, we sought to reconsider the evidence that Chomsky cited and to re-examine the purported madness in his assessments of American Democracy and what really threatened it.

After the initial rhetorical assaults on Iraq that laid the groundwork for what we then felt was an unwarranted military invasion, the years that followed, filled with rhetoric of Orwellian proportions,[3] provoked us to examine the media processing procedures that political realities undergo before they are offered to the public. Before long, the nation's humorists began picking apart the incongruities — the distressing differences between the seriousness of war and the short-sighted silliness in the Bush Administration's planning for it, let alone even waging it. Standing in the midst of the rhetorical disorder, many

---

[3] Steven Poole refers to this phenomenon as 'Unspeak' and argues that it is important to call attention to " ... the ways in which politicians [and the pundits who abet them] attempt to cloak dubious policy in the language of virtue, to challenge the Unspeak at its source" (2007, p. 8).

wondered whether the plain truth was being restrained or just hiding out somewhere.

Over the course of a year, after satirist Stephen Colbert had long been calling attention to an alternative conception of truth and how truths appeared to be undergoing a re-engineering in the public discourse, The American Dialect Society honored "truthiness" as "Word of the Year" for 2005. In the Society's executive summary, readers found that "'truthiness' refers to the quality of preferring concepts or facts one wishes to be true, rather than concepts or facts known to be true" (American Dialect Society, 2006). To illustrate the level of absurdity he was referring to, Colbert remarked with Swiftian irony, "I don't trust books. They're all fact, no heart" (2005).

At the heart of this book is an examination of discourse practices, the workings of ideology and power, that lead to the public's acceptance of certain questionable truths in these times of " ... belligerent, uninformed posturing" (Krugman, 2007). Here, "consent" means the fairly widespread, uncritical acceptance of certain 'truthiness' claims as produced by national media for mass consumption. For example, how did a certain portion of the American public come to buy the notion that invading Iraq was, at least to some extent, part of a necessary and patriotic undertaking? What mass media techniques prevailed during the sale of this military "operation"?[4]

Drawing on Norman Fairclough's work in the field of

---

[4] Worth noting is the predominant metaphor used for military invasions: In medical terms, an operation is generally necessary to save the patient's life, or at least preserve his or her health. Yet, here the so-called "operation" was more like "elective surgery." It seems ironic that countless literal surgical operations have become necessary as a result of this nation-saving, freedom-preserving operation.

Critical Discourse Analysis[5] (CDA hereafter), this book rests upon the premise that we tend to overlook or underestimate the significance of language in the production, maintenance, and change of social relations of power (1989, p. 1). To this point, we wish to emphasize that not only is the influence of language underestimated but also its semiotic signs,[6] such as, say, the meanings of color, notions of national exclusivity, or the power of verbal repetition. These signs, we suggest, may be understood to contain discrete meanings beyond words, such as images, gestures, scents, or other auditory or tactile impressions.

In the chapters that follow, we will treat language as a discursive as well as symbolic medium. Color, as one example, is symbolic and in certain contexts can be discursive. By this we mean that discursive symbols, once colored, have the capacity to heighten their meaning. Upon this understanding, we will discuss how political pundits in national media use language in conjunction with semiotic signs to condition the consciousness of consumers and cultivate their consent to 'truthiness.'

We hope to uncover at least one cause crucial to the manufacture of consent today by attending to the following questions: (a) How are patriotism and related abstractions framed by mass media appeals to our emotions? (b) How do their uses of language and semiotic signs play a role in creating 'truthiness'? While CDA provides a useful socio-

---

[5] As a resource for people struggling against oppression and domination in its various linguistic forms, CDA is an interdisciplinary framework for the study of discourse that sees language as a social practice and that focuses on ways in which social and political hegemony are reproduced by and reinforced in texts and public speech (Fairclough, 1995, p. 1).

[6] According to Danesi and Perron (1999), a sign is "something that stands for something to someone in some capacity" (p. 366).

political theory for understanding how pundits use language to manufacture consent, we will also include a widely known model for understanding how pundits appeal to their audience's economic sensibilities.

Another part of the theoretical groundwork, as elaborated in the following section, rests on Edward Herman and Noam Chomsky's work in media criticism and reveals how society's powerful elite use corporate media as tools to "fix the premises of discourse ... to 'manage' public opinion" and "mobilize support" for the particular values of the dominant culture (1988, p. xi). Herman and Chomsky's approach, when combined with CDA, allows "analysis of ... media discourses [to] impart insight into how power and meaning intersect" (Klaehn, 2009, p. 50).

Semiotic Media Filters

In their study, *Manufacturing Consent: The Political Economy of Mass Media*, Edward Herman and Noam Chomsky (1988) developed a novel "propaganda model," (PM hereafter) applicable to contemporary public discourse, useful to its analysis, and central to our purpose here. Over twenty years ago they observed, in the opening chapter, that mass media serve as systems for

> ... communicating messages and symbols to the general populace. It is their function to amuse, entertain, and inform, and to inculcate individuals with the values, beliefs, and codes of behavior that will integrate them into the institutional structures of the larger society. (p. 1)

While this model assumes the inherent influence that media institutions wield over society as swayed by market forces, it does not assume that newsroom workers or personalities are consciously "aligning themselves with the interests of the dominant elites" (Klaehn, 2002, p. 151) — the owners of the institutions. Instead, "it assumes that elite media recruit right-minded personnel to fill staff positions, ... [and] these personnel, [having conformed to remain within the system] have internalized [the 'correct'] beliefs and attitudes which, in turn, influence media performance" (p. 151). Herman and Chomsky (1988) further argued that in a "world of concentrated wealth and major conflicts of class interest, to fulfill this role [of amusing, informing and instilling the right values] requires systematic propaganda" (p. 1).

While the PM "focuses on the inequality of wealth and power and its ... effects on mass-media interests and choices, [the model] traces the routes by which money and power are able to filter out the news fit to print, marginalize dissent, and allow the government and dominant private interests to get their message across to the public" (p. 2). Herman and Chomsky provide compelling evidence of how these five filters that help process the facts fit for public consumption are employed. They cite media ownership itself,[7] funding sources

---

[7] Observes Richard Pérez-Peña, "For generations, *The Washington Post* has been a scrupulous watchdog over the capital's cozy world of power networking. For a short time, it almost became the network's host. *The Post* decided Thursday to cancel plans to charge lobbyists and trade groups $25,000 or more to sponsor private, off-the-record dinner parties at the home of its publisher, Katharine Weymouth, events that would have brought together lobbyists, business leaders, Post journalists and officials from the Obama administration and Congress." (2009, July 2). Another example of the interlocking relationships or the *quid pro quo* between pundits and government involves the scandal involving the Pentagon and former military officials. During the first four to five years of *Operation Enduring Freedom*, dozens of the latter posed as impartial "analysts" on various cable news shows, while at the same time receiving special access from the Pentagon in exchange for delivering unacknowledged talking points that

for media, sourcing for information, flak,[8] and anticommunism. While we intend to touch on all of these in use today, we will focus primarily on the fifth major filter used from the 1950s through the 1980s – "anticommunism." Since the fall of the Berlin Wall, the "anticommunism" filter has morphed into other ideologies and abstractions. For example, one key filter widely used in contemporary media discourse, Jeffery Klaehn (2009) observes, is "fear,"[9] an approach also referenced in Al Gore's book, *The Assault on Reason*. In it, Gore observes that:

> Television's quasi-hypnotic effect is one reason that the

---

the Pentagon briefed them on. Again, the "analysts" did not disclose to viewers that the Pentagon had been remunerating them in exchange for delivering the talking points, and the news shows themselves portrayed the analysts as being completely impartial. The program was discontinued after details of these unusual relationships became public in 2007. In keeping with the PM, profiteers in the military-industrial-complex (military contractors and mass media) gained handsomely from the Pentagon's talking points which always emphasized the need to sustain the two wars at a cost of hundreds of billions of dollars to the taxpayers. According to David Barstow, "Those business relationships are hardly ever disclosed to the viewers, and sometimes not even to the networks themselves. But collectively, the men on the plane and several dozen other military analysts represent more than 150 military contractors either as lobbyists, senior executives, board members, or consultants. The companies include defense heavyweights, but also scores of smaller companies, all part of a vast assemblage of contractors scrambling for hundreds of billions in military business generated by the administration's war on terror. It is a furious competition, one in which inside information and easy access to senior officials are highly prized" (2008).

[8] Here "flak" refers to targeted efforts to discredit organizations or individuals who disagree with or cast doubt on the prevailing assumptions which Chomsky and Herman view as favorable to established power structures.

[9] For a succinct description and discussion of the PM's utility and relevance to contemporary public discourse, see Jeffery Klaehn's article, "The Propaganda Model: Theoretical and Methodological Considerations" (2009, p. 46).

> political economy supported by the television industry is as different from the vibrant politics of America's first century as those politics were different from the feudalism that thrived on the ignorance of the masses of people during the Dark Ages. Our systematic exposure to fear and other arousal stimuli on television can be exploited by the clever public relations specialist, advertiser, or politician. (2007, p. 36)

We shall add to Gore's list of the "clever" a number of political pundits, "protagonists and antagonists in the struggle for hegemony" (Fairclough, p. 148), who also command the radio airwaves to exploit the masses, to play on their fears and inculcate the public with their special interpretations of "patriotism" and "American exceptionalism."

With the ever-increasing "[R]ightwing pressure on public radio and television" [10] and "the corporate ownership of media ... never ... as concentrated [as it is now]," the PM has become an increasingly relevant and useful lens to focus on the methods of propaganda at work in today's 'free' post-industrial democracies (Klaehn, 2002, pp. 172-3).

Discussions taken up in the following chapters explore how dominant sociopolitical ideologies are framed in media by various appeals to powerful symbols and abstractions. Along

---

[10] In terms of 'Rightwing' pressure on various corporate media, David Carr and Tim Arango (2010) report that in "the fall of 2008, Roger Ailes, the head of Fox News, went to his boss, Rupert Murdoch, with two complaints: he had heard that Mr. Murdoch was considering endorsing Barack Obama for president in *The New York Post*, and he had read a book excerpt in *Vanity Fair* suggesting that Mr. Murdoch was sometimes embarrassed by the right-leaning Fox News. Mr. Ailes threatened to quit, a person familiar with the conversation said. Instead, Mr. Murdoch soon rewarded him with a new, more lucrative contract — he made $23 million last year in salary, bonuses and other compensation, more than Mr. Murdoch — and *The New York Post* endorsed John McCain.

the way, we aim to answer a number of questions that form our critical examination of the punditocracy, its claims of fairness and balance, and its efforts in conflating and confusing political spin with disinterested reporting. We wonder, foremost, in what particular ways do the propagandizing efforts of "right-minded media personnel" create the kinds of consent to 'truthiness' referenced earlier. How do powerful elites use language in conjunction with other symbolic expressions to appeal to and modify our psychosocial sensibilities?

Before we begin considering the accuracy of truth claims appearing in the public discourse, it is only fair that we first recognize the skills of the Far Right and Far Left in disseminating their conceptions of truth, however revolting these perceptions of reality may, at times, appear to be. We should acknowledge, for example, Neo-conservatism and its considerable success since 9/11/01 in appropriating and redefining the concept of patriotism to fit its apparent designs for consolidating power and pressing its agenda forward — even at the expense of expressing contempt for Democracy itself.[11] We should, likewise, respect achievements of the Left

---

[11] Observes Robert Jensen, "Let's remember the basic notions behind democracy: The people are sovereign. Power flows from the people. Leadership is beholden to the people. If those ideas are at the core of democracy, Bush's recent reaction to the will of the people suggests he has contempt for the concept. Bush has a habit of praising as "courageous" those leaders who most effectively ignore their people. In the U.K., polls show more than half the public against the war, and close to a million people turned out for the Feb. 15 protest in London. In Spain, 2 million hit the streets of Barcelona and Madrid, and 74 percent oppose the war. But Bush has praised the courage of prime ministers Tony Blair and Jose Maria Aznar in remaining fanatically pro-war in the face of massive public opposition.
Silvio Berlusconi is another favorite of Bush. The Italian prime minister has to ignore the 80 percent of his people who object to the war, and on Feb. 15 the largest demonstrations in the world were in Rome, where police put the crowd at 1 million and others estimated

in fostering a monumental sociopolitical paradigm shift in thought and language use. Political correctness (PC) has undoubtedly reshaped public and private discourses and attitudes in profound and likely lasting ways.[12] Nevertheless, part of the problem of adopting the PM to examine the work of the Left and Right to control public opinion is separating two planes of criticism: Noam Chomsky's earlier critiques of Walter Lippmann and Clare Sparks' recent critiques of Chomsky.

Criticism of the Propaganda Model

Herman and Chomsky's Propaganda Model is not without its critics. Since its appearance in the literature, the PM has received criticism for its supposed methodological and ideological weaknesses, which Klaehn and Mullen (2010) challenge. Independent researcher and scholar, Sparks (2009) suggested that Chomsky and his followers crucify, in effect, the wrong man. More than being some Jewish cultural elitist who had allegedly been able to help employ sinister designs for mind control on the masses, Walter Lippmann was, in fact, a respectable scholar who advocated for truth in the news. In desiring to distinguish between the two, Sparks argues that

---

two to three times that many. But perhaps the most courageous leader in Bush-speak is the prime minister of Turkey, Abdullah Gul. The Bush team found that it took some convincing (and $15 billion) to secure the ruling Justice and Development Party leadership's support for U.S. use of bases for a war. In that effort, as a former Pentagon planner and ambassador to Turkey explained, "the biggest problem is that 94 percent of the Turks are opposed to war." (2003)

[12] Arguably the effects of PC efforts have been mixed. On one hand, it is laudable that pejoratives such as the "N-word" or "G-word" to describe people of Asian descent have disappeared from mainstream discourse, yet on the other it could be said that "utility hole" for "manhole" and "synthetic" for "manmade" (among many others) constitute real absurdities of an otherwise commendable movement.

Lippmann clearly came down on the side of correcting misconceptions propagated by media rather than furthering them:

> ... news and truth are not the same thing, and must be clearly distinguished. The function of news is to signalize an event, the function of truth is to bring to light the hidden facts, to set them in relation with each other, and make a picture of reality on which men can act. Only at these points, where social conditions take recognizable and measurable shape, do the body of truth and the body of news coincide. (Lippmann, [1922] 1997, p. 358)

Sparks further calls attention to the offending passages from Lippmann that form part of the critical foundation of Herman and Chomsky's famous theory about how and why media appear to operate on the public as they do: "manufactured consent .... The public's role is to be spectators, not participants, and that is the sound of the trampling roar of an obedient herd." As counterevidence to this apparent elitist view of the 'herd', Sparks cites a number of examples from Lippmann that contradict his own seemingly condescending view of people to even make use of the great power of Democracy that they hold within their hands. Among his perspectives, Lippmann observed that the established

> ... leaders of any organization have great natural advantages. They are believed to have better sources of information. The books and papers are in their offices. They took part in the important conferences. They met the important people. They have responsibility. It is, therefore, easier for them to secure attention and to speak in a convincing tone. But also they have a very great deal of control over access to the facts. Every official is in some degree a censor. And since no one can suppress

> information, either by concealing it or forgetting to mention it, without some notion of what he wishes the public to know, every leader is in some degree a propagandist. Strategically placed, and compelled often to choose even at the best between the equally cogent though conflicting ideals of safety for the institution, and candor to his public, the official finds himself deciding more and more consciously what fact, in what setting, in what guise he shall permit the public to know. (Lippmann, 1997, p. 247)

While not formally trained as historians, Chomsky and Herman are, in Sparks' view, somewhat ill-equipped to adequately understand the social milieu of the early 1920s when Lippmann wrote and are, thus, unqualified to use him as the 'bogeyman' for all that is wrong with the mass media. But, are Chomsky, a linguist trained in the scientific method to examine human discourse, and Herman, an economist trained to examine the processes of production, distribution, and consumption of goods, really unqualified to undertake even basic research in the social sciences? Sparks' criticism in this regard seems to be a trivial objection that does little to weaken the soundness of the PM. The evidence produced from the PM and presented in *Manufacturing Consent* cannot be drowned in a swell of attacks on Herman and Chomsky.

We would contend, instead, that elitist control of mass media and the ongoing efforts to create in audiences the right kinds of opinions cross cultural and generational divides. This sort of control is neither part of some fictional Jewish conspiracy nor part of the lingering effects of the counterculture revolution of the '60s but really more about maintaining the hegemony. What's more, a rejection and relegation of the PM to a conspiracy theory today is merely a convenient label applied to dismiss discomforting logic and evidence that doesn't align with one's political bent (Klaehn, 2003). The PM remains more than ever a useful lens for assessing the power that shapes society. We suggest that the promise of a greater Democracy through the astonishing growth of mass media has, paradoxically, forced the owners of capital into anti-democratic discourse practices whose effects we can now witness and learn from.

Central Aims

Our core intent is to interpret truth claims in ways that are free from any political party or special interest. Our analysis rests upon evidence born of a simple observation: thought most often precedes action. As such, we shall argue the proposition that various logical fallacies communicated from the media machines of both political extremes emerge from oversimplifications – of thought processes fallen victim to blind, uncritical acceptance of ideologies that serve powerful political interests. In effect, neither extreme as construed by its supporters is necessarily fully committed to propagating truth as much as it is to propping up its perception of the way things ought to be. Those things range from issues of the social, political, religious, and the economic.

This subterfuge is precisely the sort of self-serving double-standard practiced by both the Right and the Left, in which both sides purport to be critical thinkers, yet conveniently ignore the vices of their "anointed one" (George W. Bush for, say, Rush Limbaugh and Barack Obama for Ed Schultz).

The sort of naïve and uncritical acceptance of the agendas of the politically powerful, we further argue, contradicts the premises upon which the framers of the US Constitution had based their views of a responsible citizenry informed by a free and unbiased press committed to checking all forms of power.

In *Necessary Illusions* (1989), Chomsky cites a 1975 study of the "governability of democracies" conducted by the Trilateral Commission which concluded that "moderation in democracy" (p. 2) was necessary in order to mitigate the so-called excesses of democratic actions, much like those that shook up the nation during the 1960s when the struggle for equal rights became a modern revolution in American political and social thought. What this "moderation" means for us today as media consumers is that the "general public must be reduced to its traditional apathy and obedience,[13] and driven from the arena of political debate and action if democracy is to survive" (p. 3). Thirty-five years since the Trilateral Commission's study we find that Democracy has survived, but the pressing questions are what kind of Democracy and at what cost to the profession of journalism?

Sean Hannity's periodic on-air reminder that journalism is dead in America is a view we share but, doubtless, for some very different reasons. The irony in this incisive observation of his, offered almost daily to his radio audience,

---

[13] To illustrate this apathy and obedience, consider that until very recently, some 98% of incumbents in the House of Representatives routinely won reelection — percentages more reminiscent of, say, Saddam Hussein's government than of America, and percentages that belie the fact that public confidence in the House as a whole is generally quite low. Why were the percentages so high? In part because the system is rigged: incumbents can vastly outspend challengers thanks to the money they raise from lobbyists and other special interests. Yet where was the public outcry at this undemocratic system? Stories surrounding Michael Jackson's death, for example, received perhaps a thousand times as much media coverage as a story that affects the very essence of our Democracy, yet citizens tend to obediently acquiesce to these media priorities and remain essentially apathetic about entrenched corruption in American politics.

appears to have, evidently, escaped even him. To his charge, our answer is to exhume the corpse and perform a more precise postmortem so as to get to the bottom of who exactly perpetrated the "drive by"[14] and put some bullets in the back of disinterested journalism.[15] Anecdotal observations have encouraged us, so far, to reckon that the unusually strident tone appearing in today's political discourse is a symptom of widespread efforts in corporate media to exert greater control over the events that shape the Democracy.

Before we undertake an examination of key figures in the punditocracy, we must acknowledge the efforts of scholars past and present in the areas of media studies, communication theory, sociology, and linguistics who have written extensively about the uneasy tensions among mass media, special political interests, and government whose concepts of truth compete for mass acceptance in the public arena of discourse. Insights gleaned from the scholarly work of George Lakoff, Noam Chomsky, Edward Herman, Norman Fairclough, Robert W. McChesney, Herbert Schiller, Michael Parenti, Nancy Snow, Mark Crispin Miller, Jeffery Klaehn, Andrew Mullen, David Miller, William Dinan and many others who have opened up new ways of enhancing our understanding of the intricate interplay among corporate power, media, and discourse practices. Where best to begin surveying the media landscape spread before us is from a place of shared understanding of a few key words.

---

[14] An allusion to Limbaugh's contemptuous characterization of the corporate media that he routinely denies he's a part of.

[15] Regarding its validity, we acknowledge the Chomskyan view that all journalism is biased in the sense that it emanates from a journalist with a subjective viewpoint and a certain socioeconomic and historical perspective, yet this is precisely why polarizing punditry is so corrosive to the goal of creating an informed electorate.

"Whoever controls the language, the images, controls the race."

—*Allen Ginsberg (1968, August 24)*

Key Words

What exactly is a "pre-dawn vertical insertion"? To some, it may sound strangely pseudo-sexual, to others, it may sound simply mystifying. Turns out, this expression defines what happens when you launch an invasion of another nation or region just before dawn breaks and the paratroopers can find their way to the ground. Terms like these are Orwellian indeed and part of the reason why we feel this section is necessary for some clarification of the otherwise ambiguous terms we use throughout the book. Apart from stipulated and newly defined terms as well as textbook examples, all meanings can be found in *The Compact Oxford English Dictionary* (1989), *Merriam-Webster's Tenth Collegiate Dictionary* (1990), Merriam-Webster's Online, Dictionary.Reference.com or Wikipedia.

1. Black-and-White Reasoning (n.) - In *Taking a Stand*, Irene

Clark suggests that black-and-white reasoning is a process that presumes only two possibilities exist in confronting a dilemma (1996). In her book *The Structure of Argument*, Annette Rottenberg points out that black-and-white thinking creates false dilemmas, reflecting the unfair or ill-advised oversimplification of a complex problem. She observes that the false dilemma is at times "... offered out of ignorance or laziness, ... to divert attention from the real explanation or solution that the arguer rejects for doubtful reasons" (2009).

AUTHORS' NOTES: While these are useful definitions that clarify the danger of oversimplifying complex problems, the definitions include only two possible motives behind over-simplifications. In the cases we examine throughout this book, we feel it is necessary to elaborate three additional motivations. In the section that follows, titled "Added Motivations," we expand on possible alternatives beyond "ignorance" and "laziness," as discussed by Rottenberg.

2. Conservative (n., adj.) – a term that characterizes those like George Will and Pat Buchanan who tend to be isolationist in foreign policy, opposing wars and nation building abroad and illegal immigration at home, but who agree with the Neo-conservatives about the need for a smaller national government with fewer regulations on business, fewer social programs, lower taxes, and a greater emphasis on self-sufficiency. It is worth noting that many in Congress who called themselves Conservative in fact presided over a then-unprecedented increase in Government deficit-spending during George W. Bush's two terms, as the Conservative-led Republican majority passed a 700-billion dollar Medicare drug bill, founded a colossal new bureaucracy (Department of Homeland Security), and waged two enormously costly wars abroad.

3. Frame (n.) – A schema of interpretation consisting of collections of anecdotes and stereotypes that individuals rely on to understand and respond to events. In simpler terms, a person has, through life, constructed a series of mental and emotional filters. These filters help people make sense of the world. The choices they, then, make are influenced by their frames or emotional filters. Other useful descriptions appearing at Wikipedia are as follows:

Framing a political issue, party, or opponent is a strategic goal in politics, particularly in the United States. Both the Democratic and Republican parties compete to successfully harness the power of persuasion. In his article, *The Framing Wars*, Matt Bai writes that even before

> ... the election, a new political word had begun to take hold of the party, beginning on the West Coast and spreading like a virus all the way to the inner offices of the Capitol. That word was 'framing.' Exactly what it means to 'frame' issues seems to depend on which Democrat you are talking to, but everyone agrees that it has to do with choosing the language to define a debate and, more important, with fitting individual issues into the contexts of broader story lines. (2005)

4. In-group (n.) – A small group of people, within a wider context, whose common interest is to exclude others.[16] An "in-group" is a social group toward which a member feels loyalty and respect.[17]

5. Liberal (adj.) – someone who believes in using government to achieve social reform — for example, creating a public option to make the insurance companies more competitive in terms

[16] OED, 1989, p. 849
[17] Wikipedia

of rates and services; and establishing strong government regulations and regulatory agencies to prevent the kind of financial bubbles that led to the recent economic crisis. Liberals also tend to oppose nation building abroad in favor of spending more on domestic programs that narrow the gap between rich and poor. And finally, Liberals believe in enforcing constitutional protections even for those suspected of terrorist crimes (e.g., the notion of getting a fair trial in a public setting, as opposed to a military tribunal). It is worth mentioning that, according to Elizabeth Warren (overseer of the TARP funds), the bills passed by Congress to address the banking and credit crises did not constitute substantive reform but were, rather, so porous that by the time the new regulations were passed into law, the industries in question had already devised eight methods of circumventing the new checks. Furthermore, so-called Liberals, like Barack Obama, have not pushed for reforms such as allowing Americans to buy lower-priced medications from Canada.

6. Manichean (*adj.*) – descriptive term for an adherent of the dualistic religious system of Manes, a combination of Gnostic Christianity, Buddhism, Zoroastrianism, and various other elements, with a basic doctrine of a conflict between light and dark, matter being regarded as dark and evil.

AUTHORS' NOTES: We use this adjective throughout the book to refer to the tendency to divide all people into two camps: the "good" and the "bad." "Good" refers to anyone in "our" camp, and "bad" refers to anyone in any other camp. The judgment of who is "good" and who is "bad" rests principally on camp membership rather than on any moral or ethical valuation.

Corresponding modifiers thought to best describe

"good" people include beautiful, bright, brilliant, joyful, informed, engaged, obedient, loyal, and honest. Modifiers that commonly describe "bad" people are unattractive, dark, dim-witted, unhappy, ignorant, disengaged, unruly, disloyal, and corrupt. Actions ascribed to "good" people are always acceptable, even if universally denounced — such as aggression, murder, torture, or theft. The goal always justifies the process. Actions ascribed to "bad" people are always unacceptable since, as members of the "other camp," these members are themselves bad. As the world presents an ongoing struggle between "good" and "bad" people, crimes such as aggression, murder, torture or theft must be punished. So, "good" people kill "bad" people to preserve "peace" or "to protect national interests." Glenn Greenwald elaborates on this feature of reasoning in his book *A tragic legacy: How a good vs. evil mentality destroyed the Bush presidency*, pointing out that the Manichean perspective assumes the

> ... need to wage war against perceived evil and the shared hatred of common enemies. This is sufficient to maintain unity because it provides a tonic to a morally ambiguous, uncertain, and complex world — a world perceived to be filled with dangers in every facet of life. All of these factions, like the devotees of Manicheanism are in thrall to promises of a comforting and liberating moral simplicity, a framework that provides refuge from a complex, confusing, and frightening world. A unified crusade against evil enemies bestows purpose, excuses failure, alleviates confusion, and enables sensations of power. (Greenwald, 2007, p. 54)

7. Moderate (adj.) – A term the media uses to describe Republicans who agree with the Democrats on the need for healthcare reform (e.g., Olympia Snow) or Democrats who

oppose the public option but still seem to want some sort of healthcare reform (e.g., Ben Nelson, Kent Conrad, etc.).

8. Neo-conservative (adj.) – a Conservative who supports a muscular foreign policy and nation building efforts wherever American interests may be threatened in the world. A key document of this group is the so-called Bush Doctrine promulgated in 2002, which gives the president the right to wage so-called "preventive war" against a country if he or she thinks that a country may eventually pose a threat to U.S. interests. Neo-conservatives tend to oppose domestic spending programs (except for when they benefit powerful corporate benefactors of the Republican Party, such as firms dealing with homeland security, big pharma, or big oil) but enthusiastically support spending for large weapons systems such as missile defense (e.g., "Star Wars"). They tend to be very pro-Israel (regardless of the policy Israel takes), and do not mind if the U.S. goes deeply into debt fighting wars abroad. Neo-conservatives, like Conservatives, tend to be for fewer regulations and lower taxes on business. But unlike Conservatives, Neo-conservatives tend to support the unitary executive notion that gives the president sweeping powers and fewer checks thereon (e.g., allowing the president to hold post-9/11 detainees without charge indefinitely).

9. Non-zero sum (adj.) - refers to a relationship that benefits all parties. For example, treaties on arms limitations represent society's perception that all sides affected by the treaty have a mutual interest in reducing the number of destructive weapons. (see #12. for the antonym of non-zero sum: zero sum)

10. Out-group (n.) – Those people not necessarily forming a

group themselves, who are excluded from or do not belong to a specific in-group.[18]

11. Pundit (*n.*) – 2. a learned man [or woman], teacher. 3. a person who gives opinions in an authoritative manner usually through the mass media.

AUTHORS' NOTES: Connected to notions of learned wo/men are notions of authority and opinion. Since human expectations often shape the ways in which humans receive and perceive ideas and since pundits are not always necessarily learned, it is crucial to expand upon the term pundit and offer a few extra varieties. We suggest the following modifications to the term.

11.1 Pundigandist (n.) – 1. a neologism referring to a political commentator posing as a fair-and-balanced pundit whose work largely propagandizes the company's and/or party's socioeconomic and/or political philosophy.

11.2. Pundificator (n.) – a neologism referring to a pompous political pundit posing as a fair-and-balanced commentator preaching a media organization's social economic, and/or political philosophy.

11.3. Punditocracy (n.) – a group of powerful and influential political commentators.

12. Zero sum (adj.) - refers to a relationship in which the parties perceive their interests as inversely correlated. For example, without an arms control treaty, each side has incentive to accelerate its arms buildup, lest its opponents gain a strategic edge.

---

[18] OED, 1989 p. 1235

Added Motivations (Behind B & W Reasoning)

Beyond the definitions of key terms, we also wondered early on about other reasons for the apparent prevalence of black-and-white reasoning, a key process of (il)logic appearing in the Manichean worldview. What follows are two additional rationalizations that some might argue underlie black-and-white reasoning.

One popular belief is that rampant black-and-white reasoning is merely part of some effort to conceal certain intellectual weaknesses? One way, after all, to cover up a particular flaw is to project, in its place, an air of supreme confidence. Playground bullies are believed to do so with physical force to sometimes mask the pain of past intellectual or physical assaults on their psyches or persons. It certainly seems that pundits do so at times with the force of their rhetorical attacks on those from opposing ideological camps.

Pundits realize that humans cannot know everything, so may gloss over possible gaps in knowledge and flaws in logic with rhetorical flourishes. Sometimes the conscience prods us to fight for or flee from personal beliefs in the face of a hostile audience. Anxiety develops, though, when we realize we should flee or concede but for private or professional reasons determine to stay in the fight. Bill O'Reilly's periodic tendency to dig in and do verbal combat on air with his guests is one example we shall later broach.

Hubris is another possible motivation for treating issues in black-and-white terms. Some pundits seem to take pride and pleasure in being able to take command of an issue's theoretical complexities, straining out details they feel are unimportant, and, thus, presenting a presumably synthesized set of competing alternatives, easily understood, easily accepted. We humbly propose, though, that we are all guilty of feeling and deriving some amount of pleasure in pride.

One of us may see Pittsburgh, Pennsylvania, for example, as the only place on earth to find a proper sandwich. Sure, there are sandwiches, but then there are Primanti Brothers' sandwiches, which, one of us feels, are certainly deserving of their own special category. All others to be found on all other menus in all other restaurants are merely, uh, sandwiches. It likely never registers to those commentators who never enjoy meals in other parts of America or the world that excellent sandwiches can be found elsewhere.

Nevertheless, we would submit that the very ability pundits display in cutting through what they seem to see as overgrown jungles of unimportant newsworthy details is itself an admirable intellectual exercise which, we infer, must be rather gratifying on some level. We could borrow as a starting point from Proverbs some deeper understanding of this human idiosyncrasy and one of its negative effects: Pride only breeds quarrels ... (13:10).

One possible reason for the appearance of pride in public discourse is elaborated in *Doing Our Own Thing* (2003). In it, John McWhorter observes that since sometime around the late 1960s, messengers themselves, much more than the substance of their message, have moved front and center in the public discourse. That is to say, the personality of the speaker has now come to outshine the essence of the story. A reason why has been offered also by a number of other media critics. Mark Crispin Miller, for example, sees "corporate meddling with the news" (2006) as one among various culprits. The corporate model of profit-driven "news" having subsumed large "news" organizations and the profession of journalism has meant the promotion of media personalities who deliver the infotainment at the expense of disinterested reporting.

This squares with McWhorter's observation that image has become vastly more valuable to profits than message. There was a time in fairly recent American history, he notes, that speakers

> ... largely presented self-standing treatises — they recited a written text. And this was a manifestation of formality — formality suppresses the individual in favor of group norms; informality means letting our uniqueness hang out... by the seventies, this up-close-and-personal tone becomes a standard modus operandi in public addresses. (2003, p. 54)

What this means for contemporary media consumers is that we are able to witness the making of news stars. We get to be addressed in this intimate personal tone as, say, a collection of curious neighbors 'dying' to hear the new gossip about various people from far-flung corners of earth. In the process, we can also witness, for example, Bill O'Reilly unabashedly let his hostility for certain guests hang out as he declares that they just "shut up" — a recurring rhetorical tactic to be elaborated on in later discussions.

Since we are so often reduced in status as an audience, from conscious citizens seeking relevant news to passive consumers soaking up media narratives, we can be addressed by media personalities in this informal and pseudo-personal way. It, thus, becomes easier for us to conclude that it's only our easily-provoked Uncle Bill and his foolish pride that goads him into such a passionate rage at times of heightened tension between himself and his occasionally unsympathetic guests on air. To be fair, though,

O'Reilly does appear to be that rare powerful ideologue who occasionally, at least, invites opposing viewpoints to his show, which we discuss in forthcoming chapters.

Yet, we find these rationales lacking, believing instead that propaganda, say, Limbaugh style is intentional and calculated. To admit that an issue like healthcare reform is much more nuanced than, say, mere G-d-less Socialism vs. patriotic Capitalism would inhibit the efficient delivery of propaganda and instead produce thoughtful listeners who are comfortable with the gray areas of life. Instead, we have rabid Obama-haters (say, so-called Dittoheads) or equally inflamed Bush-bashers (say, Schultz followers). Since, in times of economic distress, people seek out talk radio or TV hosts who give voice to public anger and frustration and offer easy scapegoats for those anxieties, black-and-white reasoning is both good for ratings and for reinforcing audience preconceptions about, say, Obama's "questionable" birth certificate or Bush's "questionable" military service record.

Preliminary Speculations

In light of the PM proposed by Herman and Chomsky and of what the powerful have at stake in terms of social and political positions, we speculate that pundits will use polemics to frame issues in order to manufacture a consensus for the zero-sum policies they advocate. Therefore, we wish to explore the following question: Are popularity and pay necessarily driven by polemics? Since salaries tend to be a function of listenership (or viewership), a correlation should appear between the level of controversy in the rhetoric and the size of the audience. Furthermore, are there more productive approaches to framing issues than through narrowly partisan lines of reasoning?

Underlying this investigation is a call for more reasoned discussions of important political issues where talk-show hosts ensure balance by inviting two or three viewpoints on a given issue and granting one's opponents time and certain points when appropriate. In a related vein, we would like to see and hear more in the media of what the late Howard Zinn referred to as "the countless small actions of unknown people." Zinn added that he wanted to write history books that gave citizens "an idea of what ordinary people have suffered ... I wanted to be remembered as somebody who gave people a feeling of hope and power they didn't have before" (NPR.org, 2010).

Similarly, we support pundits who resist the urge to pontificate for hours or interview only prominent guests and instead use their shows to give voice to the many unknown people who call in so that these listeners are empowered to help frame the debate rather than being brow-beaten by an agenda-driven host. After all, as noted earlier, broadcast corporations are practically given the public airwaves for free; the least they can do in return is to repay the public by taking as many calls or reading as many letters as is feasible, given the need to attract listeners/viewers.

Yet instead of such democratization of the airwaves, which would likely result in more diversity of views, ever since Fox News was created and cable TV became the news viewer's medium of choice, for example, two trends appear to have emerged:

(a) the balkanization of news-viewing audiences. In the age of network news, newscasters sought the broadest possible audience and, thus, emphasized qualities of objectivity such as counter-posing Liberal and Conservative interviews, or offering two or three sources to substantiate statements. Nowadays, cable broadcasts seek a niche audience usually ideologically homogenous and hungry for some impassioned rhetorical "red meat."

(b) the need to fill a 24-hour news cycle, which is one characteristic of cable news. Whereas network news tends to occupy only half an hour per day and strives merely to summarize key events in an objective tone (since it reaches a diverse and diffuse national audience) cable news, catering to its niche audience, tends to melodramatize, over-sensationalize and overanalyze events, as it strives to keep viewers tuned in for as much of the 24-hour cycle as possible. Hence, the excesses of demagoguery[19] on cable talk shows compared to network talk shows.

How do these trends currently apply to the real world of politics and discourse? A look back at the first invasion of Iraq will provide some perspective. It is worth noting, for example, that Limbaugh's popularity initially peaked during the Persian Gulf War (1990–1991), according to Wikipedia, and reached its overall apex during this most recent Iraq War (2003–present). Similarly, Hannity and Fox News, in general, have thrived since the recent economic crisis and particularly since the election of an African American President middle-named Hussein — an occurrence that Hannity's

---

[19] Observes Ken Auletta, "As media outlets multiply and it becomes easier to disseminate information on the Web and on cable, the news cycle is getting shorter – to the point that there is no pause, only the constancy of the Web and the endless argument of cable. This creates pressure to entertain or perish, which has fed the press's dominant bias: not pro-liberal or pro-conservative but pro-conflict" (2010, p. 38).

introduction hyperbolically dramatizes for this new radical age in America. (In fact, Obama ran as a mostly centrist Democrat — well to Hillary Clinton's right, for example, on how to wage war in Afghanistan and whether to send more killer drones into Pakistan — and has governed accordingly.)

Our conviction that Neo-conservative talk shows thrive on fear seems to be supported by the latest ratings out for the second quarter of 2009, which "show the top-rated FNC having one of the best quarters in its entire history with prime-time ratings jumping an astounding 34%, presumably few of them Obama fans. That 8-11 PM slot is crucial for viewers — and advertisement revenue — which includes Fox's showcase *The O'Reilly Factor*.[20]

Having cleared the groundwork with definitions of key words and a critical discussion of our rationale and theoretical framework, we begin our analysis with the figures themselves, their backgrounds, and their programs.

---

[20] " ... Throughout the viewing day, Fox News did even better with its 1.2 million viewers, on average, more than doubling CNN's 598,000 and more than tripling third-place trailer MSNBC's average audience of 392,000." Retrieved September 5, 2009 from http://latimesblogs.latimes.com/washington/2009/07/obama-fox-news-msnbc-cnn-.html

PART II.
MILLION-DOLLAR PERSONALITIES

"The radicals have taken over!"
—*Sean Hannity [2008]*

THE SLANT HEAD

The orienting epigraph at the top of this page implicitly urges listeners of Sean Patrick Hannity to contemplate running for the hills.[21] Why would Mr. Hannity, a former high school jock, college-radio controversialist, and NYU dropout, aim to engender such paranoia in his audience? Is he really serious about his observations, and, if so, should *we* take him

---

[21] It should be noted that in this climate of paranoia over proposed changes to healthcare and allegations about "death panels," Hannity has recently (as of September 2009) changed his announcer's introduction to his radio show from hyperbolic accusations about 'radicals taking over' to a more inductive, subtle soft sell preface in which two troubled women voice their concerns about Obama's proposed 'radical' changes to the nation's healthcare system. And, it seems to work. This inductive approach may be more effective than Hannity's earlier over-the-top conclusions about a radical coup d'état because he is now letting people's authentic-sounding stories speak for themselves and, thereby, inviting listeners to conclude that Obama is a bully for forcing his sweeping changes onto damsels in distress.

seriously?

Before answering these questions, we feel that a biographical sketch of the man and his theatrics is in order. Hannity is described as a second-generation Irish-American, his grandparents having legally emigrated from Ireland. The 48-year-old was born and raised in Long Island, New York. By all accounts, Hannity has led a very conventional life, having delivered newspapers as a youngster, scrubbed pots and pans, and flipped burgers. By his own admission, he was, like most other young lads, a curious and mischievous rascal.

It's reported that in high school Hannity was known to be a loudmouth who tended, fairly easily, to launch into heated debates with his schoolmates. His apparent proclivity to hone his quarreling skills at every turn as a youth has no doubt served him well as an adult. Beyond his reported contentious disposition, he was known to combine his secondary schooling with extra-curricular work on boats as a young maintenance man and in bars as a tender. During his abbreviated college career, he also worked outside of class to help fund his education.

What motivated Hannity to pursue a career in talk radio? Well, according to the man himself, one year, after enduring a semester of insufferable lectures from a professor who proclaimed his allegiance to Communism, Hannity claims he could no longer bear his teacher's views and, thus, began to challenge him openly in class.[22] Hannity alleges that his grades

---

[22] Of course, it should noted that this is the same Sean Hannity that characterizes Barack Obama as a socialist and says that Obama's victory means that the radicals have "taken over" even though Obama won 53% of the vote significantly more than Bush won in either of his two elections.

in that course began falling precipitously from excellent marks to average.[23] Perhaps he is spinning his earlier experiences at NYU to justify his current antipathy toward academia and Liberalism in general. In any event, it is ironic that Hannity has turned out to be like the very professor he abhorred as dissent on his show is not easily brooked.

Since his days at university, Hannity has gone on to establish quite a foothold in the (dis)information industry. Though he effects the image of having moved up through the professional ranks by the sheer force of his own polemical talents and hard work, from local radio annoyance to national notoriety, he has no doubt benefitted from serving as a rhetorical goon for the GOP. He seems, in fact, sycophantically stuck to powerful Neo-conservatives, giving considerable airtime almost exclusively to shock jocks such as Ann Coulter and Laura Ingraham and giving Sarah Palin her 'comeback' interview where he served up softball questions.

Like his mentor, Rush Limbaugh, Sean Hannity is renowned for his incendiary rhetorical tactics. In his first radio show at a college station in California in 1989, he was fired for allegedly discriminating against gays.[24] In keeping with his self-evident inclination toward intolerance, Hannity has also been roundly criticized by various media outlets for having provided a forum on his WABC radio show for self-described neo-Nazi Hal Turner in the late 1990s. WABC's program director, Phil Boyce, acknowledged that Turner's views were inappropriate.

---

[23] Borrowed from http://www.netglimse.com/

[24] Hannity's public disapproval of gays seems ironically to be betrayed by the dating service now run from his website that seeks to match both conservative heterosexuals and homosexuals.

The passing years appear to have done little to soften Hannity's hard line against others outside the socio-cultural center as he perceives it. In an October 5, 2008, "special edition" of *Hannity's America* entitled "Obama and Friends: History of Radicalism," Mr. Hannity featured Mr. Andy Martin as an expert on Obama without signaling to his audience Martin's well-established history of anti-Semitism. Fox Senior Vice President Bill Shine later apologized for the show, acknowledging that Fox should have done more comprehensive research on its guests. For a sampling of the public's diverging reactions to Hannity, please see Appendix A.

His Political Theatre

Hannity hosts the 2nd most listened to radio talk show in America, garnering 13.25 million weekly listeners. As a consequence, he was able to sign a contract in July of 2008 worth 100 million dollars over five years. He has also received many awards, including two Marconi Radio Awards as network personality of the year from the National Association of Broadcasters (in 2003 and 2007) and three consecutive awards from *Radio and Records Magazine*. However, it is worth noting that these awards do not appear to be given for the quality of commentary but, largely, for the quantity of ratings points.[25]

In spite of these accolades, the means by which he has achieved such popularity and prestige is certainly

---

[25] According to WKDZ, The criteria used by the Marconi judges include ratings, community awards and recognition, events sponsored by the station, continuing community service broadcasts, and staff involvement in the community.

controversial. Indeed, the controversy itself is what may well drive his popularity; sensationalism, in Hannity's case, undoubtedly sells. In their book, *Common Ground*, Conservative Kal Thomas and Liberal Bob Beckel, characterize Sean Hannity as the most polarizing of political broadcasters. And, his Manichean perspective (e.g., pitting the "Radical Obama" vs. the "Great American" Hannity himself) is abetted by the very structure of his radio show, which takes far fewer calls than Colmes' does and devotes the first 20 or so minutes of each hour to Hannity's tightly focused hyperbolic monologue.

At the outset of the show, a baritone voice intones: "This is a special edition of the Sean Hannity Show: The radicals have taken over. Hold onto your wallets; your taxes are going through the roof."[26]

So, before Hannity has even commandeered the microphone, his show has launched pre-emptive *ad hominem* attacks on Obama and the Democrats while begging two key questions: (a) is Obama a radical? and (b) are taxes going to skyrocket? These two questions prompt us to pose others. Would taxes have gone up any less if George Bush or John McCain, both of whom Hannity supported, had been in office, since both politicians were proponents of the TARP and the principle of massive deficit spending to stimulate the economy? Bush cut tax revenues 2 trillion dollars while hiking spending, yet we do not recall Hannity complaining that such

---

[26] It's worth noting Hannity's tendency to dress up banal nouns with fairly meaningless modifiers: Regarding the news he reports, it's not just an edition, it's a special edition; regarding the brilliant minds he assembles, it's not just a panel; it's a great American panel; regarding the man himself, it's not just Sean Hannity; it's Sean Hannity the great American.

budget-busting policies would eventually lead to tax increases. What's more, we ask, have the radicals really "taken over," as Hannity has claimed, or have they merely been voted into office democratically — unlike in the General Election of 2000 when Mr. Bush was literally swept into office by Supreme Court edict in a 5—4, partisan vote. Rather than ever address the complexities of questions like these, Hannity prefers to create an atmosphere of fear and paranoia, invoking 1930s Germany.

It is also worth noting that this kind of opening monologue ensures that Hannity remains "on message" for the entire hour as callers are expected to respond to his observations. Since his monologues are designed to invoke fear and paranoia — as advertised, for example, in the announcer's declaration that "The radicals have taken over!" — the callers are quite motivated to echo Hannity's given themes.

Hannity's show occasions a number of ironies. The idea of a "take over" is ironic in that Hannity truly takes over and controls the agenda — not only in terms of the emotion established in his hyperbolic introduction, but also because of the format itself. As he opens the show by building his case, he tends to feature exclusively Conservative guests who only serve to reinforce his position. Furthermore, callers who seem to stray off topic or dare defy his will are interrupted then brow-beaten or berated. In his interview with Michael Moore, for example, Hannity isn't interested addressing the problems of inadequately regulated Capitalism; instead, he belabors the point *ad infinitum* that Michael Moore is a multi-millionaire. In fact, Hannity repeats versions of the terms millionaire or multi-millionaire in reference to Moore a dozen times or more in the space of a minute or two. So, the one-sided structure of the show belies the Democratic ideals and freedoms Hannity claims he champions.

Ironically, too, although the opening theme music for the show is Martina McBride's "Independence Day," and Hannity titled his first book *Let Freedom Ring* and sponsors numerous "freedom" concerts, his show features a range of predominantly Conservative guests, Conservative callers, and scarce criticism of the Bush Administration while it was in power. His show seems almost like an arm of the Republican Party as Hannity scarcely ever criticizes the GOP establishment.

A further irony in the above is that Hannity's format and tenor are more akin to a totalitarian's than to the small "d" democrats he implicitly identifies with in his opening teaser. He is G-d-like in his authoritative tone, smooth in delivery, and totally self-controlled during his opening act. Indeed, much like Reverend Jeremiah Wright's openings, Hannity's are passionately delivered and are like the Truth — no counter-truth is presented, no nuance admitted — from which the callers deviate at their peril. The "great American" callers, in turn, tend to verbally genuflect before Hannity, praising him with the same moniker he uses for those who compliment him during the first few moments of their call to the show.

The intended effect of Hannity's sermons on listeners, we infer, is intellectual sedation. Scant critical thinking is even necessary since the primary members of his audience are learning "the truth" about "the radicals" that have taken over. Such black and white reasoning makes it all the more easy for listeners to identify with the forces of good (Hannity and his Neo-con allies) and to revile the evil radicals in Hannity's daily morality play. Each day, we are presented with this uncomplicated Manichean fight between G-d and his angels.[27] That is to say, Hannity and the angelic Neo-cons versus the Satanic Obama and the Mephistophelean Liberals whom he (Obama) pals around with.

After the show's first commercial break, Hannity's announcer intones, as is customary, "A great American," Sean Hannity, is on the air. In this way, the announcer fulfills an important role that serves to verify the "social proof" of correct behavior for a given situation. His words serve as a model for guests to echo (Cialdini, 2001, p. 100). Soon thereafter, and quite in keeping with the principle of "social proof," Hannity's callers pick up on this theme and publicly salute him as a great American. Not surprisingly, after Alan Colmes left *Hannity and Colmes*, Mr. Hannity decided to replace Colmes with a "Great American Panel." Thus, "Great American" becomes like an *ad populum* mantra chanted throughout the show.

To his callers, Hannity consistently presents easy

---

[27] While Hannity's interviews with Sarah Palin during the presidential campaign were virtually sycophantic, with questions designed to help Palin strike back at the press, a recent interview about the 2009 success of her book was unswervingly servile. Rather than reminding Palin about "death panels" being voted 2009's "Biggest Lie of the Year," Hannity furthered the lie by allowing Palin to note: "If the health care bill goes the way Obama wants it, we're gonna have something very much like foreign countries' systems of health care like the British, and it's the American people — if we have our health care paid for by the bureaucracy, by government — depending on our health condition, depending on our age — we're gonna be subject to bureaucrats deciding, panels and commissions deciding — just like they do overseas — who will be worthy of receiving the health care that government is going to provide." ... So that is the death panel that I referred to, and I won't back off on criticizing that aspect of the health care bill." (2010, January 6)

dichotomies: we can either agree with the "radicals" who have "taken over" and are going to try to take our wallets (in the form of higher taxes) or we can agree with the "great American" — Hannity. Each issue is sifted through this polarizing filter. Thus, those few iconoclastic callers lucky enough to slip past the presumably rigorous screening are, almost by definition, anti-American (and pro "radical" and "take over") when they challenge the "great American" host. Indeed, it's as if they are challenging America itself — much as Hannity and others equated criticism of the war in Iraq with criticism of America and questioned the patriotism of war critics.

"I never let my kids or grand kids use the word 'hate,'
but I want you to know, I *hate* you!"
—*A caller to Colmes' Show*

"Genius, scholar, and war hero though he is, you have to admit – or maybe you should think about admitting – that George Bush might have rushed things a little in invading Iraq."
—*Alan Colmes*

THAT 'SQUIRRELY' GUY

He may be a master of understatement, as illustrated in the second epigraph, but Alan Colmes' irony sometimes eludes the understanding of his Fox News radio audience. Perhaps, too, because of his snarky ironies, he polarizes his listeners and often engenders both rage in his Conservative, Fox-faithful audience (note the vitriol in the first epigraph — part of his own promo no less!) and delight in his ideological allies. Colmes, like Hannity, has created a space in the public discourse wherein people feel moved to vent polarized emotions about Colmes himself and the ways in which he treats the issues. He "[m]anages to be [as] doubly stupid as he is ugly by claiming OJ is innocent...." [28] He is "[a] sane, reasoned, Liberal yet

[28] Borrowed from JuliusW (March 18, 2007) at http://www.rate

independent thinker who does more for this cause by articulating non-extremist, logical positions in a classy, non-abrasive way. Sean Hannity could sure learn a lot from you"[29]

Like Hannity, Colmes was raised in New York, New York, yet he was initially more focused than Hannity, a college dropout. At 16, Colmes graduated from high school and set off for university at Hofstra. He finished in 1971, and thereafter pursued a career as a stand-up comedian — rather fittingly, considering how often he would later become the butt of Hannity's and various guests' jokes as well as the butt of his own self-deprecating wit.

Ironically, despite the accelerated pace that marked his academic development, Colmes, 59, did not rise to prominence as quickly as Hannity and Limbaugh had. After his fledgling stand-up career, Colmes turned to radio, taking a succession of jobs at various stations in the Northeast. He became prominent in New York when WABC chose him to fill its morning drive slot, calling the show *W. Alan B. Colmes* to reflect the station's call sign. [30] He became prominent nationally when he and other regional radio hosts formed a cooperative called Daynet, which syndicated his show nationally. Colmes has kept his own show, now distributed by Fox News, ever since. In 1996, he was hired by Fox News CEO Roger Ailes, who was looking for a partner for Sean Hannity. After 12 years on the highly popular *Hannity & Colmes* show, Colmes left at the end of 2008 but remains on his daily 3-hour Fox News radio show.

---

itall.com/i-13581-alan-colmes.aspx

[29] Borrowed from Underspin (February 11, 2005) at http://www.rateitall.com/i-13581-alan-colmes.aspx

[30] Wikipedia

Colmes' radio persona differs from that of the other hosts we are studying, as he reveals a measure of open contempt for many of his callers — somewhat ironically, perhaps, given the contempt with which he was held on *Hannity & Colmes*. Yet, the contempt here is in reverse from the anti-intellectual Hannity. Whereas the other Fox hosts — not to mention most of the hosts we are studying, with the exception of Olbermann — seem contemptuous of intellectuals, Colmes seems to embrace intellectual values. Indeed, he graduated from high school two years early, married an Associate Professor at Rutgers, routinely reads the *New York Times* (a paper he refers to frequently on the show), and seems most comfortable talking to highly intelligent guests such as Professors Noam Chomsky and Bertell Ollman and former Professor Newt Gingrich, as opposed to his callers, whose time he generally limits to 20-30 seconds, and whom he often cuts off, calling some of them narrow-minded, even bigoted, Conservatives — or simply stupid.

In fact, he often embodies the stereotype of the East Coast elitist Liberal who is uncomfortable among and irritated by the masses. Indeed, Colmes has an intermittent segment called "Sudden Death," in which he or his producers unilaterally cut off callers — often after a few seconds — for such "sins" as saying they like the show or asking Colmes how he is doing. He considers this segment a "workshop" or tutorial in which his audience members learn to be better callers. (After the caller has been cut off, Colmes lectures the audience on the sin that was committed.) One almost expects Colmes to admonish his listeners that a pop quiz will be forthcoming. This sort of condescension may partly explain why so many of his callers express outright hostility toward Colmes, who, in turn and with great relish, cuts them off or screams back at them. The result is undeniably entertaining, though at the expense of the smooth, air-tight control of subject matter and emotional tone that epitomizes Hannity's radio style.

Given Colmes' embrace of the life of the mind, so to speak, is it not ironic that he has published only one book, compared to the many published by his anti-intellectual rivals on the Far Right? Unlike the more prolific O'Reilly, Hannity, and Limbaugh, Alan Colmes has to his credit the 2003 treatise, *Red, White & Liberal: How Left is Right and Right Is Wrong*.[31] Note that the title Colmes has chosen is cut from the same cloth as his radio show: both seek to redefine stigmatized concepts, in that "the Left" has traditionally had negative connotations since the McCarthy Era, and Fox itself arguably connotes a Rightwing perspective — except for Colmes' show.[32] Rush Limbaugh argues that Liberals are running away from their philosophy by camouflaging it in euphemistic terms like "progressive,"[33] yet

---

[31] It's worth noting that Colmes seems to view his media career quite differently than O'Reilly or Limbaugh does. Whereas Colmes has only published one book and was only too happy to quit the highly profitable Hannity & Colmes Show to focus on just his radio show, O'Reilly is a veritable media assembly line, cranking out 8 books (5 of them on the NYT best seller list), writing his weekly syndicated column, and airing his 5-days-per week television program and his 3-hours-per day radio show. Even Limbaugh, whose journeys into the world of TV have proven unsuccessful, seems to live for his radio show, which at 20-plus years has outlived all three of his marriages combined, and he has written best selling books as well.

[32] It is worth noting that Ed Schultz too is redefining the left — offering his listeners a "down home" dialect from a conservative state yet touting liberal ideas. However, Schultz seems more prone to the phenomenon that Limbaugh speaks of. Whereas Colmes proudly calls himself a liberal and member of the left, Schultz shies away from the L-word, styling himself as a straight-talker hailing from the heartland. He will use the word progressive on his show, but rarely, if ever, uses "liberal."

[33] Yet, the term has actual concrete literary meaning in that *The Progressive* magazine has been advocating for progressive values for

Colmes explicitly calls himself a member of the "Left" and his website "Liberal-land."

Furthermore, note that Colmes has taken in recent years what has been a Conservative symbol—the flag—and tried to turn it into a Liberal symbol. Indeed, this seems to be a preoccupation of Colmes'—changing the enemy from within. He has taken a largely Conservative news medium—Fox News—and sought, however unsuccessfully, to redefine it through his Liberal radio show and has chosen the image of the flag, which is usually associated with Conservatives in recent years, and sought to redefine it as a Liberal emblem. For a sampling of the public's diverging reactions to Colmes, please see Appendix B.

A Colmesian Approach to Talk

Colmes begins his show with what he refers to as "First Word," a segment in which he lets his callers determine the topic. Of the other pundits we have examined, Colmes appears to be the most explicitly interested in creating a true democratic public discourse. Indeed, Colmes acknowledges as much, pointing out to his audience, that

> We barely screen; we put you on hold; we just want to know what's in your head, give us a sense of where you're at, at the top of the show because *you* [speaker's emphasis] are the focus of the show. Not me. I am simply your humble facilitator, your enabler, giving you air time, urging you to be a part of the program, interviewing guests, just sitting here pressing buttons. I am basically just a telephone operator ... (Colmes, October 21, 2009)

---

the past 100 years.

However, whereas Limbaugh or Hannity may spend a couple of minutes with a given caller, Colmes keeps the calls brief, allowing no more than twenty to thirty seconds for each call — even when his ideological allies call. After 15 to 30 minutes of "First Word," Colmes will generally interview a guest for about 15 to 30 minutes and then end the hour with "Third Word" in which the audience once again can determine the subject at hand.

Colmes, it seems, is Hannity's near-polar opposite in terms of self-deprecation. Whereas Hannity's announcer refers to Hannity as a "great American," Colmes' announcer suggests to Colmes, "I think you should really find another line of work." Thus, if Hannity is an authoritarian, Colmes is very much a postmodern ironist, poking fun at his own authority, encouraging the callers to question him. In stark contrast to the careful, over-produced choreographing that often characterizes Hannity's theatrics, Colmes' tend to be preternaturally democratic — indeed, his "First Word" ensures that his *callers* control the first part of his show, and his "Third Word" ensures that they get the last word after Colmes has interviewed some newsmaker or other guest.[34]

---

[34] On the other hand, Colmes' format may reflect his relative laziness. Whereas O'Reilly, Hannity, and Limbaugh all tightly control the structure of their shows and put in the hours to amass "evidence" for their carefully constructed arguments, Colmes appears to prepare little, preferring a more impromptu approach. Similarly, as aforementioned, Colmes has published only one book while, say, O'Reilly has published more than a dozen. Furthermore, it is worth noting that Colmes often appeared underprepared on *Hannity & Colmes* and was easily outmatched by the better-prepared Hannity. Nevertheless, whatever motivates Colmes' free-style format, the effect is to further democratize the caller-host relationship, allowing many more callers than the more

If Hannity portrays his show very much as a kind of Sermon on the Mount, with Hannity delivering the message, Colmes patterns his show after the democratic ideal — a collision of his usually Liberal leanings with his audience's mixture of Liberal and Conservative ideas. Approximately, 60% of Colmes' callers disagree with him, usually from a Conservative perspective. The effect on the audience member is jarring, as he or she is forced to decide between the frustrated host, who often loses his temper at his Conservative callers, and the often quite articulate callers, whose talking points — Colmes claims — seem to come from the other Fox shows they watch. (Colmes remains the lone Liberal among Fox's deep roster of talk show hosts.) The listener is also jarred by the dizzying array of issues broached on the show, as Colmes keeps each call relatively brief and individual callers raise a variety of topics. Indeed, as many as eight new discussions are hatched in a given ten-minute segment versus Hannity's laser-like focus on his issue *du jour*.

Colmes' show is also unique in that the call screening is minimal, and arguably a majority of the callers hotly disagree with Colmes on the issue they had called to discuss. In fact, on a recent show, a listener praised Colmes for his limited call screening, comparing it to the much more extensive call screening on shows such as Limbaugh's and Hannity's:

(Shaquelle from Durham North Carolina)

Caller: The reason you have a great show and the people who get through like from another universe makes the show very good ...

---

authoritarian Hannity and Limbaugh allow.

Colmes: You mean the crazies who call me?

Caller: ... but if you call like Rush or one of those guys, you have your conversation with them before.

Colmes: Yeah, we do very light screening on purpose to keep it fresh and keep it real on this show.

Caller: Because all they ask is —

Colmes: ... we purposely do a minimum of screening to get to real reactions and to keep the filter as unfiltered as possible; we think it makes for a much more interesting and entertaining show. Now sometimes we get criticized for that [they] say why do you put on so many crazy people but that's what's out there. This is what exists. We are the true reality show.

It is possible, of course, that the caller was a plant but not likely. Colmes seems genuinely surprised by the call, and the caller himself was quite ungrammatical and did not seem the least bit canned or prepared. To underscore what the caller Shaquelle is saying, the subject of Colmes' show, unlike that of the other talk show hosts we are studying, is the very combat between Colmes and his callers — this sort of polarizing, internecine battle is what makes the show interesting.

Thus, we can see the irony that many of those who call in to praise the show are Colmes' ideological detractors — yet they love the aforementioned combat and Colmes' mock rage. In other words, Colmes has never stopped being a stand-up comedian, whereas the other hosts, even the pseudo-vaudevillian Limbaugh and the somewhat silly Schultz, generally keep the focus on a given issue about which they provide evidence and sound-bites, etc. (exception: Limbaugh lets the callers control the agenda on Fridays only).

The excerpt from Shaquelle is revealing on another level as well. Note Colmes' cynical attitude toward his audience whom he simply labels "crazies." He fatalistically observes "that's what's out there," yet Colmes has not sought to replace his distributor, Fox News, with a more neutral or Liberal carrier whose callers may be more likely to echo Colmes' sentiments.

Only Colmes begins his show *en medias res*, as he takes calls without any introduction or preface, hence the bumper-pool effect of the discussions that send listeners bouncing in various new directions. The best analogy may be to two opposing teaching methods: Hannity, Limbaugh, *et al* are classic authoritarian teachers — they control the agenda, screen the calls carefully, strike an authoritative tone, and reward obedient "brownnosing students" (the starry-eyed callers who, say, call Hannity a "Great American" or say "dittoes" to Rush).

Colmes, by stark contrast, initially appears to be the post-sixties professor who has empowered his callers/students to set the agenda and determine the direction of the show, as various callers respond to each other as much as they do to Colmes, who often has nothing to say, merely thanking the caller for his call. Indeed, even when he receives that rare helpful caller who tries to clarify a point Colmes was awkwardly making, Colmes is still largely indifferent, merely thanking the caller. If his show were a classroom, the desk arrangement would likely be an oval, so that the callers/students could face and speak to each other, as Colmes doesn't shape the dialogue so much as he merely responds to some of the callers, especially if he strongly disagrees. Limbaugh *et al* would, by contrast, maintain a traditional seating arrangement with the host/teacher at the lectern using the "textbook" (their scripted propaganda) as if it were a Bible and treating callers as if they were blank slates to be imbued with Divine logos by the all-knowing [H]ost.

Yet, notice we suggest earlier that Colmes "initially appears to be." This is because, as we have argued with respect to Shaquelle, the actual direction of the show is not determined by the callers — in fact there is no direction, apart from the highly entertaining verbal combat between Colmes' largely Conservative, usually ill-informed callers and the hyper-sensitive, histrionic host who often screams at his Rightwing callers (yet, interestingly doesn't block them from calling, since the combat and Colmes' subsequent frustration are precisely what stimulate the listener.[35]

The show is like a dysfunctional household that we can, like with so many other reality shows, voyeuristically peep into, fascinated by the excitement as Dad screams at Jr. for the 18th time that day. Colmes routinely treats his audience to his personal venting as he expresses frustration with the withering disdain of his Conservative callers: "You know what I can't stand; I can't even stand the tone of their voices; I'm in the wrong job."[36] By contrast, Hannity's shows, like his rightwing allies', are like 1950s sitcoms where father's authority largely goes unquestioned and father himself is viewed as the infallible leader of the family.

If Colmes has any shortcomings, they are in his occasional presumptuousness and dogmatism. For example, in reply to Conservative callers' claims that Obama's response to the recent incidents of piracy, off the coast of Somalia, shows

---

[35] Listeners occasionally call in to inquire about Colmes' state of mind and mental health with one member of the audience recently asking "how much aspirin you go through and what brand?"

[36] Borrowed from an August 11, 2009, Colmes' show podcast.

that foreigners aren't respecting America's sovereignty, Colmes snarled, "That's a Rightwing talking point... It's ridiculous."[37]

But, Colmes offered no evidence that represents what he felt was an exclusively Rightwing topic. While he did suggest that Obama didn't want to over-react or disclose too much to the public when a secret mission may have been on the way, Colmes made no attempt to empathize with the caller or acknowledge that there might be a plausible alternative to Obama's response to piracy.

Oddly, for a host who is typically quite careful and conscientious enough to present opposing points of view on his show, Colmes seems utterly tone deaf much of the time. For example, on his November 19, 2009, show, he makes a purely Constitutional argument for closing GITMO when his listeners, many of them Rightwingers, surely don't support extending rights to foreign terrorists. What's more, in that same show, Colmes says to a caller that he wouldn't be interested in marrying Sarah Palin and asks why anyone else would [want to marry the gorgeous goddess Palin]. Yet, if Colmes sometimes lacks empathy for his hostile callers' views, he still plays the non-zero-sum game more than any other pundit.

---

[37] Perhaps after 12 years of fending off rightwing talking points from Hannity and his fellow conservatives, Colmes has been conditioned to reflexively attack his opponents.

"The only way to reduce the number of nuclear weapons is to use them."

—*Rush Limbaugh*

THE LORD OF THE DITTOES

Rush Limbaugh has been renowned for his use of Conservative bombast and acerbic wit for over two decades. Born in 1951 in Jefferson City, Missouri, Limbaugh did not enjoy the kind of meteoric rise one might expect from someone with his silver-tongued voice. Indeed, Limbaugh dropped out of college and was allegedly even on welfare (ironic, given his contempt for government handouts) for a time while he was trying to determine what career path to take.[38] Later, he began a succession of radio stints. But his career did not really take off until his talk show became nationally syndicated over twenty years ago.

[38] For more, see the satirical "interview" between Al Franken and Limbaugh wherein Franken satirically arranges Limbaugh's own statements over the years. (1999)

Limbaugh's struggles with marriage (thrice divorced) and drugs (apprehended for possessing thousands of illegally acquired OxyContin pills) are well publicized. What is less well-known is his charity work. Limbaugh's 16th annual telethon for cancer research raised $1.7 million in 2006 and $15 million overall since its inception.[39] And, Limbaugh himself contributed between $100,000 and half a million (or 0.2% to 1% of his yearly income) from 2000 – 2005 and 2007.[40]

With his massive audience of 20 million listeners, his 40-million-a-year salary, his massive ego (he says he has talent "on loan from G-d"), and his equally huge girth,[41] Limbaugh is so influential in the ever-shrinking GOP that he is arguably the *de facto* leader of the party, much to the consternation of more moderate Republicans such as George Bush's former presidential speech writer David Frum who characterized Limbaugh as

> ... aggressive and bombastic, cutting and sarcastic, who dismisses the concerned citizens in network news focus groups as "losers." With his private plane and his cigars, his history of drug dependency and his personal bulk, not to mention his tangled marital history, Rush is a walking stereotype of self-indulgence (2009, ¶7).

Despite Limbaugh's cartoon-like flaws, he wields tremendous influence in a currently rudderless Republican Party. Indeed,

---

[39] Retrieved September 9, 2009, from "Annual Reports" at Leukemia & Lymphoma Society at http://www.leukemia-lymphoma.org/all_page?item_id=9556

[40] Rush Limbaugh Show transcript April 28, 2005

[41] One wonders whether there is some malign significance to his expanding waistline, audience size and influence in the GOP and the ever-shrinking size and influence of the GOP.

when GOP Chair Michael Steele, speaking to CNN's D. L. Hughly, criticized Limbaugh for his "incendiary" and "ugly" tactics, Limbaugh's counterattack was so intense that Steele was forced to apologize to Limbaugh — an unelected political vaudevillian. For all his efforts to persuade the public that he is truly an entertainer, Limbaugh's own remarks regarding Steele's apology reveal Limbaugh's true power as not only an enforcer of the Republican agenda but also a key co-manufacturer of it.[42] For a sampling of the public's diverging reactions to Limbaugh, please see Appendix C.

Limbaugh's Style

For all of its purported sophistication and carefully controlled message focus, *The Rush Limbaugh Show* oozes with unintended irony as it opens with an inadvertently eco-friendly soundtrack [*The Pretenders'* "My City Was Gone"] which castigates Cuyahoga Falls, Ohio, for marring its once-beautiful landscape with strip malls. Limbaugh's listeners hear only the melody but not the lyrics that sharply contrast with Limbaugh's often hyperbolic opposition to environmentalists, whom he routinely and famously derides as "environmental whackos."

Limbaugh has amply earned a reputation as a rhetorical bomb-thrower, famously saying on January 16, 2009,

---

[42] When prompted to comment on Steele's abject apology, Limbaugh observed: "Well, you'd have to ask him why he apologized. But, the reason I went after him is not because he said those things about me. It's because he's off-message! Michael Steele should be out there raising money and planning more ways to get people to vote for Republicans. For further details, see http://thinkprogress.org/2009/10/12/limbaugh-steele-leader/

that he hoped Barack Obama failed [to revive the economy]. Indeed, he has rankled the punditocracy (Washington journalists and TV news commentators) with a full arsenal of inflammatory remarks about a range of political issues, public personalities, and ethnic and gender identities.[43]

Despite his image as a tactless and mischievous rascal, Limbaugh, true to his lawyerly heritage (his father, brother, grandfather and an uncle all practiced law), is the consummate preparer and closer, addressing his audience as though it were a jury and he were giving concluding remarks, all with the flair of Perry Mason table-pounding passion.[44] In light of his

---

[43] The following string of quotations characterize some of Limbaugh's outrageous claims: "Feminism was established so as to allow unattractive women easier access to the mainstream of society." "The NAACP should have riot rehearsal. They should get a liquor store and practice robberies." "They oughta change Black History Month to Black Progress Month and start measuring it." "Look, let me put it to you this way: the NFL all too often looks like a game between the Bloods and the Crips without any weapons. There, I said it." "Sorry to say this, I don't think he's been that good from the get-go. I think what we've had here is a little social concern in the NFL. The media has been very desirous that a black quarterback do well." (Rush's comments about Philadelphia Eagles quarterback Donovan McNabb, while working as a commentator on ESPN) "I mean, let's face it, we didn't have slavery in this country for over 100 years because it was a bad thing. Quite the opposite: slavery built the South. I'm not saying we should bring it back; I'm just saying it had its merits. For one thing, the streets were safer after dark." "[S]he's smart enough to know she can't feed herself. She's actually [a] very smart cat. She gets loved. She gets adoration. She gets petted. She gets fed. And she doesn't have to do anything for it, which is why I say this cat's taught me more about women than anything my whole life." (Three days after judging the Miss America Pageant, Rush Limbaugh is asked if it's still fair to compare women to his cat.) (DailyKos.com)

[44] Indeed, his grandfather, Rush Limbaugh Sr., was a diplomat and lawyer who practiced law until his demise at age 104. Ironically, Rush Limbaugh III, the man with the golden EIB microphone, is on one hand an extension of his grandfather, a lawyer making a case for a point of view

juridical background, isn't it ironic that Limbaugh so often rails against defense attorneys? He likely does so since this constituency overwhelmingly supports Democrats.

Nevertheless, Limbaugh moves seamlessly from earnest "prosecutor" to a sort of crude version of a Swiftian satirist. Again, he engages his audience in a way that makes members feel accountable to his interpretation of "law." The sound-bites of the "accused," which he offers as evidence, are like smoking-gun exhibits in a high-profile double murder case. By stark contrast, though, Ed Schultz and particularly Alan Colmes seem to meander through the hour, letting the callers drive the show's direction and preparing little in advance to steer the discourse.

Limbaugh's format is similar to Hannity's, except that Limbaugh controls the topic his callers can discuss not just at the top of the show, but throughout the show and throughout the week, except for Fridays, when callers can broach their own topic. Whenever he takes callers, he limits the number to a meager few. Among those who do get through, many supply the secret handshake, referring to themselves as Dittoheads or echoing Rush's subsequent commentary by saying, "Dittoes Rush." Also, like Hannity, Limbaugh's Bo Snerdley enforces a strict call screening and rarely invites a Liberal caller.[45] And for that rare

---

and on the other a decidedly undiplomatic public figure.

[45] In theory, the caller has to ask a question or state a comment to a person who determines whether or not the caller's question or comment adds value to the program before allowing the caller to interact directly with the radio or TV host. In reality, impotent cowards like Rush Limbaugh use it to make sure some intelligent caller with an opposing view or facts to disprove the stuff he makes up doesn't one-up him on the air and threaten his authenticity, or lack thereof, or make him appear stupid to his listener base.

brave caller who opposes Limbaugh, the rotund rhetorician will browbeat and then cut off the caller, trying to use him or her as an object lesson for what is wrong with the Liberals/Elitists/Democrats/Feminists/Environmentalists.

Nevertheless, perhaps partly because of his ego and partly to maintain message focus, Limbaugh rarely entertains guests and devotes precious little time to audience calls, save for Fridays. Yet there may be an ulterior motive to his apparent egocentric madness. The refrain that he has "talent on loan from G-d," even if meant tongue and cheek, may serve much the same purpose as Hannity's "Great American" self- proclamation.

To criticize Limbaugh is, by extension, to criticize G-d and is, thus, taboo. Just so, Limbaugh's characterization of his network as the "Excellence in Broadcasting Network" or EIB, which he repeats at every commercial break, may mislead his audience into thinking that his show has been recognized for its journalistic excellence; Limbaugh gives no disclaimer that this is a mere trademark, not a critical recognition of excellence. The absence of a disclaimer may further serve to discourage listeners and callers from criticizing or even questioning Limbaugh. This method of self-aggrandizement is typical of Limbaugh's style of innuendo. He will intimate something — in this case, that his network is critically acclaimed — and through incessant repetition fit that "fact" into his audience's mind.

Yet, when we peek behind the Wizard's curtain, fascinating ironies appear. For example, Limbaugh incessantly accuses the Democrats of being anti-family values and anti-responsibility — while he himself, as aforementioned, has terminated three marriages, was arrested[46] for illegally buying

---

[46] Yet, never convicted.

thousands of tablets of the prescription drug OxyContin, and was allegedly living with his parents as an able-bodied adult.[47]

Ironies also emerge in Limbaugh's stand on the Vietnam War and his anti-elitism crusade. Limbaugh fervently supported the Vietnam War but failed to show up for the fight due to either an old football injury or a severe case of Pilondial disease.[48] Though his repeated castigation of Democrats as "elitists" paints him as a hard-working, run-of-the-mill Joe-the-plumber every-man, Limbaugh, nonetheless, rarely fails to call attention to his excellent taste in fine cigars, his improving handicap on the golf course, and his flat in that bastion of cultural elitism, New York City's Manhattan.

In addition to the ironies concerning his personal life, it is worth noting his double-standards concerning politicians. For example, he is sure to chide Barack Obama for using a teleprompter or using "ums" when speaking extemporaneously, yet conveniently ignores the teleprompter dependence and lexical troubles of his fellow Neo-conservative George W. Bush. Limbaugh would argue, though, that what appears to be a double-standard is really Limbaugh's attempt to present an alternative perspective from what the national media are portraying. Thus, if mass media portray Obama as eloquent and Grammy- and Nobel-worthy and Bush as illiterate and remedial-reading worthy, then Limbaugh will emphasize

---

[47] For alleged facts about Limbaugh's welfare status, see Al Franken's book *Rush Limbaugh Is a Big Fat Idiot*.

[48] According to Wikipedia, Pilondial Disease is an "abscess near or on the natal cleft of the buttocks that often contains hair and skin debris." It must be noted too that Limbaugh's birth date was ranked as 152 in the Vietnam War draft lottery. No one was drafted above 125. He was classified as '1-Y' (later reclassified '4-F') due to either a football knee injury or a diagnosis of Pilondial disease.

Obama's flaws and Bush's virtues.

Ironically, though the self-described "Doctor of Democracy"[49] frequently chides the Democrats as being un-democratic and the media as being biased, Limbaugh's own program rarely features an opposing viewpoint, either from the celebrities or media personnel he interviews or from callers (who apparently are carefully screened). Indeed, many of Limbaugh's listeners identify themselves as "ditto heads," pledging, in effect, their allegiance to the self-proclaimed anchor man of America, which makes Limbaugh most akin to the very authoritarian régimes (Cuba and North Korea) he has so passionately railed against.

His refrain, uttered daily at the outset of each program hour, that he has "talent on loan from G-d," further implies that he is something of a prophet, whose audience is expected to imbibe his "truths" rather than to challenge or at least reflect upon them. Although that deistic allusion may be intended somewhat tongue-in-cheek, it is clearly in keeping with those exceedingly rare occasions when Limbaugh acknowledges that his opponents may well be right or that their positions have any redeeming qualities whatsoever. Indeed, his labels for those opponents — drive-by media, Dingy Harry (for Senate Majority Leader Harry Reid) Bela Pelosi (for House Majority Leader Nancy Pelosi), femi-Nazis (for feminists), etc., all imply his utter contempt for those who disagree with his views.

Source of Appeal

The root of Limbaugh's popularity is, perhaps, best

---

[49] (Limbaugh, The Rush Limbaugh Show, October 30, 2009)

explained through an analogy to high school. We all remember the hyper-strict, supremely un-cool teacher whom we dared not cross openly but privately made fun of. Limbaugh, who was, in fact, a mediocre student academically and who dropped out of a community college, has created the persona of the wise-guy student who "whispers" into the ear of his audience snide jokes about this ultra-powerful, ultra-detested teacher — that is, the enforcer of what Limbaugh and his audience would call "political correctness" and of the Progressive values that, say, some whites feel have diminished their socio-economic power. The class, of course, detests very strict, hopelessly "un-cool" teacher.

Critics may also infer from Limbaugh's rants against elitist intellectuals and bureaucracies that his more rabid listeners may tend to lack higher education. Thus, they cheer Limbaugh when he declares that global warming is a hoax, contradicting some 20,000 of the world's preeminent scientists who compose the Intergovernmental Panel on Climate Change, not to mention contradicting every other major scientific organization – the National Science Foundation, American Meteorological Society, The American Geophysical Union, NASA, etc. Similarly, this may explain his appeal when he extols the virtues of the US healthcare system even though the most recent World Health Organization study ranked the United States 37th in the world in overall quality of healthcare. So, Limbaugh is not the most empirical of reasoners nor his Dittoheads the most scrupulous in his weighing claims. Love is indeed blind.

"Olbermann is a ... *sick* pupp[y]! The way [he] treat[s] my son and anybody that's opposed to [his] point of view is just horrible."
—*George H.W. Bush*
(October 16, 2009) CBS Radio

Der Olbermann Kopf

Keith Olbermann, 51, took an unusual route to his current perch as political commentator and host of the left-of-center news show, *Countdown with Keith Olbermann*, on MSNBC. He moved from sports broadcasting to the more serious world of political journalism.

Born in New York City to a commercial architect and a preschool teacher, Keith Olbermann was a precocious child with an earnest passion for baseball card collecting, about which the youth published a number of articles. After graduating from Cornell at 20 (like Alan Colmes who graduated from high school at 16), Olbermann spent 20 years in sports casting and sports commentary, winning numerous awards, including 11 Golden Mike awards for his work as a sports anchor and 3 awards from the Associated Press as best sportscaster in California. Yet, despite his intellectual credentials and career achievements, there is a prickly, career- threatening side to Olbermann. In fact, ironically as much as Olbermann despises Bill O'Reilly, who is often his "Worst Person in the World" and with whom he has feuded for years, the two share one important trait: They have not spent their careers being company men.

Whereas Limbaugh, Colmes, and Hannity, who stand as straight-talking, fearless iconoclasts, have avoided controversy with their corporate bosses since appearing on the national stage, Olbermann, by his own admission, has burned many corporate bridges. Even his career with his current employer MSNBC has not been smooth. He first began anchoring a news show with the cable network in 1997, when he aired "The Big Show with Keith Olbermann," a prime-time program that discussed three or four news topics within the one-hour framework. But when the Monica Lewinsky scandal broke, the show became White House in Crisis, and eventually Olbermann grew tired of the tedious hyping of that "crisis" (compare the national impact of that "scandal" with that of the current banking and subprime crises, the recession, and the Bernie Madoff Ponzi Scheme). In 1998, according to Michael Hiestand, Olbermann stated that his work at MSNBC "would make me ashamed, make me depressed, make me cry," and shortly thereafter he left the network for Fox Sportsnet.

Similarly, while he was at ESPN in 1997, according to Wikipedia, that network suspended Olbermann for two weeks because he had made an unauthorized appearance on The Daily Show on Comedy Central with then-host and former ESPN colleague Craig Kilborn. During the show, he referred to Bristol,

Connecticut [ESPN's headquarters], as a "'Godforsaken' place."[50] Later that year, he abruptly left ESPN, angering the network's management. The feud between the network and Olbermann continued for some ten years, marked most notably by an essay he published in Salon.com in 2002 in which he quoted his former ESPN bosses as saying that Olbermann had "too much backbone," a charge that is ironically factual, as Olbermann has six lumbar vertebrae instead of the normal five.

It is worth noting that Olbermann could have quietly left ESPN and MSNBC but chose that path of a messy, noisy departure from both. It is also worth noting that both networks, though initially angered by his abrupt departure, would later rehire him for significant anchoring duty. So, despite his inconsistent loyalties, he is clearly able to attract a significant following. For a sampling of the public's reactions to Olbermann, please see Appendix D.

His Methods

For all the ostensible animus Keith Olbermann has for Bill O'Reilly, his show essentially mirrors O'Reilly's in many important respects: the proliferation of *ad hominem* attacks; the leading questions he asks to guests; the fact that he usually has political allies as guests. In fact, Olbermann is arguably more polarizing than O'Reilly, since O'Reilly at least has *some* antagonistic guests; Olbermann rarely has any. What's more, Olbermann's "Worst Person in the World" segment — an "honor" often bestowed upon none other than Bill O'Reilly — suggests that *ad hominem* attacks are built into the very structure of the show.

---

[50] *Seattle Post-Intelligencer* article (May 8, 1997)

As with Hannity's acidic tone, Olbermann's may help explain the surprising growth of his audience. The exact size of his audience is somewhat difficult to ascertain. According to tvbythenumbers.com, he attracted 1.24 million viewers for Thursday, September 3, 2009, but, for the full month of September, according to Olbermann himself, he garnered 1.782 million viewers, which, is not only more than any other Liberal talk show host has tallied, but more than O'Reilly's 1.44 million viewers for September 3rd.[51]

Not only is the show by its very structure replete with *ad hominems*, but it is intrinsically melodramatic, with the daily Countdown to the Worst Person and the Best. This daily countdown forces Olbermann to do precisely what no "objective" traditional newscast dares to do: make explicit judgments and wear its biases on its sleeve. Indeed, the inveterately self-righteous Olbermann revels in such judgments, pausing dramatically before revealing the worst person of the day.

What's problematic about this approach is that it invariably means that a given newsmaker or story cannot be explained in its complexity but rather must be oversimplified into Olbermann's own version of "thumbs up" or "thumbs down" assessments. Extending this movie analogy in regards to guests, Olbermann tends to feature only one-dimensional newsmakers, those representing bad guys or those embodying the very height of virtue but no in between, no nuance. For example, when he castigates Rush Limbaugh, which is almost daily, Olbermann will not only excoriate Limbaugh verbally but also will two-dimensionalize the attack by featuring a looping video clip of

---

[51] http://tvbythenumbers.com/2009/09/04/cable-news-ratings-for-thursday-september-3-2009/26296

Limbaugh's head bobbling bizarrely atop a rotund body in the corner of the screen. Thus, much like Fox News, Olbermann's show features a Manichean structure to enter- tain an audience that shares his personal biases, but it is also ideally unsuited to provoke deeper critical reflection on issues and newsmakers or to challenge his audience's knee-jerk assumptions about politics.

On the other hand, Olbermann's polarizing approach does have an upside: a refreshing candor. Whereas "objective" commentators subtly convey their judgments by the way they cover stories (e.g. by calling the Iran-Contra combatants "freedom fighters" while calling, say, the Iraqi "insurgents" or "terrorists" or by interviewing Israel officials for comment on the Israeli-Palestinian conflict but not interviewing Palestinian officials in kind), Olbermann *explicitly* presents his biases and judgments for public scrutiny. There is no caveat emptor: buyers know exactly what they are getting when they tune in. That is to say, Olbermann does not hide beyond the moniker of "No Spin" or "Fair and Balanced" or "Straight Talk from the Heartland" commentary, as O'Reilly and Hannity at Fox News and Ed Schultz at MSNBC tend to do.

He begins the show by counting down the top five stories. Generally, he starts by introducing video, then interviews an "expert" (usually a left-of-center journalist) for commentary on the story occasioning the video. His questions are almost always leading ones. For example, on August 7, 2009, he asked Jonathan Alter, a *Newsweek* journalist, whether Alter believes that the Republicans' strategy has really changed that much since the Presidential election primaries. At that time the Republicans, according to Olbermann, were saying, "If you vote Democratic, you'll die because of terrorism

[but] that seems to have waned [and] now, it seems, if you vote Democratic you'll die because of health care reform" and the guests, as Alter does, generally reaffirm the thrust of his leading questions.

Another characteristic part of *Countdown* is cross-pollination, as two of the three guests on the day in question come from Newsweek (Alter and Senior Editor Dan Gross), which, like MSNBC, is owned by General Electric. So, not only are you getting a narrowly ideological point of view, but you are receiving *Newsweek*'s "brand" of that ideology.

Three other aspects of Olbermann's style bear mention. First, he occasionally reads his scripts at breakneck speed and without taking a breath, as if anxious to show that he's the smartest student in the class. Second, he loves to point out ironies that diminish his — usually Republican — targets on the personal level. For instance, Olbermann describes the founder of Blackwater (now named Xe Services LLC), Erik Prince, as a born again Christian who says he was motivated by Christian principles and views himself as a crusader tasked with eliminating Muslims and the Islamic faith from the globe. Olbermann then ironically points out that the religiously faithful Prince had had an affair with his nanny, but that Prince "did the right thing — he married her."

Third, he likes to enumerate overwhelming amounts of evidence or details with blitzkrieg rapidity. For example, during his Special Comment on healthcare in the October 6th 2009, episode, he decries the Senate Democrats' healthcare compromise but adds that "I bless the Sherrod Browns and Ron Wydens and Jay Rockefellers and Sheldon Whitehouses and Anthony Weiners and .... " Is this part of some latent need to show off the sheer speed of his screeds? If you'll excuse the alliteration.

In light of Olbermann's provocative approach to political commentary, it behooves us to end this section with assorted colorful critiques of his show from both fans and detractors. Robert Cox, who contributes to the blog Olbermannwatch.com, criticizes the commentator's one-dimensional guests and lack of fact checking. "Olbermann is what's wrong with journalism today." Cox adds, "Far from being the Edward R. Murrow he likes to present himself as, he's the Walter Winchell of journalism. He stacks the deck with his point of view and he flat out lies."[52] And *Miami Herald* television writer Glenn Garvin said, "To me, he's simply the flip side of Bill O'Reilly, a guy rewriting the wires and sprinkling it with random political

---

[52] Cox's comments should be viewed within the context of his apparent one-man crusade to rid the airwaves of Countdown. The following farewell letter to his readers reflects Cox's blatant bias against Olbermann: "There is no disguising the fact that we have been extremely unhappy with the recent decision of NBC Universal not only to retain Keith Olbermann for four more years but to elevate him in an unprecedented fashion. We had held out hope that MSNBC would allow Olbermann's contract to expire even up until the last few weeks. But the deal is done and our Countdown Clock expired at midnight on March 1, 2007. Given this, we have come to the conclusion that we have done more harm than good over the past 2+ years in keeping Olbermann in the public eye at a time when few were watching his show and even less cared about his assault on the journalistic standards we hold dear. So, after careful consideration and consultation with the entire staff, we have decided the time has come to retire OlbermannWatch.com. It's been a great run. We certainly had a lot of fun running the site but it's just been increasingly difficult to maintain our enthusiasm as Olbermann's ratings have increased and a compliant media has done everything to boost Olbermann and his show. We wish all of you the best over the next four, painful years." Sincerely, Robert A. Cox Managing Editor, Olbermann Watch.com

rants, better gag lines, but a more predictable point of view."[53]

Conversely, he garners rave reviews from *Chicago Sun Times* TV critic Phil Rosenthal who observes that "Keith Olbermann is onto something. Something big ... Countdown flows from funny to poignant in connecting the seemingly random dots of a day's events, important and trivial, steadfastly clinging to basic tenets about what is and isn't news without being bound to traditional approaches." And *American Journalism Review* writer Mark Lisheron says, "Watch *Countdown* on any given night, and you'll be treated to deft wordplay and a clever juxtaposition of the serious and the sublime. Olbermann has a news sensibility and gravity that suggests Eric Sevareid and an ability to stand apart from and skewer the ridiculous that channels Groucho Marx."

---

[53] Borrowed from *American Journalism Review* at http://www.ajr.org/Article.asp?id=4268

"It's almost as if every one of these town meetings is turning into the Jerry Springer Show."
—*Ed Schultz (2009)*

Big Eddie

Don't fall for the Joe Everyman persona of "Big Eddie." Belying his folksy charm and down-home good-ole-boy radio persona, Ed Schultz was actually born into an upper-middle class, well-educated family in Norfolk, Virginia. His father was an engineer, his mother an English teacher. After he graduated from high school, the younger Schultz accepted an athletic scholarship to Moorhead State University, a Division II college in Minnesota, where he achieved All-American honors as a quarterback.[54]

[54] Schultz keeps personal information about his formative years private; indeed, his website emphasizes only biographical information about his college years and beyond. Nothing about his somewhat privileged upbringing graces The Ed Schultz Show homepage. By omitting his place of birth and his parents' educational and professional background, the website implies that he is a stock Joe Midwesterner — a man of real men. Perhaps Schultz is aiming to avoid being typecast as an East Coast, limousine liberal, which would likely limit his national appeal as has been

Unfortunately, his brief career with the Winnipeg Bombers detonated prematurely when he could not adapt to the Canadian football rules. Fortunately for Schultz, he later found work as a play-by-play announcer and color commentator for North Dakota sports teams and eventually became an anchorman for WDAY in North Dakota.

Ed Schultz has perhaps the most eclectic interests of any of the pundits we are examining. He has acquired a private pilot's license, and engages in hunting, fishing, and golfing. Indeed, isn't it interesting that his pastimes seem calculated to attract both rural and upscale listeners, just as he combines a Liberal ideology (typical of the Northeast and West Coast) with a southern drawl?

One caveat is in order here: Published biographical information about Schultz, who fairly recently rose to national prominence, is scarce, so we are relying mainly on Schultz's Wikipedia entry, which appears to have been written or influenced by Schultz himself. For example, it describes Schultz as a "devoted family man" (though on his second marriage) and, in general, lavishes praise on him ("Why is the *Ed Schultz Show* hotter than a polar bear in Pensacola? Because ... he's a straight-talking, no-nonsense voice of reason in unreasonable times. While others preen and pontificate, Ed Schultz keeps the lines wide open for his listeners — making good on his boast that the *Ed Schultz Show* is Where America Comes to Talk. No radio talk show is as accessible ... ") Not exactly the most objective encyclopedia entry! In spite of this, we did manage to supplement the entry with some neutral details that we will describe as

---

the case with that other East Coast liberal, Alan Colmes, whose audience ratings are not as high as Schultz'.

necessary.

Schultz' improbable rise to national prominence—from a fairly obscure Fargo, North Dakota TV-radio personality to a host of his own show on MSNBC (the *Ed Show*), not to mention the highest ranked nationally syndicated Liberal talk show on radio, garnering three million listeners per week in 2007, according to *Talker's Magazine*—arguably began in 1992 when Schultz launched a regional talk show called *News and Views*, which was subsequently syndicated in other regions. Then in 2004, Democracy Radio and Jones Radio launched the *Ed Schultz Show* on two stations, which is now on over 100 stations nationwide.

What is the source of Ed Schultz's appeal? A combination of factors. Schultz combines an aw-shucks, folksy, Midwestern, blue-collar charm with a talent for ingratiating himself with the powerful (his was one of the few talk shows that Barack Obama appeared on when he was running for president). Also, as noted, he has the advantage of belying the usual stereotypes of a Liberal.

Whereas Alan Colmes, a New York Jew, fits that stereotype snuggly, Schultz is a former Conservative, a former jock, and a hunter-fisherman with a pseudo-Southern drawl. Thus, he may appeal to a broader audience at just the time when formerly iron-clad "red states" like North Carolina and Nevada are beginning to turn blue and open up to a broader spectrum of voices. Also appealing to a "red state" audience is the fact that Schultz is a small businessman himself as he owns a portion of the syndicate that airs his show. Thus, when he speaks of healthcare concerns, he sounds not like a Liberal ideologue, *á la* Colmes (who, echoing Michael Jackson's "Never-land," calls his website "Liberal-land") but someone at the "ground zero" of healthcare issues — an employer actually paying for his employees' healthcare. So, Schultz has credibility on the socioeconomics of, say, healthcare that many Liberals may lack.

In terms of host-audience rapport, Schultz tends to be kinder to his callers than Colmes is, rarely hanging up on callers or calling them names — perhaps because they tend to be more aligned with Schultz's left-of-center ideology. (Remember that since Colmes is the resident Liberal on what is otherwise a Conservative stable of Fox radio hosts, his callers tend to be conservative and thus more combative toward him.) Schultz shares *more* in common with MSNBC's Liberal host Keith Olbermann: Both have predominantly Liberal guests and callers and a background in sports broadcasting. But, unlike Olbermann, who has continued his sports commentary in addition to his *Countdown* news show, Schultz now focuses almost exclusively on political news. And, just as Schultz moved from sports journalism to political discourse, so he underwent a considerable ideological transformation.

He saw himself as an anti-tax, anti-big-government Republican in the mid-nineties, but says that after meeting his second wife Wendy, a psychiatric nurse who now produces his radio show, his views evolved, and he now views himself as a pro-union, pro-single-payer-healthcare Progressive.

Paralleling his move to the Left, his audience reach has become increasingly larger. From his modest beginnings in Fargo, he now operates out of New York City, being heard via XM radio's Air America and Serius Satellite's Left, and, as earlier noted, attracts several million audience members per week, making him the number one Liberal talk show host and, according to *Talkers Magazine*, ranked number five among radio talk show hosts in the country in 2007.

Additionally, he has won a number of journalistic awards, including three Eric Sevareid Awards (for highest ratings for a talk show in a large market), a Marconi Radio Award for News/Talk/Sports station of the year, and a Peabody Award.

Despite the critical recognition, Schultz's career, like those of Olbermann's and O'Reilly's, is not without controversy. As a play-by-play announcer in North Dakota, Schultz was suspended for calling a hockey coach "a jerk" and "bush league." He also created ill-will when he disparaged the mascot of the University of North Dakota Fighting Sioux football team while he was play-by-play announcer for the team. As a consequence, in an article in *Sports Illustrated* in 2004, he was voted second only to Brett Favre as North Dakota's "Enemy of the State."[55]

Schultz has published one book, *Straight Talk from the Heartland*, in 2004, and given the unvarnished remarks he gave that endangered his job status, he does seem to value plain spoken-ness. He seems to pattern his image and book title after O'Reilly's and the latter's "No-spin Zone." We can infer both strive to appeal to angry and/or skeptical audiences that feel they have been mislead or lied to by the national media. This is a clever tack for a progressive seeking cross-over appeal. His listeners can see him either as an antidote to the rightwing bias of Fox News or as a moderate Midwesterner who counter-balances the oft-alleged Leftwing bias of the national media. By contrast, Colmes' only book, *Red, White & Liberal: How Left Is Right & Right Is Wrong*, does not presume the public's distrust of the media. Thus, it is not surprising in a time of economic turmoil and public

---

[55] See Wikipedia for more details

anger that Schultz, whose book title reflects that public cynicism, appears to be more popular than Colmes, who seems oblivious to the widespread public cynicism. For a sampling of the public's diverging reactions to Schultz, please see Appendix E.

BIG ED'S ENGINE

Schultz's show is structured much as Colmes' — with many callers, a guest or two per hour and, unlike Limbaugh and Hannity, not much of a monologue. Yet, despite his claim that his show features hardly any call screening, he rarely seems to have a Conservative caller, leading one to believe that either Conservatives don't call the show, or that the screening is more rigorous than he lets on. Two more differences from Colmes' show are worth noting.

First, whereas Colmes' show limits calls to ten to twenty seconds, Schultz's draws the callers out with probing questions, often using callers' stories to expand on larger points. For example, recently a caller complained that he could not acquire healthcare coverage because of a pre-existing medical condition. Schultz spent a minute or two discussing the caller's plight then used the caller as an example of why Congress should pass a healthcare plan that prohibits insurance companies from denying coverage for those with pre-existing conditions. So, Schultz seems to have a well-conceived game plan for handling callers while Colmes sticks to the more scatter-shot, impromptu approach.

The second difference involves their attitudes toward sports. While Colmes is indifferent to sports, Schultz, a former jock, will sometimes engage in minutes-long digressions on football or golf (his son, as he often boasts, is on the professional golf tour). So, the structure of his show is not as tight as Hannity's or Limbaugh's — or even Colmes' rapid-fire conversations. Yet, these periodic digressions may actually be shrewd rhetorical maneuvers. As his enthusiastic references to sports may belie the image of an East Coast intellectual, *a la* the sports-indifferent Colmes, Schultz's show can appeal to a stereotypical Midwesterner, and he can cast himself as having conventional family values. These allusions to sports may also add some lightheartedness to what otherwise may seem too serious and ideological a show. While Conservatives might be more sports-oriented, broaching sports is a shrewd means of identifying with Conservatives resistant to his Liberal ideology.

And calling himself "a shameless self-promoter," he frequently plays his own comments on a recent cable TV show or encourages the audience to watch him on an upcoming cable show — which begs the question of why he can't simply make those points anew on live radio? Does this redundant practice speak of some underlying insecurity?

In contrast with this ironic redefinition of a Conservative icon, Schultz's only published book, *Straight Talk from the Heartland*, seems patterned on O'Reilly's "No Spin" USP. In both Schultz and O'Reilly, the explicit emphasis is not on ideology, but on Midwestern plain-spokenness which itself has become a kind of ideology. Thus, in an age turned off by ideology and partisanship, it is not surprising that O'Reilly and Schultz enjoy higher ratings than does Colmes.

At last, despite his efforts to present 'straight talk', Schultz does appear to observe the demands of Democratic Party. A February 2, 2010, broadcast illustrates our point.

Schultz opens the show with suspense and drama, thanking Norman Goldman for guest-hosting this past Thursday and then explaining that he (Schultz) had been on special assignment to the White House and couldn't host for part of that day. Then he explains that he met in the White House basement with David Axelrod and several other operatives where Axelrod scolded him for being too hard on the Administration — whereupon Schultz appeared to do exactly what Axelrod wanted: Mr. Obama's bidding. Schultz presented the Administration's perspective uncritically — praising the State of the Union address, explaining how the Administration says it hasn't given up on healthcare reform, how the public option is still on the table — it was almost as if Obama's press secretary were doing the talking.

Such a display of "carrying the President's water" (a phrase Limbaugh used to describe how he'd been carrying water for the Bush Administration a few years ago) served several purposes for Schultz: (a) it shows his national audience that he is an influential pundit whose words can impact on the Administration; (b) it shows, conversely, that he now intends (at least for the moment) to be on his "best behavior" from the Administration's perspective, (c) it shows that he has access to the White House (which he described in great detail, noting that the floor he was on seemed like a shrine to Obama, with dozens of pictures of Obama and his family on the walls, but he added that it was really good that Obama's staff has such warm feelings for him that they would put up so many pictures. Note Schultz's assumption that it was the staff's decision to create the shrine-like atmosphere).

From Schultz's assessment of his White House experience, it may appear as though the Administration wants

Schultz to act more like a propagandist than a pundit. What's less clear is whether he plans to do so indefinitely.

"The 'shut up' line has happened only once in six years."

—Bill O'Reilly [2002]

Bill O'

Like Madonna, Cher, or Charo, Bill O' has achieved international diva-like status and is widely recognized simply by his first name. Yet, his reputation may be based on a false premise. Bill O' consistently attempts to present himself as a sort of clever but crusty down-to-earth friend of the working man. Indeed, his book *Who's Looking Out for You?* implies that he can empathize with the little guy, while one of his other books, *Culture Warrior*, implies his opposition to the elitist elements in American society. His no-spin motto, too, suggests that he alone levels with the average Joe Sixpack about how things really are.

Yet, O'Reilly's own background reflects the very elitism he rails against, belying his carefully cultivated working-class persona. The son of an oil company accountant, O'Reilly grew up on Long Island, attended Catholic schools and pricy Marist

College in Poughkeepsie, and went on to spend his junior year abroad at the upper-crust University of London. The studious O'Reilly also holds graduate degrees in broadcast journalism from Boston College and in Public Administration from that bastion of east coast elitism, Harvard's Kennedy School of Government. So much for his anti-elitist bona fides.

Prior to his mega-star status at Fox News, the ambitious O'Reilly experienced his share of journalistic setbacks and triumphs. In the 1970s, he worked as a reporter at a variety of TV news outlets in such places as Scranton, Pennsylvania; Dallas, Texas; and Denver, Colorado. In 1980, he was given his own program on WCBS-TV in New York, and did well enough to be promoted to the national network as a CBS News correspondent, where he covered the wars in El Salvador and the Falkland Islands.[56]

Thereafter, O'Reilly became a correspondent for *ABC World News Tonight*, and in 1989, he was hired as a senior correspondent and back-up anchor by the nationally syndicated tabloid/gossip show *Inside Edition*, where he soon became anchor. Yet, he was abruptly replaced as anchor in 1995 — which ironically may have been his serendipitous break. For O'Reilly, who then earned a quick Master's from Harvard, was therefore available a couple of years later when Roger Ailes was

---

[56] According to Wikipedia, O'Reilly left his CBS news position after a dispute in which fellow correspondent Bob Schieffer used footage shot by O'Reilly's crew without crediting O'Reilly or the crew. O'Reilly later wrote a novel depicting a television reporter who exacts murderous revenge on his network colleagues after a similar dispute. Might this be a sign that O'Reilly, publishing the novel some 15 years after the Schieffer incident, does not forget slights very easily? Anyone who still doubts that O'Reilly is wired very tightly should see the variety of clips that show his meltdowns over the decades, most notably his *Inside Edition* eruption over a mal-functioning teleprompter.

looking for a seasoned journalist to anchor a new show on the then-startup Fox News Channel.

O'Reilly's career hasn't been without controversy. Perhaps the most famous incident involves a sexual harassment complaint filed against O'Reilly by former *O'Reilly Factor* producer Andrea Mackris, who accused him of making sexually explicit phone calls, including a "vile and degrading monologue about sex." Eventually, O'Reilly and Fox News agreed to pay Mackris an undisclosed sum — said to be in the millions of dollars by the *Washington Post* — and the charges were dropped. Yet, the event certainly casts O'Reilly's family-friendly persona — burnished by his best-selling children's book — and his penchant for black-and-white moralizing in a new light. While it is true that he has co-authored two children's books (*Kids are Americans Too: A Survival Guide for American Families* and *The O'Reilly Factor for Kids*), one wonders how can a self- proclaimed expert on the American family can write about proper parental role models while reaching a multimillion-dollar settlement in a sexual harassment suit?

O'Reilly has also had highly publicized disputes with many Liberal personalities, including Jon Stewart, Phil Donahue, Richard Dawkins, Bill Maher, Bill Moyers, George Clooney, Eminem, Rosie O'Donnell, Barney Frank, and many others. He is also considered the basis for Stephen Colbert's pompous Conservative persona on "the Colbert Report," which is essentially a shrewd parody of O'Reilly's show. Yet, these controversies, much like those that have beset David Letterman, have not hurt O'Reilly, who now has more viewers than ever, according the Nielsen Ratings featured on

TVbythenumbers.com.[57]

Ideologically, O'Reilly has been somewhat dis- ingenuous, which perhaps has likely enabled him to attract a politically diverse audience. According to Wikipedia, he has long claimed that he does not identify with a particular political party, but the *New York Daily News* reported on Dec. 6, 2000, that he had been registered as a Republican in the state of New York since 1994. In response, O'Reilly explained that New York ballots provide no option to register as an Independent, but it turns out that the form *does* contain a box that reads: "I do not wish to enroll in a party." About two-thirds of O'Reilly's audience members identify themselves as Conservatives, compared to 24% Moderates and only 3% Liberals.[58] For a sampling of the public's reactions to O'Reilly, please see Appendix F.

B. O's Theatrics

Although O'Reilly is best known for his eponymous *Factor*, he has actually excelled in four media formats: television, radio, newspapers, and books (fiction and nonfiction). *The O'Reilly Factor*, originally named *The O'Reilly Report*, began in 1996 and is now the highest rated show on cable TV. Meanwhile, O'Reilly's radio show has 3.26 million listeners and is carried by more than 400 stations. O'Reilly is rated as the 11th most important talk show host in the country, according to *Talker's*

---

[57] From September to October 15th 2009, ratings for both commentators have been trending upwards, approximately 20 to 25% (about 3 million to 3.5 million) for O'Reilly and 20 to 50% (about 1 million to 1.5 million) for Olbermann.

[58] Further details of audience demographics can be found at http://people-press.org/report/?pageid=834

Magazine, the talk radio industry publication, and as the 2nd most important host in the nation, according to *NewsMax*, a Conservative internet news site. O'Reilly also contributes to a syndicated weekly newspaper column carried in many newspapers, and he has authored or coauthored eight books, including several best-sellers. In addition, the 60-year-old New Yorker has earned a couple of Emmys, an award for his investigative journalism, and various other awards.

Despite his successes in these other media, most people associate O'Reilly with his cable television show, *The O'Reilly Factor* — the most successful talk show in the history of cable. The show is taped in the late afternoon and airs at 8:00 PM eastern time. It is an ideal time of day for a show that presents blunt black-and-white reasoning with fiery editorials. Many of his viewers have just come home from work an hour or two earlier and may seek out a show that on the one hand demands little from them intellectually and on the other allows them to vent some pent up tension vicariously through O'Reilly's daily diatribes. Consider this illustrative fulmination from a 2005 *O'Reilly Factor* broadcast:

> If I'm the president of the United States, I walk right into Union Square, I set up my little presidential podium, and I say, 'Listen, citizens of San Francisco, if you vote against military recruiting, you're not going to get another nickel in federal funds. Fine. You want to be your own country? Go right ahead. And if Al Qaeda comes in here and blows you up, we're not going to do anything about it. We're going to say, look, every other place in America is off limits to you, except San Francisco. You want to blow up the Coit Tower? Go ahead!' (Bill O'Reilly, after San Francisco voted to ban military recruiters from city schools, Nov. 8, 2005)

Another of his observations reflects his penchant for scoring cheap political points at the expense of important international institutions.

> I just wish Katrina had only hit the United Nations building, nothing else, just had flooded them out, and I wouldn't have rescued them. (Bill O'Reilly, on his radio show, Sept. 14, 2005)

Consider the implications of this irresponsible statement. With his influential perch (bully pulpit?) at Fox News, he is essentially rooting for the deaths of thousands of UN employees whose mission is to prevent another world war and alleviate poverty worldwide. In addition, he is channeling the memory of the 9/11 attacks, in this case advocating, Osama-like, the wholesale destruction of another New York edifice filled with innocent people, and inciting the latent xenophobia of many in his Fox News audience.[59] Despite statements such as these, it is still difficult to situate O'Reilly in a single political camp.

More recently, the bombastic host made a rather notable policy pronouncement on a recent show: he supports the creation of a government-managed healthcare plan if it provides working Americans with an affordable option to other private insurance plans. He is somewhat unpredictable compared to his more orthodox Republican colleagues, Limbaugh and Hannity. That is, O'Reilly's stance sometimes leans according to the political winds. For example, as the so-called "public option" polls increasingly well in national surveys, O'Reilly, not wanting to alienate his fairly diverse audience, jumps onto the bandwagon

---

[59] That he is so popular in spite of — or perhaps even because of — such xenophobic comments indicates *ipso facto* that his audience shares or at least condones his xenophobic ideas.

and supports the public option.

Yet from another perspective, O'Reilly is once again demonstrating his willingness to challenge his employer, in this case opposing the Conservative (Fox-centric) party line on a public option opposed not just by all of Fox's opinion shows but by every Republican in the Senate and the House. It should be noted, though, that O'Reilly chooses to offer tentative support for the option precisely at a time when he declares the option politically dead, so that he has little to lose by supporting a policy that has become, at least in his mind, purely hypothetical. As evidence for our claim, we offer the following exchange borrowed from O'Reilly's *Factor* between O'Reilly and the Heritage Foundation's Nina Owcharenko:

O'REILLY: The public option now is done. We discussed this, it's not going to happen. But you say that this little marketplace that they're going to set up, whereby the federal government would subsidize insurance for some Americans, that is, in your opinion, a public option?

OWCHARENKO: Well, it has massive new federal regulation. So you don't necessarily need a public option if the federal government is going to control and regulate the type of health insurance that Americans can buy.

O'REILLY: But you know, I want that, Ms. Owcharenko. I want that. I want, not personally for me, but for working Americans, to have a option, that if they don't like their health insurance, if it's too expensive, they can't afford it, if the government can cobble together a cheaper insurance policy that gives the same benefits, I see that as a plus for the folks.[60]

The sketches we've drawn of the pundits and their varied approaches to propping up their party would not be complete without references to those key figures who protect them — the undervalued but indispensible screeners.

[60] For more, see DailyKos' Jed Lewison at http://www.huffingtonpost.com/2009/09/17/bill-oreilly-backs-public_n_2906508.html

The Paradox of Putative Politeness

When we glance at them as though we were tourists, totalitarian societies may seem gentle and harmonious, but only because, as outsiders, we don't see the secret police and censors that enforce the social harmony appearing on the surface. So, in a sense, with certain talk shows. Here, the censors are call screeners who can eliminate dissonant voices, ensuring that the callers are almost always friendly since, of course, any subversive call will disrupt the "social order" of the airwaves. This reliance on screening leads to what we term the Paradox of Putative Politeness.

Alan Colmes, for example, can appear extremely brisk and impolite to many, if not most, of his audience members, yet this perception is inversely proportional to how accessible he is to his hostile callers. Indeed, the theme of the show, not so unlike his tenure on *Hannity & Colmes*, is his palpable frustration with the unceasing flow of hostile callers from the Neo-conservative camp. The collision of ideologies combined with Colmes' frustration with the consequent disharmony of the dialogues make for rather entertaining radio, yet Colmes comes off as an off-putting, overly emotional, often rude host — precisely because he employs so little call screening and, thus, receives more hostile calls than any of the other hosts we examined.

We find Colmes' approach entirely commendable. While the other five hosts are preaching mainly to their ideological choirs and changing hardly any minds, Colmes largely reaches precisely the audience he needs to persuade. The result is a much rockier rhetorical road, but that road also reflects the true diversity of opinion in that melting pot we call America — if you'll pardon the mixed metaphors. Conversely, the other five hosts create an ideological pressure cooker they dare not burst.

For example, Rush Limbaugh is even-tempered and congenial with his callers — precisely because his call screener, Mr. Snerdley, employs a fairly tight filter, allowing mainly those callers whose views connect with or reflect Limbaugh's. Recall the example discussed earlier from Shaquelle who claimed that Colmes' call screener is far more lenient than Limbaugh's or the other Conservative hosts'. Yet rarely do we see behind the curtain of the Great and Powerful Radio Oz. Instead, we see only the surface effect — the host behaving graciously to his many adoring callers.

Except for Colmes. Indeed, ironically, Colmes tends to complain on air to his producer about how open his call screening policy is and rhetorically questions whether he should alter the policy. The question itself creates a noteworthy parallel between Colmes' customary irritation and Democracy itself: Fascist and Communist societies often appear, on the surface, to be much more cohesive and orderly than do Democratic ones.

The trains ran on time in Mousillini's Italy, and, from our perspective, Kim's Democratic People's Republic of Korea appears very smooth running right now, with virtually no public dissent over the difficult socioeconomic conditions. Contrast these features of social compliance and business-like efficiency with the ever-present frustration shown in the United States Congress, where the Democrats and Republicans appear in a constant tug of war that makes any real progress on solving, say, healthcare issues or the banking crises highly unlikely.

Nevertheless, at the very least, we can witness two or more contrasting points of view in a Democracy (and with Colmes), and it is this messy interplay of opposing ideas that makes Democracy (and his show) superior to the Stalinistic uniformity of, say, Communist North Korea, or Rush Limbaugh's show. In other words, precisely because no political issue ever gets solved on Colmes' show — the Right and Left are in constant cut-throat conflict — his show's political stalemate mirrors that of, say, the United States Senate. Yet, at least all sides generally receive a fair hearing and a fair invitation to be heard. As Donald Rumsfeld so aptly observed, despite his penchant for sophistry, "Democracy is messy." [61] But only Colmes' show strives to embody this process in all of its glorious messiness.

---

[61] It should be noted that Rumsfeld used this quote not to justify acrimonious arguments in a democratic body but to shrug off the rampant corruption then plaguing Iraq's incipient democratic institutions in the aftermath of the toppling of Saddam Hussein's autocratic régime.

UNCOMMONALITIES

Notwithstanding the apparent differences in filtering calls, other interesting contrasts abound. For example, all of the pundits, except Colmes, have a sports background, with O'Reilly and Schultz actually playing professionally — a semi-professional baseball pitcher and a Canadian football quarterback respectively — and Olbermann, who published numerous articles on sports-card-collecting as an adolescent has gone on to spend more than twenty years in sports broadcasting and commentary. This may partly explain why only Colmes, who has professed complete ignorance of sports, brooks dissent.

A team tends to enforce conformity, all the way down to the mandatory uniformity in its uniforms. Hence, the five pundits with sports backgrounds [62] all create essentially dissent-free programs. In most cases, the "game plan" is hatched and controlled by the "coach," and those who disagree or digress either don't make the cut (are screened out) or are benched, that is to say cut off by the hosts, or chewed out (brow-beaten). By contrast, Colmes never has a game plan, lets the "players" control the first part of the game, and endures ample doses of dissent daily. This may explain why Colmes' ideologically diverse listeners, as Shaquelle had indicated, seem to tune in to be entertained while the more partisan listeners who patronize the other five pundits' shows may do so for ideological reinforcement.

With the exception of Colmes and Olbermann, most of the hosts cultivate a blue-collar persona that belies their elitist upbringing. Limbaugh, as noted earlier, grew up in an

---

[62] While Limbaugh didn't play sports, he worked as a sports announcer with the Kansas City Royals and as a commentator ESPN.

upper-middle-class, lawyer-laden family (his brother, father, uncle and grandfather were all lawyers). By contrast, Olbermann and Colmes each seem to pride themselves on their erudition and may appear to be effete elitists to their neutral viewers/callers, not to mention to the Conservative hosts, who often ridicule the affluent East Coast punditocracy. Which is certainly ironic.[63]

Indeed, although all of the Conservative pundits we're studying disparage the "elitist" lifestyle, Hannity and O'Reilly grew up and currently live or work in New York, while Limbaugh has or had an apartment in New York (he's been threatening to leave New York because his taxes are rising). Limbaugh also smokes cigars and has a passion for golf — not the most blue-collar sport! Furthermore, all of the hosts are extremely wealthy, Limbaugh, Hannity, and O'Reilly being at the top of the media food chain and very likely living in the lap of luxury.

Yet unlike many prominent fat cats, e.g. the Bushes, the Kennedys, and the Gores, all six of our pundits, except perhaps for Hannity, achieved their national prominence and personal affluence relatively late in life, with Schultz gaining his national talk show after he'd passed age 50. Even O'Reilly was about 40 when he became the host of *Inside Edition*. Limbaugh was close to forty before he received a national show.

That Limbaugh was something of late-bloomer sharply contrasts with the relative precociousness of O'Reilly, Colmes, Olbermann, and Schultz. As we have earlier noted, O'Reilly and Colmes enjoyed academic success with Colmes graduating high school at sixteen and O'Reilly attending the prestigious

---

[63] For example, Colmes frequently alludes to the 'elite' *New York Times* while Olbermann reads scripts with exceptional speed interspersed with sesquipedalian terms. Olbermann also quotes noted philosophers, past and present, and other distinguished figures.

University of London. Olbermann published articles while barely in his teens and later graduated from Cornell. Schultz is also a university graduate. Then, there's Limbaugh. While surrounded by a family of distinguished lawyers, Rush failed to finish junior college and couldn't sustain steady employment until well after his formative years. When he finally achieves center stage, he appears very unwilling to share the spotlight with anyone else. [64]

By contrast, Colmes relies more on gimmicks and banter with his producer and screener. For example, he has an occasional feature, as we've noted earlier, called "Sudden Death," in which callers can be cut off suddenly for any reason by Colmes and cohorts. In light of Colmes' fairly heavy reliance on guests, gimmicks, and caller-driven agendas, we can conclude that (a) Colmes is clearly more impromptu than Limbaugh. As befitting his stand-up comedian background, Colmes seems to enjoy the serendipitous interactions between himself and his audience. And, (b) Colmes is more comfortable than Limbaugh is in sharing the stage. (Remember that Colmes became nationally famous as the other half of Hannity.)

Besides their financial transformations and the ways they choose to shine in the limelight, some of the hosts changed ideologically as well. Of the six commentators, Schultz and O'Reilly have grown beyond their ideological roots — Schultz, heretofore an anti-tax Conservative, becoming more Liberal after meeting his current wife, a psychiatric nurse, and O'Reilly, a rather nonpartisan journalist, becoming more identifiably Conservative

---

[64] Indeed, might this desire to shine exclusively also explain why none of his three marriages has worked out? After all, he appears to be blissfully wedded to his daily show and, thus, the spotlight it shines on him — and only him.

after leaving network TV for Fox News.[65] As for Olbermann, since he had a sports broadcasting background, his ideological views were not widely known until he began his Liberal TV talk show.[66] Yet, his views were certainly surprising since the stereotype of a white male sports guy, particularly one who delivers football commentary, is of a red state Conservative.

Another surprise exhibited by some of our pundits is between their public personas as John Wayne tough guys and their professional spinelessness. Hannity and Limbaugh tend to present themselves as straight-talking shoot-from-the-hip iconoclasts who like to stir up a hornet's nest of controversy, yet ironically they exhibit poodle-like obedience to their pay-masters. There is no public record of controversy between Limbaugh and Hannity and their bosses; indeed, Limbaugh has worked for the same employer for twenty years while Hannity has worked harmoniously for Fox News for the past twelve. To our present knowledge, neither Limbaugh nor Hannity has criticized his employer.

By contrast, O'Reilly and Olbermann not only specialize in controversy on the air, but seem most comfortable in a contested relationship with their bosses. Indeed, Olbermann has quit a number of shows and compounded matters by

---

[65] It could be that O'Reilly has always been conservative, indeed even alleged to have been registered as a Republican in New York for many years, but he maintained a neutral public persona until he joined Fox News. O'Reilly was employed for many years as a network journalist striving for ideological neutrality.

[66] It is true that Olbermann did have an earlier news show on MSNBC called *The Big Show with Keith Olbermann*, but to our present knowledge, this show did not lean Right of Left ideologically, but reflected a neutral perspective. Olbermann was employed as a sports journalist for many years as a sports commentator, so his concern was not political.

subsequently slamming his former employers. Similarly, as we footnoted earlier, O'Reilly left CBS in a huff over its airing of footage from O'Reilly's camera crew while failing to credit O'Reilly's contributions. The result of O'Reilly's ire was not a verbal airing of grievances, like Olbermann's, but a literary one.

Ed Schultz, too, has not avoided controversy with his bosses. As a substitute host on a Minneapolis-based sports talk show, he is noted for calling the head coach of the Sioux hockey team a "jerk" and "Bush League" and was suspended for two weeks.[67] Colmes, on the other hand, tends to defend his employer Fox News, even after he quit *Hannity & Colmes*. When his occasional Liberal callers criticize his employer, Colmes generally rushes to the network's defense. For example, he has argued that there is a strict division between Fox's new anchors and their opinionated hosts and that the former are scrupulously fair and balanced.[68]

Neither Hannity nor Limbaugh is anxious to challenge his corporate boss and thus endanger his lucrative salary. While it is true that Limbaugh was fired by ESPN, he wasn't fired for challenging management but for questioning whether Donovan McNabb was purposely over-rated by the media who, Limbaugh claims, were rooting for a black quarterback to succeed. Conversely, Olbermann, O'Reilly and, to a lesser extent, Schultz seem more willing to challenge their bosses. Inspired by the examples of the latter three pundits, we decided to challenge all four radio hosts "on their own turf" so that we could complement

---

[67] For more details, see http://en.allexperts.com/e/e/ed/ed_shultz.htm

[68] It should be acknowledged that Colmes did finally have the chutzpah to quit his presumably lucrative and stable position as the apparent milquetoast Mr. Bill of *Hannity & Colmes* — thus finally showing some spine and integrity.

our more detached, analytical approach with a more spontaneous and participatory method. We thus turned to that most technologically sophisticated of communication devices, the telephone.

"So, you want the first word?"
—*Alan Colmes' screener (2010)*

TALK-RADIO SCREENS

Since we critiqued the members of the punditocracy from our offices in Japan and had conjectured that their methods of call screening are largely part of the control of the discourse they feel they need to wield, we knew that we also had to mount a calling campaign to test our theory. After all, as Anderson Cooper famously observed in a promo for his news show, it's not enough to simply sit on a set and report the story. You have to see it, feel it, touch it. So inspired, we wanted not merely to report second-hand on our pundits' call-screening processes but to experience them first-hand, so to speak. So, in the misty early morning hours of January 13, 2010, toting a bandolier of two freshly ground bags of potent Starbucks java, we scaled the locked iron gates of our local campus and made our way to the office where the calls soon commenced. Since we are in Japan and fourteen hours ahead of the East Coast of America from where all of the shows broadcast, we had to employ a pre-dawn vertical insertion onto the campus quad. Unlike the heroic preliminaries in our initial nighttime assault, the actual calling process was interminably boring and frustrating, but certainly necessary.

We had also taken some inspiration from Paul Cartledge who suggested that whether we are historians, philosophers or just plain citizens, we are all interested in better understanding the political process, the negotiation of concepts and their implementation in practice (2009, pp. 6-7). Call screeners, we determined, are a significant part of that process. To try to determine which screeners practiced the most democratic and anti-democratic approaches to the discourse, we devised one question (1. below) that we thought would challenge the Conservative host and another (2. below) that we felt would do the same for the Liberal.

1. Isn't 'Dingy' Harry Reed, actually, right in asserting that there is a racial hierarchy in America? No matter how smart you are, if you sound 'Ebonic,' you are not going to be taken seriously by the establishment—George Will himself said as much on Sunday. It's this reality, which is probably a relic of 200 years of slavery, that is the *real issue*, not the clumsy way Reid worded it. Similarly, Reed is right that color matters. Would Colin Powell have been taken seriously as a presidential candidate had he been a few shades darker? Would Halle Berry be considered the sexiest woman in America if she were a couple degrees deeper in color?

2. To the Liberal hosts, we put the following questions: Obama promised that if we passed a stimulus package, this would lower the unemployment rate that was then about 8%. Now it's over 10%. This is one of many promises he's broken from his others to televise the Congressional healthcare debates on C-SPAN to his promise to accept campaign spending limits to his promise to close Guantanamo, etc. If he's broken all of those promises, why should we trust his current promises not to raise taxes for the healthcare plan and to start returning the troops from Afghanistan in 2011? It seems to me that Obama was what Barbara Streisand was singing about in the song "Promises, Promises"! We can trust this man with our hard-earned tax dollars?

Limbaugh Screening

As we'd expected, several tedious efforts to Limbaugh's show were necessary before we could break through the lines. Limbaugh's producer/screener, Bo Snerdley (James Golden), was engaging but businesslike, asking for name, the nature of the call, and the city and state from where we were calling. After we offered "University Heights, Ohio" as the city name,[69] we then heard typing in the background, followed by a half-minute pause. It is possible, we later reasoned, that the typing and the pause were part of an effort to determine which region of the American

[69] We submitted University Heights, Ohio, as the city and state for the originating region during the screening process because we had imagined that a call coming from Okinawa might be taken more expeditiously and Limbaugh himself might have construed the overseas call as implicit support from members of the US military. As a consequence, the wait was tremendously costly — over two hours on the phone at international rates.

map tended to be more sympathetic to Limbaugh's ideas and which region tended to be more hostile. Since University Heights, Ohio, is predominantly comprised of middle- to upper-middle class professionals, we inferred that our moderately challenging initial question was, nonetheless, acceptable to Mr. Snerdley who, thereupon, informed us to hold the line. (Of course, we could be entirely wrong about Mr. Snerdley's methods.)

As the live show was piped through the phone line, we were treated during each commercial break to a steady stream of propagandistic satires of Gore, Obama, and other assorted Democrats. These productions would seem to prime callers for hatred of Obama and the other public figures being lampooned. They might also serve to discourage especially the Liberals who, like everyone else, must endure as much as two hours of this 'entertainment' to finally talk to Limbaugh. Nonetheless, Snerdley periodically returned to the line to make sure we were still waiting and eventually said that we were next. As Limbaugh continued droning on and playing sound bites for nearly another hour, we noticed during the entire wait that he accepted only three or four other calls (the first one wasn't present — perhaps because the wait was so long). Ultimately, we held the line for approximately 130 minutes before we were finally able to pose our queries. Only a partial transcript is offered at Rush Limbaugh's site, the remaining details of which follow:

Rush: Barry in University Heights, Ohio. Hi, Barry, great to have you on the EIB Network.
Caller: Happy birthday.
Rush: Thank you, sir.
Caller: Rush, isn't 'Dingy' Harry Reid actually right in asserting

that there's a racial hierarchy in America? Isn't that the point that George Will made over the weekend? No matter how smart you are, if you sound Ebonic, you're not going to be accepted, you're not going to be taken seriously by the white establishment. Isn't that true?

Rush: Did George Will say that?

Caller: Sure did. He implied it.

Rush: I had the George Will sound bites yesterday and I didn't get to them. I read the transcript. I know he totally exonerated Harry Reid. He said there was nothing racist about what Harry Reid had said, but I didn't know he's said that about the black dialect or Ebonics.

Caller: The point is that Reid is only calling attention to a reality that I think what should alarm people is not the clumsy comments that Reid made but the reality that he was calling attention to, namely that there is a racial hierarchy and that you are judged according to how Ebonic you speak. And it goes for color as well. Think of Halle Berry, think of Colin Powell. Can you picture Colin Powell being as presidential material if he was much blacker? Or if Halle Berry was much darker, would she be considered as sexy as she is by society?

Rush: You know, you're asking the wrong guy because I don't think this way, and that's why Harry Reid's comments here kind of - you know -

Caller: But I'm saying that is in the sub-consciousness of our society, it's a relic of 200 years of slavery.

Rush: I don't know. Since you bring this up, are you a Democrat?

Caller: I'm an independent.

Rush: Democrat, okay. I'm thinking if what you say is true, how in the world is it that any American rap star is a multimillionaire?

There aren't enough black customers to make these guys as wealthy —

Caller: Well, because white people want to flatter themselves that they really are interested in the authentic black experience.

Rush: But then why wouldn't they vote for a rapper running for president if they agree with his policies?

Caller: Well, they will vote for —

Rush: You say they wouldn't because he doesn't sound white.

Caller: Voting for someone and listening to someone's music are two very different things. Because remember that historically we saw African-Americans as entertainers, not as politicians. We saw them as athletes —

Rush: Wait a minute, what is this 'we' business? You. You know, don't tar all the rest of us with this. You're basically saying that the country is still racist. That's what Harry Reid wants you to say.

A few points are worth elaborating about the conversations between the screener and the caller as well as between the host and the caller. We had theorized that since Limbaugh seems, on the surface, to be such a pathological control freak that the process of screening would itself suggest something about this suspected pathology. Of all the other screeners we met, Mr. Snerdley, by virtue of his own notoriety, represents yet another key obstruction that potential callers, critical of Limbaugh's views, must negotiate their way past. Mr. Snerdley brings to the screening process the notable weight and girth of his relative celebrity. Not to mention, Snerdley is perceived as cantankerous, typically appearing on the show to denounce the "Liberal establishment" for some alleged violation. Indeed, while we were waiting for our turn, Snerdley issued an on-air editorial, angrily condemning Harry Reid's controversial racial remarks. To even pose a question to Limbaugh, therefore, one must first bypass the institutional gravitas of producer and screener, Bo Snerdley. (By contrast, none of the other three call screeners had significant name recognition.)

Perhaps more momentous than the screening process itself is the editing process that seems to follow relatively challenging calls. Expunged from the call transcript posted at Limbaugh's website are key words that allude to the irony of Limbaugh's own narrow-minded past comments about a certain professional quarterback, which we had referenced earlier in this book. Missing from the transcript are the words: "not as quarterbacks" (uttered as a comparison to "athletes"). We infer from these missing words that we had been edited in one of two ways: Either the transcript does not accurately represent the actual call, or the connection was cut before the words could be uttered.

Cutting off callers is a useful editing device on air because neither callers nor audience members can really hear the 'click.' The host can cut in after cutting the connection to a caller, as Limbaugh has apparently done, and create the illusion of a genuine dialogue, and after the host has driven home his point, he can cut to a commercial. Our tacit acceptance of the imperatives of commercial radio reinforce our beliefs that callers float away into oblivion for good reason: talk shows must meet their obligations to sponsors. So, a cut phone line and some well-placed advertising can become functional filters for sifting out dissenting views.

At last, the racial hierarchy that Limbaugh denies exists in America, made all the more obvious by the myopic views of those who generally disparage the linguistic differences among some blacks and whites, is all the more ironic in light of the mocking comments that had gotten Limbaugh released from his duties at ESPN. The editing done for this particular record, or the call itself, seems to illustrate another kind of control that limits details that could potentially humble the host.

Hannity Screening

To Hannity's show, we were glad to find that our first effort produced a direct hit. The unnamed screener was friendly and engaging, asking the same questions as Bo Snerdley had — but probing more deeply to try to determine, it seemed, what side of the political divide we might be on. After we offered a short introduction of name and city, the questions turned immediately to the topic where we were asked to weigh in.

Caller: Yeah, isn't the esteemed Senator Dingy Harry actually correct in what he says that there is a racial hierarchy?
Screener: Hmmmm, so, do you think there is?
Caller: Well ...., yes.
Screener: Do you want to elaborate or ....
Caller: I mean, if you sound Ebonic, you are not going to be taken seriously ....
Screener: Interesting. Please wait, don't want to lose you.
Commercials: supportyourvet.org

An eighty-minute wait produced an opportunity to hear Hannity's latest diatribe against President Obama, sound bites of a debate between Martha Coakley and Scott Brown, assorted commercials and public service announcements, and a very lively argument between Stephen Smith, a New York commentator, and another black commentator on whether Reid was correct in his observations. After listening to the on-air Donnybrook, we heard what seemed to be a totally sincere but terse apology from Hannity's screener that he would not be taking our call, even though she identified us forty minutes earlier as next up to bat. Perhaps it was the very impassioned debate Hannity had hosted that left even him speechless, that drained his interest in continuing a discussion of the Senator Reid controversy.

Schultz Screening

As with our efforts to reach Hannity's show, a fortuitous opening in the phone line appeared upon our first try. The unnamed screener, like Hannity's, was exceptionally personable and engaging. Unlike Hannity's, though, he asked only the most basic surface questions.

Screener: Hi, would you like to talk to Ed?
Caller: Yes, sir.
Screener: What's your name?
Caller: Dan
Screener: Where are you calling from?
Caller: Japan.
Screener: Dan from Japan? Wow. What's your topic?
Caller: It's about the stimulus package and unemployment.
Screener: Please hold. (Full show piped through)

Commericals: Ed personally delivering commercials.
"Stop Repair Bills"

Screener: Dan, we're thirty seconds away, and you are the third caller. You're two calls away, okay buddy?

Commercials: Auto insurance, Aqua sonic; Life insurance, Matrix Direct; Weight loss regimens – Sensa (Approximately fifty minutes wait time.)

Schultz: Dan from Japan, you're on the Ed Schultz Show.

Caller: Hi Ed, great show. Say, Obama promised that if we passed a stimulus package, this would lower the unemployment rate that was then about 8%. Now it's over 10%. This is one of many promises he's broken from his others to televise the Congressional healthcare debates on C-SPAN to his promise to accept campaign spending limits to his promise to close Guantanamo, etc. If he's broken all of those promises, why should we trust his current promises not to raise taxes for the healthcare plan?

Just as all of the other professionals had done, Schultz expeditiously produced an answer to each opposing point. The tone in his phone voice, though, seemed such a paradoxical blend of earnest invitation and brute force that it produced a degree of respect and trepidation. When he is not passionately asserting his position in a grating tone, he sounds exceedingly sincere. Despite these impressions, a somewhat unsatisfactory answer containing vague references to the routine problems of government bureaucracy was given for the reason why the healthcare debates were not carried on C-SPAN.

Schultz certainly deserves some critical applause for, at least, desiring on the surface to approximate a truly democratic dialogue. Indeed, 'dialogue' may be his middle name. Under the surface of that apparent desire for discussion, though, there seems to wait the lingering threat of Schultz's passionate verbal virtuosity. Even a determined opposition to Schultz's take on the issues risks a severe retort.

Colmes Screening

Like our efforts to reach Limbaugh, Colmes' show required numerous attempts as well. When we finally broke through, we were greeted by a soft and inviting voice from which came the simplest query.

Screener: Alan Colmes' show, you want the first word?
Caller: Yes.
Screener: Please hold.
Music: Led Zeppelin track from *Houses of the Holy.*
Screener: Okay, just make sure you keep your radio off.
Caller: Right.
Music: The Who's "Magic Bus."
Screener: Okay you're next.
Colmes: Hello.
Caller: Alan, great show. Just a quick question. Mr. Obama promised that if we passed a stimulus package, this would lower the unemployment rate that was then about 8%. Now it's over 10%.
Colmes: Well, he also said, well actually, it was up to 10.2 which is now headed down. Secondly, he said it would take probably 'til mid-2010 for unemployment to start going down. Thank you.

A couple of points are worth noting about our encounter with *The Alan Colmes Show*. The music selections that listeners are treated to while holding the line represent similar efforts to those on Limbaugh's show, only less cynical. The period (late '60s, early '70s) from which these Rock classics come recalls a time of social upheaval when student idealism and activism ruled America's college campuses. This subtle priming may remind callers of the days when, say, Colmes himself came of age.

Although the entire encounter with *The Alan Colmes Show* was approximately twenty minutes in duration, and the short talk with Colmes himself only ten to fifteen seconds, we came away feeling enlivened by the utterly free ride into the mass airwaves. Here, beyond the sophistry, we found firsthand what we imagine the ancient Athenians enjoyed, a free public airing of diverging views. Colmes' screening process is essentially non-existent. In fact, the screener herself seems more like an inviting, unpretentious maître d' who welcomes guests into the forum of public discussion.

Commonalities

Concerning message control, Limbaugh seems to be Colmes' polar opposite. While Colmes has debates between opposing sides and interviews many opponents, Limbaugh doesn't seem to enjoy sharing the spotlight, even with his ideological allies. His method represents the ultimate message control — his is the only celebrity voice heard most of the time on his show. This makes him unique among the others we've studied, for all of the others routinely have one or more guests per hour. Why does Limbaugh appear to mostly exclude other voices?

Perhaps he feels that guests will take him "off topic," which is also why he sets a given day's discussion agenda and warns his callers to weigh in only on that given topic. A former Republican operative David Brock (2003) illustrated this point in his book, *Blinded by the Right*, when he shares an anecdote about how Limbaugh would apparently use others' scripts to frame issues that appeared to be commissioned by the Republican Party. For example, Limbaugh had received a fax co-written by David Brock (2003) designed to defend Clarence Thomas and bolster the chances of Newt Gingrich to gain political power (p. 261). Limbaugh, then, read the fax virtually verbatim. It appears from Brock's book that Limbaugh did not credit the three authors but read the script as though he were extemporizing. Thus, if Limbaugh is receiving his talking points from Republican operatives, that would explain why he takes so few calls and insists on a narrow message focus, at least on Monday through Thursday.

A more Freudian explanation may be that Limbaugh's own life seemed to lack direction and structure early on, as he was not a good high school student and dropped out of junior college. So it is not surprising that finally given a chance to control not only his own destiny but also a national program, he seeks to exert maximum control. Yet Limbaugh himself would probably argue that he exerts such control not for any Freudian reason but because control works — his show is the most popular on political talk radio, and he now has considerable influence within the Republican Party. Why jeopardize these feats by letting his callers drive much of the show?

Having developed a catalog of descriptions for our pundits and their programs, we offer a review of what seems to be either an overlooked or somewhat underappreciated basic element of meaning — the use of color in certain hosts' propagandizing techniques. We will frame our talk of colors, and other related appeals, with what are known to be their psychological effects on the emotions, since certain colors have lately provoked a range of irrational observations. We'll take an unusual tack, too, by suggesting that efforts in propagandizing ideologies can also be understood in terms of marketing.

Part III.
Buying Idea Brands

"Advertising is the art of making whole lies out of half truths."

—*Edgar A. Shoaff*

IDEOLOGIES & NAME RECOGNITION

Part of the manufacturing and marketing of goods and services involves branding. If we find certain consumer brands attractive or useful, we, of course, tend or want to buy them. But, we may also do the same with various brands of ideologies. In his seminal work, *Reality in Advertising* (1961), Rosser Reeves illustrates what the term "brand" actually means to advertisers and to consumer cultures. In order to realize success in the marketplace, corporations tout the exceptional qualities of their products so as to underscore their product's distinct value when it is time to move the product into the market for mass consumption. Reeves points out that a brand must communicate a "unique selling proposition" (USP), a certain set of qualities that helps establish a conceptual category of distinctiveness that people may easily identify with, accept and, thus, buy into.

Reeves further observes that advertisements should communicate propositions not just in words, product puffery, or show-window advertising. Each advertisement must say to each audience member, "Buy this product, and you will get this specific benefit." The proposition must be one that the competition either cannot, or does not, offer. It must be unique — either a uniqueness of the brand or a claim not otherwise made in that particular field of advertising. The proposition must be so strong that it can move the mass millions (1961, p. 4).

It must also be noted that tied to the process of branding is the power inherent in the company that confers the brand name with the aim, of course, of creating and preserving the product's positive image. How is power, in this case, connected to communicating a USP and preserving the necessary public image? Power affords individuals or institutions openings in the mass market or public discourse to create new conceptual categories of right vs. wrong, in vs. out, on vs. off, etc. Power affords opportunities to define or redefine the product or ideology in light of the new categories. In contemporary consumer cultures, this approach to controlling the image and preparing the product for the mass market requires a kind of reasoning that intersects with, indeed is aided by, black-and-white thought processes.

Certainly, the sorts of pundits whose work we have so far discussed are not trying to sell the public anything in the literal, classical sense. We are not asked as audience members to exchange our hard-earned money for some durable or disposable product. However, what we *are* buying in the figurative sense, through the level of attention we give them, are ideologies, which enter the market in some ways like goods and services do. Particular political points of view, for example, with their accompanying messages about their importance, relevance, and legitimacy appear, much like effective soft-sell advertisements, as part of the national discourse.

That is to say, like the strategies used in product placement, ideologues attempt to *subtly* influence audience members to embrace particular ideologies that may even conflict with their own material interests. Ronald Reagan, for example, was skilled in using American exceptionalist language to attract trade union support for policies that, consequently, undermined the power and interests of those very unions. Rush Limbaugh, likewise, uses American exceptionalist language to attract working class support for tax policies that drain the very educational funding necessary for upward mobility.

With so many products, services, and opinions brought to us through so many media and presenting us with so many choices to make about their utility and value, we may sometimes develop the sensation that we are simply wading in viscous vats of (dis)information. Advertisers, nonetheless, fulfill an important role in reducing a product's complex features into clear bite-sized denominators of information, which helps us to make supposedly informed choices about what to buy and what not to. Black-and-white advertising techniques make it much easier for us to choose one thing over another.

There are automobiles, and then there are BMWs. There is mayonnaise, and then there is Hellmann's. There are hamburgers, and then there are Wendy's. There are the generic products, and then there are all the other distinctive brands. In some positive ways, though, we may *think* that this sort of simplified promotion of product brands can assist us as consumers to distinguish more expeditiously between the quality we may want or need and the cheaper imitations we can just afford. But, can we afford to pay attention to everything?

It may be fairly easy to infer from Reeves' work that advertising is a kind of fine art. Advertising is, in essence, part of a highly refined skill at fitting a USP into the minds of consumers in the most cost-effective ways. This is a place where advertising and propagandizing techniques meet. Though four to five specific methods used to improve ad effectiveness are generally recognized, two are worth calling attention to here: (a) be consistent in standing by a strong, solitary claim so as to avoid diluting the strength of your core intent; and (b) avoid visual gimmickry that calls more attention to itself than the intended message.

Of what relevance, though, is the USP to the argument that corporate institutions and their agents view the general public more as collections of consumers than critically thoughtful and active participants in the key affairs of the republic? Recent research, mostly in the social sciences, has helped confirm what many citizens have likely already suspected about themselves. We are all targets of propaganda. In clarifying the troubling intersection of politics and the marketing of goods and ideas, Norman Fairclough (2001) observes in *Language and Power* that advertising itself has

> ... made people into consumers i.e. has brought about a change in the way people are, in the sense that it has provided the most coherent and persistent models for consumer needs, values, tastes and behaviour. It has done this by addressing people as if they were all commonsensically already fully fledged consumers. The general point is that if people are obliged day-in day-out to occupy the subject position of consumer, there is a good chance that they will become consumers. What may begin as a sort of game, a suspicious experimentation for audience members, is likely through the sheer weight of habit to end up being for real. (p. 171)

Apart from the goods and services they present to the market, corporations have long recognized the need to manufacture increasing levels of material wants in the public to consume when the need is not necessarily present or self-apparent. How many more new editions of, say, grammar reference textbooks, popular word-processing programs, and scores of other perpetually refined and repackaged products will the public have to purchase before the ultimate versions of a product finally emerge? If there is really any lingering question of whether we are all seen more as consumers than as citizens, we need refer only to the periodic reminders communicated in various media that tell us so. Are we not all occasionally urged to reflect on the belief that mass consumption largely fuels the post-industrial economy we've all taken part in creating?

Certainly, when former President Bush appeared on national television shortly after the 9/11 outrage and urged his fellow Americans to go and shop (to send a message to the terrorists that they can't threaten our economy[70]), this is one claim that political elites reinforce. (It may be worth debating whether FDR would have enjoyed any higher political clout had he urged for the same measures after Pearl Harbor.)

If they are effective, advertisements reify society's illusory ostensible "needs," manufacturing in the minds of consumers perpetual images of unnecessary material desires. It seems reasonable, therefore, that expressions such as "conspicuous consumption" (Veblen 1994, p. 68) would need to be invented to describe the new kinds of consumer thought processes and behaviors that would emerge during a time when industry could move into the marketplace an unparalleled wealth of material goods and services.

There is also little wonder why this expression is still current even after its introduction to the discourse over 100 years ago. If we are today, as maintained by Fairclough, already "commonsensically fully fledged consumers" of goods and services, it seems only reasonable that we are also seen by corporations as consumers of ideologies.

Born into this post-industrial society and bombarded by images of its material successes, we are indoctrinated through natural exposure to various corporate media that help set some of our most basic aspirations in life on the default switch for mass consumption. Mass media help turn material consumption into a near-reflexive action by preparing minds to

---

[70] It is also worth noting that Wall Street was re-opened for business just a couple of days after 9/11. Joel Arak reported that the Bush Administration pressured the EPA to approve the reopening of Wall Street even though the air quality was extremely unhealthy. No one appears to have any data on the public health consequences of that decision despite the enormous political interest in getting Wall Street back to working order.

recognize and uncritically align with the dominant culture's norms regarding "right-minded" consumer behavior. To corporations, we are either consuming goods or consuming the "right" ideas about how to live and thrive in a society fueled principally by material consumption.

If we are, as well, consumers of ideologies, how do marketers then go about fitting their ideological USPs into our minds? We begin to explore our case by offering first another metaphor for that special category of professionals known as political pundits. In keeping with the work of Lakoff and Turner who observe that "[m]etaphors are so commonplace we often fail to notice them" (1989, p. 1), we wish to introduce another one that we, as members of the consumerist culture, may have also previously overlooked: pundits-as-advertisers.

McDonald's has its golden arches, Nike its swoosh, NBC its proud peacock, Disney its mouse ears, and O'Reilly his *The O'Reilly Factor*.[71] We understand the delicious appeal of fast burgers and fries in terms of the arches, the wonder of super-light footwear in terms of the swoosh, the wondrous Technicolor images on TV in terms of the peacock, and family entertainment in terms of Mickey's ears. For the unvarnished truth straight from the horse's mouth, we understand the *Factor* as the Holy of Holies of political straight talk.

Political pundits market their views by fitting their ideologies into easily recalled USPs. At Burger King, we can

---

[71] It is important to acknowledge the brilliant marketing strategy for information dissemination, at Fox News, developed by Roger Ailes, former media consultant for Presidents Richard Nixon, Ronald Reagan, and George H. W. Bush. The ironic play on "no spin" and "fair and balanced" from a masterful political spin-doctor seems more a self-parody than a sober journalistic philosophy.

"Have it [our] way," and, conversely, in *The O'Reilly Factor*, we can have the truth Bill O'Reilly's way. Like the presentational symbol of the Marlboro Man proposing a unique style of freedom found in a cigarette smoked in the great outdoors, the discursive symbols [72] of Olbermann's *Countdown*, Hannity's *Hannity's America*, Colmes' *First Word*, and Limbaugh's EIB, each propose to a mass audience their unique selling points.

---

[72] Susanne Langer elaborates on the differences between presentational and discursive symbols in *Philosophy in a New Key* (1979, pp. 80-93).

"There are few journalistic standards left these days as we have proven on this broadcast again and again."

—*Bill O'Reilly*
(2007, December 4)

THE 'NO-SPIN' FACTOR

Besides the unintentionally amusing rhetorical ironies he stumbles into periodically, Bill O'Reilly, at 6 feet 4 inches in stature, is a big, imposing man. When he's peeved in public, people can readily tell. A man of that mass must draw attention whenever he melts down in anger. Indeed, his tirades have become popular spectacles of attraction for YouTube gawkers who want to weigh in on his mass media (anti)charisma. O'Reilly's rhetorical style has been described as bombastic and belligerent. Others see him as a "straight shooter" type while still others see him as a pathological liar.[73] Despite these diverging responses to the man, what's clear is that when provoked, he tends to sneer and snap into an accusatory rage in order to assert his views over his guests'.

---

[73] For more, see Al Franken's political critique and satire of the Right in his book *Lies and the Lying Liars Who Tell Them* (2003).

On the surface, his USP suggests that he can be trusted because he appears to be a true champion of the masses, a working-class kind of a guy cleaned up and always ready to knock the Liberal elites down a peg or two. In effect, he is always *looking out for you* — a rhetorical tag twisted into a title for one of his best-selling books. The implied proposition in his USP is that since everyone else couches his or her news in political spin, he aims to do the opposite. So, his popular show is a well-produced stage for him to "factor" in to his political commentary a no-spin kind of a spin.

What's superficially appealing about O'Reilly is, paradoxically, what makes him repulsive. He is quick to strike an accusatory tone with guests when he smells what he thinks is bull. This rhetorical device is a useful offensive weapon as it puts guests almost immediately in a defensive posture. If invective were mud, the first one to throw it often gets the upper hand since the target must clear off the mud before mounting a response.

The message is that he's right, and we (those in the political out-group) are wrong. While a multitude of examples appear in the public record that illustrate his principal strategy, we will parse a few characteristic samples of his USP.

Captain Bill

A well-documented and much discussed January 18, 2005, broadcast on *The Radio Factor* features Bill O'Reilly spinning yarns about his previous tours of combat in Central and South America. He tells listeners that he's "been in combat, ...seen it, [and] ...been close to it." The second and third declarative utterances are meant to reinforce the first, but smooth off the edges by qualifying more precisely *his* personal understanding of what it means to have "been in combat."

This effort in slightly modifying the apparent black-and-whiteness of the surface meaning suggests that he may want to pre-empt any public challenge that might come his way about his combat experience. If you've "seen" something or have "been close to it," as Hillary Clinton begrudgingly acknowledged,[74] these are not precisely the same as being "in" something. The preposition "in" when couched in stories about combat is almost always meant to be construed as firsthand experience in the fight.

This is why, if you are in, say, the US Army and the patch on your right shoulder reflects a combat support unit that never really experienced the heat of the fight firsthand, then you don't really get to tell the kinds of stories that your brethren outside the wire do. Nevertheless, carrying a weapon as a trained warrior into combat and receiving enemy fire is likely not what O'Reilly had meant, but, he worked himself into a corner when he went further with his tale:

> And if I'm ... my unit is in danger, and I've got a captured guy, and the guy knows where the enemy is, and I'm looking him in the eye, the guy better tell me. That's all I'm gonna tell you. He better tell me. If it's life or death, he's going first.

While the tone O'Reilly strikes in this part of his story betrays

---

[74] Observes Katharine Q. Seelye, "The Clinton campaign says Senator Hillary Clinton may have 'misspoke' recently when she said she had to evade sniper fire when she was visiting Bosnia in 1996 as first lady" (2008).

the rigorous training combat soldiers undergo, it also captures the essence of the kinds of propositions that this pundit tends to put forward: I'm John Wayne incarnate, the Duke, and you [my fellow Americans] are the people I'm always looking out for. This kind of USP is highly effective, as we had seen with George W. Bush's proposition that he is the war president,[75] but the suggestion is appealing only if it goes unchallenged.

O'Reilly's proposition flew over the airwaves only briefly until Roger, a curious caller to the show, weighed in and shot it down, so to speak. After O'Reilly greets him and is likely expecting a sympathetic voice from him, Roger immediately puts Bill on the defensive, a position he is clearly not used to. Asking for clarification over O'Reilly's apparent insinuation that he'd served in the military and, furthermore, in combat, Roger forces Bill to straighten out the record. This public challenge, O'Reilly concludes almost immediately, is an unequivocal affront.

To his credit, O'Reilly surmounts his pride and admits

---

[75] Observes Paul Krugman, "America's founders knew all too well how war appeals to the vanity of rulers and their thirst for glory. That's why they took care to deny presidents the kingly privilege of making war at their own discretion. But after 9/11 President Bush, with obvious relish, declared himself a 'war president.' And he kept the nation focused on martial matters by morphing the pursuit of Al Qaeda into a war against Saddam Hussein" (2005). It is further worth noting the method of reasoning that underpins such a proposition: Like O'Reilly, Bush construed public challenges to his relative power and the position he takes on issues as personal attacks. In a public disclosure of his reasons for personally hating Saddam Hussein, Mr. Bush observed at a 2002 Republican fundraising event that he "is the guy who tried to kill my dad." Revenge, like O'Reilly's occasional defensive reactions on The Factor, seemed to be part of Bush's modus operandi — a stark contrast to Bill Maher's observation in the same year that we do not go to war "to get even" (2002, p. 129). We wonder if the rush to war was the product of this personal animus.

that he has not been in the military. But Roger pushes just the right buttons, and soon sends O'Reilly into a ballistic retort. Roger publicly questions why O'Reilly says he was in combat, reminds O'Reilly that he's just a media guy, observes that listeners might misunderstand O'Reilly, and references the irony of fair and balanced reporting, a clear dig against Fox News.

Even so, Roger does not find O'Reilly's explanation entirely credible. That O'Reilly describes himself as having been "in the middle of a couple of firefights in South and Central America" with "his pen in hand," and "people were shooting" at him seems to Roger to be just a bit phony, unworthy of being called combat service.

Since it should be self-apparent, though, that O'Reilly is a champion of the masses, he ironically doesn't care *who* you are. If you challenge him, he will rhetorically rip you from head to toe. But why should such an approach to the public discussion be admitted? We suggest that his method is merely a reflection of the rage that people of his camp likely feel. Proponents of O'Reilly's approach to discourse get to vent their outrage vicariously through him. Furthermore, he is, or pretends to be, so emotionally invested in protecting the masses from political spin that he can construe any challenge to his views as an unwarranted personal attack. This is one reason why he is so quick to tell Roger to "shove" his "snip remark" about "fair and balanced." Roger's keen observation checks O'Reilly's John-Wayne-war-movie swagger.

What does O'Reilly's principle approach here suggest? If the man and his method were one and could be reduced to a simplest common denominator, the underlying description would likely be consistency. What we can count on almost without fail is a strong, unambiguous claim of omniscience. It is not necessary that O'Reilly tells his audience explicitly so, since the tone he sets with the very level of conceit he brings to the stage already clearly implies how possessed he is of infinite awareness. Signs of this great awareness emerge in a variety of his locutions.

Most reasonable people would conclude, for example, that the exclamatory imperative, "shut up," is rude. As a know-it-all, though, Bill O'Reilly has been able to justify using it consistently to communicate to the public another feature of his USP. "Shut up" is a useful rhetorical device that neatly and authoritatively divides those who know and are, thus, fit to speak from those who do not know and are better advised to remain silent.

In the Blue Corner

Although well prepared to assert his perspective in the presence of O'Reilly on *The Factor*, Jeremy Glick discovered firsthand what level of energy is necessary to mollify an opposing point of view such as his. The now-legendary episode between O'Reilly and Glick illustrates quite well what the public has come to expect from this pundit when he is flustered.

As though Glick had been summoned to some Fox News chamber of horrors, the inquisition begins with O'Reilly recounting an apparently offensive political position that Glick had recently endorsed. O'Reilly begins one of his "Personal Story" segments by drawing the attention of his audience to an "offensive" anti-war advertisement[76] which he construes as anti-American because it allegedly "accuses the USA itself of terrorism." He begins by admitting he is surprised by both the advertisement and by one person in particular who had signed it, the son of a NYC Port Authority worker who had lost his life in the 9/11 catastrophe.

Hence, before even introducing Jeremy Glick, O'Reilly has already prepared the minds of his audience by constructing a Straw Man and setting it out as the major premise of his argument against the forthcoming guest. As if appealing to the *pathos* of his prime audience and its presumed desires for retribution, O'Reilly misrepresents the aim of the petition in order to build his empty case, proceeding as though it were already universally felt by the public that Glick is wrong, if not treacherous. He continues and recites the offending portion:

> We too watched with shock the horrific events of September 11 ... we too mourned the thousands of innocent dead and shook our heads at the terrible scenes of carnage — even as we recalled similar scenes in Baghdad, Panama City, and a generation ago, Vietnam.

Nowhere in the so-called ad (see Appendix G) can any explicit indictment of America be found except in the implicit hint, here,

---

[76] Part of the appeal of mass media for political pundits is being able to assign, virtually uncontested, labels to things, concepts and actions: Though O'Reilly refers to the petition in black-and-white terms as an "anti-war advertisement," the document's aim is to publicly challenge the logic and intent of policymakers and warmongers who are designing the plans for war. As the petition aims to persuade Americans to check their conscience and critically examine the aims of its leaders, O'Reilly over-simplifies and attempts to reduce the redressing of a flawed policy to a liberal political stunt.

that America also shares in the blame along with the world's long list of other nations that have tacitly condoned or even carried out unwarranted violence.

By glossing over facts, for example, about the misery and great causalities inflicted on civilian populations during *Operation Just Cause* (1989), and *Operations Desert Shield/Storm* (1991), O'Reilly can place Glick in the category of other radicals who have over the centuries spoken truth to power. Because he can consistently stick to a strong, if dubious, claim that doesn't dilute his core intent, O'Reilly can employ a key tactic in undermining the credibility of a witness with a point of view that doesn't square with what he sees is the norm.

In keeping with the tone one might expect to hear from an omniscient narrator able to probe the mind of any character, he proceeds to tell Glick what Glick's father would have likely thought about his son "mouthing [such] a far-Left position." At this point in the interview, it becomes even more evident that O'Reilly's intent is to turn the petition into a political tool to divide even further those still contemplating whether to support or to challenge the rationale used to make war. Instead of referring honestly to what the document is, emphasizing its intent, and re-examining for the public some of its key criticisms, O'Reilly dishonestly oversimplifies and thereby obfuscates the original purpose behind the petition.

Like Roger, the caller to *The Radio Factor* referenced earlier, Jeremy finally pushes the right buttons to put Bill on a launch pad to rage. On one hand, it is perfectly acceptable for the host to accuse the guest of acting in some egregious way, but on the other, it is unacceptable for the guest to accuse the host of acting in the same way. O'Reilly's earlier attack on Glick called attention to actions that O'Reilly had found disagreeable just as Glick's attack on O'Reilly did the same.

When Glick accuses O'Reilly of cynically evoking the 9/11 tragedy to rationalize and manufacture consent for "everything from domestic plunder to imperialistic aggression worldwide," O'Reilly begins a hasty retreat into his mental bunker, regroups and re-emerges with the only effective retort he apparently feels he can muster. He begins the counter-struggle by telling Glick to "keep [his] mouth shut," a new twist on the usual "shut up," and ends with a barrage of hostile words and threatening gestures.[77] O'Reilly's command for technicians to cut Glick's microphone moves the interview into the sort of threatening environment one might expect in a *Jerry Springer Show* grand finale. Although O'Reilly sticks steadfastly to one core message through his USP, that hostile guests ought to "shut up," he risks diluting the full strength of that message with his visual displays of physical hostility.

Nevertheless, at the center of O'Reilly's USP lies a political ideology recently elaborated in the cognitive sciences. In his book, *The Political Mind* (2009), George Lakoff observes, for example, that Conservative thought tends to differ fundamentally from Progressive thought in that Conservatives

> ... begin with the notion that morality is obedience to an authority — assumed to be a legitimate authority who is inherently good, knows right from wrong, functions to protect us from evil in the world, and has both the right and duty to use force to command obedience and fight evil. (p. 60)

---

[77] This serves two purposes: (a) it allows the outmatched rhetorician to intimidate his guest (something his hulking frame usually does; and (b) it satisfies the cable news audience's desire for combat and excitement.

While O'Reilly's generally Conservative USP embodies the *follower-leader* ideology, which suggests the masses are lost without their leader, it also speaks of two perspectives on contemporary family values. Lakoff's illuminating discussion, grounded in recent research in cognitive linguistics, provides insights into two metaphors that get mapped onto American political discourse. His analysis of national and regional political conversations in light of the *Strict-Father* and *Nurturant-Parent* metaphors provides a framework for our better understanding the different rationales at work behind Conservative and Progressive talking points respectively.

Our critiques, thus far, of O'Reilly's approach to political analysis and discussion have focused mostly on the surface effects of his apparent intentions. He's intimidating and persuasive to some observers because he comes off as a cowboy, a battle-hardened combat soldier, or a father who knows what's best for his posterity. But, what are the likely causes of these effects? What's going on cognitively beneath the surface of what we can see and hear rhetorically in the media he makes use of?

Lakoff provides some perspective. As we earlier noted, Conservative thought tends to emerge from a distinctly different view of the world and of the family than does Progressive thought. If Conservatives largely see discipline and obedience to authority as the path toward freedom, then these qualities are held up as virtues. The laws and regulations of large institutions and the free market spring from natural laws of obedience to the rules laid down for them to operate and for us to operate within them.

One positive outcome, therefore, of personal discipline and obedience, Lakoff observes, is prosperity (2009, pp. 60-7). If you are not prospering, Conservatives tend to conclude, then you are either not playing by the rules or not disciplined enough to enter the fray and fight to get ahead. Some fundamentally flawed church dogmas emerge from the latter sort of thinking as well. If you are not prosperous, then you are likely not obeying G-d. Ministers of the Word, much like political pundits of the Right, in this case ignore the systems of oppression[78] already in place that impede individuals from moving ahead within and beyond the community.

Along with sticking consistently to one strong claim of authority, O'Reilly's USP says something deeper about what the pundit values beneath his rough exterior. He likely values tough love and the notion of authoritarian protection.

This *follow-leader* ideology is convenient for talk show hosts for a few reasons: (a) it attracts to the host precisely the kind of call-in followers who are not going to challenge the host so that the host appears authoritative and admired when taking calls on the air (hence Hannity being constantly praised as a "great American" by his callers); (b) it enables hosts to attract particularly large followings in times of economic or military turmoil when a public in distress is searching for a strong leader who promises easy solutions to its problems; and (c) it reminds Conservative male listeners of a time, fondly recalled, when males — at least on the surface — were firmly in

---

[78] Who can deny that history texts have traditionally ignored or demeaned the tragic plight of women, Native Americans, African Americans, and immigrant populations? For a comprehensive, scholarly critique of American history textbooks, see James Loewen's *Lies My Teacher Told Me* (1996).

control of the family and each family member had his or her clearly defined role to play, *á la*, *Leave It To Beaver* or *Father Knows Best*.

"Deliver us from evil ... "

—*Sean Hannity* (2004)

You're a Great American

What a wonderful way of greeting someone! Or, is it really? On Hannity's show, this salute seems an almost reflexive gesture as callers genuflect before their great leader. The implications of this ceaseless refrain are that Hannity has created a Kim Jong Il-esque cult of personality. To oppose this leader is, by definition, to be unpatriotic, perhaps even a dissident or traitor like those who refused to cry out to *Herr Fuhrer, Sieg Heil!* This seemingly innocuous phrase helps to polarize callers into distinctly different categories: the Enlightened ones who agree with the Great American and the dissidents who dare question this Divine Oracle.

In their book, *Meaning*, Michael Polanyi and Harry

Prosch observe that "Fascism ... converted patriotism into a cult of brutality" (p. 28). If this were so, we wonder whether the contemporary American brand of Neo-conservatism, heralded by Hannity in recent years, has co-opted conventional Christian metaphors and twisted them to serve its own political purposes. One of Hannity's various USPs, we suggest, effectively blends images of patriotism with principles and codes of Christian community so as to create and reaffirm the black-and-white categories of good and evil, of insider and outsider, of right and wrong.

At times, our patriotic fervor for our homeland gets commingled with reverence toward the people who inhabit that land. The problem with conflating these different feelings is that a homeland and its institutions of power are not the same things as human beings. If we see them as the same, we risk valuing *institutions* over the humans who create them and periodically reassess their relevance, utility, or moral worth toward a greater common good. Yet, sometimes, even a healthy critical self-reflection occasionally meets stiff resistance from those mired too deeply in orthodoxies. John Wilkes Booth, and what became his "full-blown obsessive hatred of the North,"[79] for example, typified early American resistance to the nation's internal change and to a growing widespread desire to abolish the institution of slavery. Those who see themselves as prominent constituents of powerful institutions work to castigate or eliminate, now and then, parts

---

[79] This is an allusion to the sort of extreme behavior born in the mind of an individual with a highly unusual personal understanding of patriotism. Borrowed from *Team of Rivals: The Political Genius of Abraham Lincoln* (2006, p. 728).

of the machinery they perceive as subverting the norm or questioning rather than falling in line.

These problematic parts, whether perceived to be foreign-made threats or homegrown, are viewed by some to be fundamentally evil, a state from which certain pundits today feel we must all be delivered. Sean Hannity, for example, calls attention to this need for deliverance by handily hijacking the words of Jesus in the "Lord's Prayer" (in the preceding epigraph) to engender fear and to inspire sympathy for Mr. Hannity's own personal understanding of evil and how he feels it threatens the existing social order. Somewhat like a louder and shriller echo of Patrick Buchanan's earlier treatise[80] on the "immigrant invaders" who are now reshaping America's cultural landscape, Mr. Hannity and his colleagues at Fox News and others at CNN also supply visuals as they see the status quo in impending peril from non-assimilating "illegals."

Tarring the Outsiders

Beyond the textual information they package for television, producers also use visual imagery that carry emotional resonance to incite suspicion and sew seeds of panic and mistrust. J. David Cisneros' compelling case against Fox News, CNN, and other corporate mass media, for example, reveals the processes of dehumanization at work on migrants making their way north from Mexico. Portrayals of these migrant workers in the corporate media frame people seeking a better life in America as inorganic substances bound to

---

[80] For more, see *The Death of the West: How Dying Populations and Immigrant Invasions Imperil Our Country and Civilization* (2002).

"invade" (2008, p. 590) the host society like a pernicious strain of H1N1. Rolling images of migrants on the move taken through night-vision goggles, which are typically used to capture nighttime war footage, cast humans as glowing streams of green toxic waste.

Cisneros paints a devastating portrait of xenophobia at work in the contemptible reporting practices peculiar to both major networks. Slanted coverage of these migrants and the patriotic "Minutemen" who arm themselves and volunteer to survey the landscape in search of the "invaders" is, according to Cisneros, evidenced in the way immigrants tend to be characterized metaphorically. Rendered in the media as biological "infestations" and "infections" (p. 572) as well as sociological "pollutants" and "contaminates" (p. 583), this class of immigrants, Cisneros argues, manifests metaphoric

> ... understandings of the immigration 'problem' [that] create conceptual and societal hierarchies that lend themselves to particular solutions. The best option to deal with the mobile threat presented in news media discourse is to corral and quarantine the pollutants. (p. 593)

The primary patriotic duty, thus, becomes protecting the homeland at all costs. Nevertheless, despite these warped depictions of humans in mass media, the lessons of history remain in place. Even a cursory glance back through the pages of the human narrative will show that no empire has prospered long without the necessary assent of a patriotically animated and intellectually tranquilized citizenry. The rise of Nazi Germany illustrates, for example, the development of consent whipped up by men able to appeal to certain levels of nationalistic pride. "As the status quo was threatened," writes Daniel Goldhagen (1997),

> those opposed to the civil integration of Jews into German society mustered their energies, intellects, and considerable polemical talents to sway their countrymen to resist and to turn back the tide of perceived Jewish infiltration that threatened to break the moorings of Germans' social and cultural identities. The result was a societal conversation of ever-increasing emotion that focused ever more on the definition, character, and valuation of Jews .... (pp. 55-6)

What we can witness today in the name of patriotism are some parallel rhetorical assaults carried out in certain media that aim to resist what seems, at all costs, any sort of social change. Since real fears of unknown quantities and qualities can freeze intellectual curiosity and suppress the natural development of empathy toward others, media can choose either to stoke or smother fear.

They All Look the Same Anyway

Fairly recent research in cognitive linguistics provides some perspective on why change, or even the perception of it, generates such committed and vociferous resistance. The fear of change has much to do with outward appearances rather than with the inward essences of individuals or groups who represent the "other." Long-held conventional wisdom speaks of this tendency of people to assess a book by seeing only its cover. What we see on the surface, though, often betrays what really *is*. In *More Than Cool Reason*, Lakoff and Turner parse the important differences between ways of perceiving a reality whose deep and surface distinctions sometimes, quite naturally, go unnoticed. They observe, for example, that both

> ... the essence and appearance are inalienable to the object, but the essence is more important. Add to that the commonplace knowledge that, typically, only the outsides of things are directly accessible to perception ... while appearances, of course, are not. Since we can perceive the appearance but not the essence, the question arises, can we determine the essence of something from its appearance? (1989, p. 148)

Well, in the case of socially privileged citizens who have been more apt, historically, to hastily assess others on society's periphery,[81] the traditional answer remains, as it always has been, no. Pundigandists who play on this natural tendency to judge first by outward appearances use it to underscore what they construe as core differences between those of the in-group and those of the out-group.

Because of their obvious outward appearances, members of the out-group have traditionally encountered various forms of resistance from others unwilling to share power or, even, access to it. One fashionable way of preventing those on the periphery from entering the center, nowadays, is

---

[81] Robert Jensen observes in his book that the "United States ... at the beginning of the twenty-first century ... is a white supremacist society. By 'supremacist' [he means] a society whose founding is based in an ideology of the inherent superiority of white Europeans over non-whites, an ideology that was used to justify the crimes against indigenous people and Africans that created the nation. That ideology also has justified legal and extralegal exploitation of every non-white immigrant group, and is used to this day to rationalize the racialized disparities in the distribution of wealth and well-being in this society" (2005, pp. 3-4).

to rhetorically blend images of patriotism with those associated with the enforcement of the nation's laws. For society's advantaged, any action that advances the interests of the hegemonic classes is construed as patriotic and, thus, "legal" — be it water-boarding a detainee to extract a "confession" that "WMDs" exist or invading a sovereign nation for reasons that make little sense beyond enormously enriching oil and defense interests.[82]

Indeed, Neo-conservatives appear to have defined themselves not by what they *are* but, rather, what they *are not* — traitors to what they perceive is America's exceptional role in the world. Thus, policy objectives have come to feature one over-riding goal:

> ... destroy and/or kill the enemy, potential or suspected, often including everyone nearby .... It is a movement in a

[82] These examples of questionable ethics epitomize Dick Cheney's interpretation of the term "morality." Indeed, in the summer of 2001, before 9/11, Dick Cheney convened a meeting of his energy task force, apparently attended by a number of prominent oil company executives, in which Cheney displayed a map of the location of the oil reserves in Iraq. Since Iraq was a sovereign nation and Hussein had kicked foreign oil companies out of the country and nationalized his oil industry, the only explanation for the meeting and the object of inquiry is that Cheney and the executives were looking ahead to a time when Hussein would be removed from power and the U.S. could, then, privatize the oil fields to the benefit of U.S. oil companies — as indeed is happening right now; western oil companies were just "invited" back into Iraq for the first time since Saddam kicked them out. This meeting seems to square with observations made in the white papers of the Neo-conservative think tank The Project for the New American Century. Section V of Rebuilding America's Defenses, entitled "Creating Tomorrow's Dominant Force," includes the sentence: "Further, the process of transformation, even if it brings revolutionary change, is likely to be a long one, absent some catastrophic and catalyzing event — like a new Pearl Harbor" (Wikipedia).

> permanent state of war. All matters, foreign and domestic, are framed in terms of that war and ritualistic attacks on the enemy du jour—the terrorists, the Communists, the illegal immigrant, and most of all, the 'liberal.' (Greenwald, 2007, p. 53)

Nevertheless, it is important to distinguish what we mean between two levels of hegemony at work today: (a) the truly powerful (e.g. defense contractors, oil interests — those with billions in assets) who are rational actors playing upon racial fears to advance their own interests, and (b) those who are not financially powerful (whites — who as a group have historically enjoyed social power over non-whites) but do respond to racial appeals, unconsciously desiring to preserve a racial hierarchy that continues to grant them a modicum of social status.[83]

It is crucial for us to underscore the difference between the manipulators and the manipulated — between the cynical actions of powerful actors such as Cheney *et al* and the unconscious latent prejudices harbored by a fair number of

---

[83] For example, after 9/11, (even as early as the mid- to late-1990s) Cheney and cohorts, as part of the "Project for the New American Century," sought to invade Iraq for strategic and oil-related reasons (Chrichton, 2004); they were able to conveniently use 9/11 as a pretext for doing so, perhaps reasoning that Americans largely sought to 'kick some brown ass' (not necessarily the asses of the perpetrators, whom we couldn't find or bring back to life). This might explain why American mass media haven't made much of the fact that an estimated 700,000 Iraqis have died as "collateral damage" through June of 2006, according to the British journal *Lancet* (2006) and 4.7 million have been displaced by the war, according to Amnesty International (2008). Yet given our largely media-driven stereotypes of Arabs as terrorists (think of how Hollywood has largely portrayed Arabs as such, as opposed to representing the overwhelming majority), it may be difficult for us Americans to identify with Arab casualties of the U.S. war in Iraq—particularly since their deaths may be indirectly related to the war.

Americans, especially those of privilege.[84] As concentrated political power and social station imply reasonable and moral authority, these positions can also serve as catalysts to legitimize in the eyes of the masses the agendas and actions of the powerful, however dubious the designs of the privileged may be.

From the perspective of the advantaged classes, the members of marginalized groups pursuing their own interests are construed as "illegal" and, thus, unpatriotic — a Mexican peasant living on a dollar per day seeking a better wage just north of the border is just a common criminal even though his plight largely parallels that of our ancestors who likely came to America to escape persecution and/or poverty. Indeed, were the pilgrims "legal" in the eyes of Native Americans? To the contrary, it was the pilgrims, who eventually viewed the Native Americans as subhuman and who illegally pushed them onto reservations.

It is, therefore, not necessary to dig any deeper for the essence of individuals and groups on the periphery since it is already self-apparent that the periphery is radical and wrong given its inherent social position in society. Just listen to Sean Hannity pontificate daily with his media megaphone about how Obama and his "radical" cohorts have taken over. Accepting Hannity's premise forces us to realize that it would be against our interests to dig any deeper to empathize[85] with others

---

[84] Nobel Prize winning economist, Paul Krugman expands upon this point in his seminal work *The Conscience of a Liberal* (2007).

[85] It is worth noting the ironic charge that was leveled against Supreme Court Nominee Sonia Sotomayor. She was accused of the "e-word," having "empathy" for society's downtrodden. Strangely, her 17-year history on the Appellate Court does not reveal a distinct pattern of empathy toward any given group, yet those privileged classes that accuse her of having too much empathy had no problem empathizing with their own groups and their class interests. Indeed, those groups who were exclusively represented on the Supreme Court showed 180+

since doing so would, in turn, force us to acknowledge our equality and, thus, undermine our sense of privilege. It's no wonder why, too, socially powerful pundits can so easily help manufacture consent for "patriotic" policies, given their inherently powerful positions.

Last year's "tea" parties of April, 2009, for example, coordinated by Fox News, thrown in various regions of the United States and attended by, some say, a modest number[86] of tax-paying malcontents,[87] are purported to illustrate widespread waning consent for the economic policies of Mr. Obama. The governor of the Lone Star state even issued a veiled threat to secede from the Union unless Obama acts more like a tax-cutting Conservative Republican and rescinds the programs he has proposed to stimulate the economy.

Neo-conservative pundits portrayed the grass roots[88] "revolt" as a patriotic duty to protest what many of their

---

years of empathy toward white male citizens seeking to maintain their socio-economic supremacy. The denial to grant Dred Scott his freedom, the denial of basic civil rights, voting rights, land rights, integration etc. all illustrate the terrific amount of empathy with the classes that stood to benefit most from those decisions.

[86] Nate Silver reports 311,460 in 346 cities across the nation.

[87] *The Economist* reported that "[t]he biggest cause of anger is Mr. Obama's willingness to bail out everyone with a tin cup ... People who have borrowed prudently and lived within their means are livid that they are being asked to bail out neighbours who [had] splurged on McMansions and giant televisions" (2009, May 5).

[88] "It turns out that the tea parties don't represent a spontaneous outpouring of public sentiment," observes Paul Krugman, "They're AstroTurf (fake grass roots) events, manufactured by the usual suspects. In particular, a key role is being played by FreedomWorks, an organization run by Richard Armey, the former House majority leader, and supported by the usual group of Rightwing billionaires. And the parties are, of course, being promoted heavily by Fox News" (2009, April 12).

like-minded brethren have construed as the government's unjust fiscal policies. Throwing off the shackles of an unjust ruler, so to speak, has meant exercising a patriotic duty to save the Republic from a "fast approaching era of big government spending." But, are these protests genuinely patriotic or just elaborate episodes in which to bemoan the power of an office one's party could not attain? Or, have these constituents suffered a sudden, convenient case of amnesia created by the relatively minor monetary and human costs of war waged on two fronts?

FATHER COUNTRY: HALLOWED BE ...

Protest is a G-d-given right and duty, though evidently acceptable and valid it appears, only when the Right exercises it. The hypocritical disapprovals leveled at the Left for calling into question the ethical problems posed by, say, a pre-emptive war in Iraq are now conveniently swept under the Neo-conservative carpet when Liberal policies hold sway.

Perhaps most striking about these sorts of pretentions are the Neo-con commentators who report on and champion this duplicitous behavior yet who clearly see themselves as Christian, or at least claim to be connected on some level to G-d. We wonder, though, how G-d got tangled up in this human-made mess. Are we guilty, in the words of Reverend Jeremiah Wright, of "Confusing God and Government"?[89] We suspect that Leo Tolstoy's turn-of-the-century observation of the powerful still resonates with clarity today. He observes that

[89] For more on Fox's repeated deceptive use of Rev. Wright's sermon, see http://www.youtube.com/watch?v=QOdlnzkeoyQ&NR=1

> ... in their dread of the Christian conception of life which will destroy the social order, which some cling to only from habit, others from interest, men cannot but be thrown back upon the pagan conception of life and the principles based on it. ([1893] 2006 p. 97)

Of the various social peculiarities that a growing number of so-called Christians have exhibited in the mass media since 9/11, jingoism, crudely disguised as patriotic passion, has become the most perplexing. Adopting the former ideological frame seems evidently easy when the latter can be negotiated, in this case, by powerful Neo-conservatives who can employ the machinery of mass media to redefine important social or political concepts. To be fair to the Right, though, we are not suggesting here that present-day Conservatives are exclusively guilty of employing the power of corporate media in attempts to re-engineer what they feel should be the public's understanding of key terms, but regarding the unceasing campaign for warped concepts of patriotism, the Neo-conservative punditocracy has certainly out-performed their political counterparts as of late. How have they been able to do this?

Fairly late scholarship has investigated this phenomenon. In his book, *Living in the Number One Country* (2000), Herbert Schiller provides some further insights from his perspective as a critic of American hegemony. He argues that the power inherent in one's social station can further legitimize one's personal understanding and communication of key terms in the culture.

That is to say, power provides individuals and the institutions that enjoy it much greater opportunities to wield, or attempt[90] to gain, a significant kind of control over basic meanings and key concepts. According to Schiller, one of the " ... most tested and effective means of keeping order in the ranks comes from 'definitional control': the ability to explain and circulate, [say,] the governor's view of reality, local or global" (2000, p. 152).[91] Doris Graber also suggests that executives and legislators, and we would add pundits, strive to define situations and project images in their own way to influence information that media pass on to the public so as to gain or retain support and maintain power (2010, p. 226). From

---

[90] Populist commentator, Jim Hightower observes that even "giant corporations are trying to co-opt the meaning of one of our important words: 'local.' It's important, because small businesses all across the country have created a very positive, grassroots economic movement, based on being local producers, providers, and marketers. Over 130 cities have 'local business alliances,' with 30,000 businesses enlisted. The movement has been phenomenally popular with consumers, who like the flavor and personality of local enterprises and like the fact that their consumer dollars stay in their community. So, now other businesses want in on the action – such outfits as Frito Lay, Wal-Mart, Starbucks, CVS, and Barnes & Noble. These global brands are using TV ads and other promotions to hawk their mass-produced stuff as 'local.' The sprawling Barnes & Noble chain, for example, ... asserts: 'All bookselling is local.' Hellmann's, a division of Dutch-owned Unilever, is claiming that its mayonnaise is local because most of its ingredients come from North America." (2009, December 30)

[91] Borrowed from page 152 in Schiller's book, *Living in the Number One Country*. Also, by framing the current issue of voluntary end of life counseling, Rush Limbaugh, for example, has been attempting to control how healthcare reform is defined by the media and has created a no-win situation for Obama, whose very denials that he is proposing a death panel only reinforce the frame of Obama as death panel proposer in the public's mind — just as Richard Nixon's insistence that "I am not a crook" only reinforced his image as a crook (or why would he have to deny it, as George Lakoff astutely explained).

friendships to families and corporations to nations, all institutions strive to maintain certain norms whose interpretations are occasionally challenged. Who can indulge in what and how, as well as what should be denied, are all part of the negotiation of meaning within and across the various relationships we build or that touch our lives.

Definitional control "serves to bulwark, or at least minimize threats to, the prevailing order" (Schiller, 2000, p. 152). Though they are not governors of state, pundits still manage with great power the special meanings they broadcast over the airwaves. Like the public's interest in and reassessment of its understanding of Democracy after WWII, patriotism is just another concept that undergoes periodic renegotiation and refinement.

For the secular world and, apparently, for the world of the "saved," appeals to patriotism are ingenious inventions of minds intent on preserving power and allegiance to secular constructs, such as social, economic, or political ideologies and institutions. Without patriotism living and working in the populace, governments are unable to stand. Nevertheless, wherever power is at stake, self-preservation and self-interest also congregate. An explication of the term can reveal the absurdities that could, potentially, develop in the minds of those ensnared by the forces of heightened patriotic fervor.

Contemporary notions of patriotism spring from harmless and humble beginnings, as in the Latin *pater* for father. This root meaning is useful for our purposes here. It is also interesting as it connotes feelings typically associated with a father figure ultimately interested in the welfare of his posterity. But how, if you adopt the ethical positions of Christ, can you embrace also the things that patriotism in Hannity's mind calls for?

To signal, first, the self-evident, patriotism can be a very powerful means of extending allegiance or expressing obedience to a surrogate father — in this case, the state. Second, and perhaps not so obvious to Hannity *et al*, are the words of Jesus who once reminded his witnesses to call no one on earth 'father,' for they have only one, and He is in heaven (Mat. 23:9). As the reference here that the Christ uses is to a spiritual father, it is, nevertheless, important to note the near-spiritual levels to which the nation has been lifted up in recent years by certain Neo-conservative commentators. Either join them in their special ceremonies of public praise or face their condemnation.

Perhaps more importantly, though, if we dare to parse the meanings of patriotism a bit further, we find that it, like Democracy and freedom, is entirely subjective. George Orwell reminds readers in "Politics and the English Language" (1949), for example, that words such as "democracy, socialism, freedom, [and] patriotic ... " have many different meanings which "cannot be reconciled with one another" (p. 308). He goes on to observe that it is

> ... almost universally felt that when we call a country 'democratic' we are praising it: consequently, the defenders of every kind of régime claim that it is a democracy, and fear that they might have to stop using the word if it were tied down to any one meaning. (p. 308)

Patriotism is as subjective a feeling as religious awe, the

numinous one feels when humbled in meditation in the presence of his or her Creator. Its effects on our attitudes and actions toward others are what make it concrete. Nonetheless, no scientific instrument exists, or likely ever will, that provides a universal metric by which patriotism can be weighed internally. And, yet, despite the problems of such an abstraction, Neo-conservative pundits such as Hannity and Limbaugh want to define it for the ostensible convenience of their audiences. This, at least, seems on the surface to be the case.

Further philosophical insights can be gleaned, at last, from the work of Alasdair MacIntyre who argues that modern politics has no place for patriotism, because there really is no fatherland *per se*. Although there can be jingoism and propaganda, there can be no genuine affection for the nation or for our fellow citizens since we have no shared project that connects us one to another or to the nation. It would be strange for us to feel affinity for the state on one hand as it frustrates our personal projects while on the other it permits no effective voice, and fails to provide a unifying vision of the good life (1998, p. 227).

In their public promotions of this mythical "good life," which, evidently, only "true" patriots can and should enjoy, religious pundigandists[92] extol in one breath a purely secular notion of patriotism and in another breath reject that "good life" referenced, ironically, by their master teacher executed on a

---

[92] In an exclusive interview on Fox with Rev. Jeremiah Wright, Sean Hannity acts as a pundigandist who suggests that he (Hannity) also possesses an informed understanding of the Holy Scriptures through his study of the Gospel at seminary, which causes us to wonder what seminary propounds faith in American hegemony over faith in the sacrificial Lamb.

cross at Golgatha. To the Christ who had declared to "give life and that more abundantly," Neo-conservative pundits who presently value patriotic passion as highly as they do, ironically, enjoy the very material benefits[93] of the wider society that multitudes of their fellow citizens still have no equal access to.

As more common criticisms of contemporary socio-economic inequalities go, people tend to say that it is easy to support and defend a status quo that, by virtue of your class or race, inherently affords you greater opportunities to share in its material wealth.[94] Interestingly, during George W. Bush's presidency, Neo-conservative pundits and politicians who were the central champions of war as an instrument of patriotic duty failed themselves to ever serve in this "patriotic" capacity. The Bush-Cheney project for the Middle East was bought by the mass media[95] and sold to an unwitting portion of

---

[93] This is a reference to Pierre Bourdieu's concept of "cultural capital" that children are endowed with by virtue of socialization in their families and communities. Bourdieu argues that, through their familial socialization, children of the socioeconomic elite receive both more of and the right kind of cultural capital for school and life success (1977, p. 73). Uncommon exceptions to this cultural phenomenon such as college dropouts who later became billionaire software magnates or popular radio talk-show hosts should not be counted as representative examples of the wider culture.

[94] It is worth noting George Lakoff's critical analysis of the term "freedom" and its contemporary uses. He theorizes that the differences between our acknowledging or ignoring inequalities may arise from the fundamentally different ways in which we construe causes and effects at work in society: conservatives tend to impute class differences to direct causation whereas progressives tend to attribute differences to systemic causation. Regarding our ability or inability to get ahead in society, the former consistently point to the personal failures or low ambitions of individuals while the latter point to the social, financial, political or economic failures of the system (2006, pp. 112-8).

[95] Then *New York Times* "big foot" Judith Miller accepted and promoted wholesale the self-serving WMD narrative of such

the public as America's project for the spread of freedom and democracy on foreign shores. We reference once again the words of MacIntyre. Why, he observes, if the State is purely instrumental, to be used to advance one's own projects, would anyone be willing to die for it, since death means the end of all such projects (1998, p. 236)?

For those pundigandists who profess themselves to be on one hand great Americans and on the other hand children of G-d, it is worth calling attention to some insightful observations from the past that contradict those who presently "worship created things rather than the Creator." The spirit of Isaiah once moved by G-d proclaims that heaven is [His] home, and earth [His] footstool. We suggest that the United States is but a part of that metaphorical footstool. Any efforts to reinterpret that hierarchy sit outside the spiritual borders these pundits claim to be bound by. Patriotism is a "heretical religion," Franz Werfel reminds us in *Between Heaven and Earth*, "based on [the] erroneous doctrine that nations have a soul and that this soul is more permanent, more 'eternal', so to speak, than the soul of an individual" (1944).

Nevertheless, serious contradictions abound. We recount the words of earlier commentators who have professed a certain closeness to G-d but whose words appear to betray any sort of intimate proximity.

"un-named sources" as Ahmed Chalibi who turned out to be on the CIA's payroll, who'd been groomed to be the new Iraqi Prime Minister, and who was wanted for embezzlement in Jordan. When the WMD's couldn't be found, Chalibi's replacement narrative was just as creative: the weapons were conveniently smuggled into Iran. So much for the Times' scrupulous vetting of sources. It must also be noted, though, that the *Times* did publish an unprecedented mea culpa for such a catastrophic blunder.

> On this earth you must belong to the church militant or get the hell out of it. That's the right word. You're either with me or against me. There is no middle ground in this battle between Christ and the Anti-Christ. If you step out of [the battle], you're no worse than those boys who ran off to Norway, Sweden, those boys who deserted the government. You're deserters, rotten deserters (11 June 1973).

These observations may sound surprising to those unfamiliar with the views of Father Charles Edward Coughlin, a so-called "man of the cloth" at the time. Broadcasting his disdain for military men who, like Christ, would dare critically self-examine their hearts and choose not to participate in war was, during the height of Coughlin's influence, a major feature of his own quasi-political ambitions. Father Coughlin, it could be noted, was quite adept at using rhetorical schemes like those employed by George W. Bush decades later: America-at-war as Christ; rotten-war-deserter as Anti-Christ. Hence, the implied comparision is that Christ-as-America is the Eternal Soul while the Anti-Christ-as-a-deserter is the soul-less wretch.[96] This kind of intellectual construct, though antithetical to peace, nonetheless seems to pervade the thoughts of many so-called peacemakers. Why should war or the prospect of it strike such a chord with those who claim faith in a Rabbi made globally famous for preaching about ways of achieving an eternal peace?

---

[96] It should be noted that ironically as Rumsfeld began to notice Bush's initial support for the war begin to wane, Rumsfeld cynically resorted to using Biblical passages as a lure to re-energize and re-focus Mr. Bush, to reinforce the pious president's support for the war effort. Rumsfeld's ruse seems utterly cynical.

NON-ZERO-SUM SOLUTIONS

Robert Wright (2009) provides an alternative perspective to peacemaking in his book, *The Evolution of God.* While he discusses how sacred texts can be and too often are interpreted today as polemics, Wright could, as easily, be discussing how contemporary pundits and the news events and documents they tend to emphasize are just as polemical. Is it not somewhat ironic that pundigandists consistently rail against mass media's tendency to stress the negative in events, yet those same hosts emphasize the negative in, say, Muslim cultures and ignore the overwhelming majority of Muslims — and legal or illegal immigrants — who do not wish the US ill and who are productive members of society?

Wright notes that successful religions "have always tended to salvation at the social level, encouraging behaviors that bring order because civilization was constantly threatened by chaos in pre-Abrahamic religions." He goes on to note that the contemporary

> ... social system [is] an incipiently global social system, ... again threatened by chaos. But now religion seems to be the problem, not the solution. Tensions among Jews, Christians, and Muslims — or at least among some Jews, Christians, and Muslims — imperil the world order. And the tensions are heightened by the scriptures of these religions — or at least by the scriptures as they're being interpreted by the people who are heightening the tensions [just as pundigandists heighten tensions between, say, 'blue staters and red staters' or Democrats and Republicans' or 'Mexicans and Americans' or other insiders and outsiders]. Three great religions of salvation

have helped put the world in need of salvation (p. 409).

So, how can we achieve that right sort of salvation today? Wright notes that underlying the scriptures are maps of both religious tolerance and intolerance. The key to the world's salvation is to convince people that they are in a non-zero-sum relationship with other people because "when people see themselves in a zero-sum relationship with other people — see their fortunes as inversely correlated with the fortunes of other people, see the dynamic as win-lose — they tend to find a scriptural basis for intolerance or belligerence. When they [conversely] see the relationship as non-zero-sum — see their fortunes as positively correlated, see the potential for a win-win outcome — they're more likely to find the tolerance and understanding side of the scriptures."

Such is the case with political partisans who certainly *could* help lay the social groundwork for cross-cultural and political understanding — tying people's outward differences to non-zero-sum solutions that emphasize patience and goodwill.

"Not on your life. If it was good enough for the founding fathers, it's good enough for me, and I'll fight in defense of our Pledge of Allegiance."

—*Sarah Palin, 2006*

Pledges to the State

When confronted by a question in a 2006 gubernatorial survey concerning whether she was offended by the phrase "Under God" in the Pledge of Allegiance and if she was, why or why not, Sarah Palin decided to cite the Founding Fathers as her inspiration for protecting the pledge. Who knew the Founding Fathers also gave birth to the Pledge of Allegiance — a document drafted over a hundred years after the nation's founding and whose reference to G-d was inserted only half a century ago? So, what is it about the Pledge that engenders such an immediate connection to the US Constitution and those gentlemen who drafted it? A quick Google search of these key terms nets a first hit at Wikipedia featuring a description of this much-debated oath of loyalty.

Tied to the intellectual act of consent to power is the

stock that society puts in pledges and oaths. At the very least, some tacit pledge of allegiance to an ideology, for example, is necessary for society's consent to the policies and laws shaped by that doctrine. But, why does the recitation of a pledge sometimes evoke such strong emotion? Perhaps pledges and oaths remain fashionable because of our collective convictions that words themselves are solemn or pseudo-sacred tools of our swollen intellects — that they somehow speak of our power over those things we routinely identify, name, and define. In her book, *Verbal Hygiene*, Deborah Cameron likens this sort of behavior to "magical thinking" — when there is a symbolic connection deeply embedded in human culture between exerting control over language and exerting control over things and events in the world (1995, p. 219).

Another way to reinforce a political USP is to speak about it publicly — to repeat it as though it were an incantation, such as the necessity of paying allegiance to a flag, an ideology, or other symbol of state power. Reiterating to the public the seeming necessity for everyone to repeat the pledge also sets up a simple frame for marking off the stark differences between the "good" people and the "evil" people. Those who fail to fall in line with the call to pay allegiance to some social or political construct can, themselves, help clear the groundwork for their own public destruction as well as a perfect opportunity for political enemies to voice their outrage. But, is such an outrage warranted?

One recent entry to the public discourse that deserves elaboration is the concept of "manufactured outrage." According to *Urban Dictionary*, it is a kind of

> ... falsified righteous outrage at things that are basically

> unimportant and meaningless, frequently employed by politicians, political activists, or the media. Politicians and talking heads use it to garner support for their causes, to claim the moral high ground and to tar their opponents; the media often just use it in a cynical bid to increase ratings.

Given, say, Father Couglin's level of ire discussed earlier, we wonder whether his was no more than a manufactured variety, a sort of falsified contempt for things that don't, or shouldn't, much matter to a man who has already pledged allegiance to his master, the Christ.

So, what is the Pledge and why does it matter so much to some people — particularly to certain political pundits? In September of 1892, Francis Bellamy, a Baptist minister ironically enough, published the "Pledge of Allegiance" in *The Youth's Companion* magazine.[97] His original intent had been simply to mark the 400th anniversary of Columbus' voyage to the "new" world.

One might imagine that the Pledge would have been an instant hit with the relatively young nation. It wasn't, and it wasn't until fifty years later, in 1942, that Congress officially recognized the Pledge. Interestingly, during that period, despite the anxieties and tensions generated at home by the nation's war efforts abroad, the resulting internment of Americans of Japanese descent, and other assorted injustices introduced to the populace,[98] a Supreme Court ruling, only a year later,

---

[97] For a brief history of the Pledge of Allegiance, see http://dls.virginia.gov/pubs/briefs/brief28.htm

[98] In *A People's History of the United States*, historian Howard Zinn discusses the bizarre treatment of African American soldiers segregated into the bowels of the Queen Mary enroute to the European

prohibited school children from being forced to even recite the Pledge.

How popular are pledges to other nations worldwide? Besides the United States, only one other nation, perhaps then under the influence of America's intoxicating colonial power, devised its own pledge to its national flag — the Phillipines.[99] In light of the relatively unpopular practice of creating and encouraging the recitation of pledges throughout the rest of the world, why do they even exist? Why is it considered necessary for the citizens of any nation to take an oath of allegiance to a particular nation?

Conventional wisdom has shown, after all, that even under oath people lie and that words mean nothing to those intent on hiding their true intentions or the beliefs they actually hold. Aren't men's mouths full of deceit anyway (Psalms 10:7)? Perhaps it is not entirely surprising that Father Coughlin decades ago as well as some commentators today, who profess some religious conviction, esteem pledges to higher powers as highly as they do. The Higher Power that the faithful invoke in prayer can apparently appear to some to be quite like the higher powers of government that wield temporal forms of control over our lives. This apparent confusion over who or what truly rules the lives of men has not prevented some political pundits from making hay out of the issue.

Consider the position of a fifth grader and his older sister whose actions precipitated two Supreme Court rulings,

---

theater of combat, the segregation of blood donations for military blood banks, as well as the Fascist marginalization of American women employed in droves in the Homefront's war industry (1995, pp. 406-9).

[99] For more, see http://w2.eff.org/Censorship/Academic_edu/CAF/civil-liberty/pledge.history

the last of which set today's precedent prohibiting the state from compelling anyone to recite the Pledge.

> 'I do not salute the flag because I have promised to do the will of God,' wrote ten-year-old Billy Gobitas to the board of the Minersville (Pennsylvania) School District in 1935. His refusal, and that of his sister Lillian (age twelve), touched off one of several constitutional legal cases delineating the tension between the authority of the state to require respect for national symbols and the right of individuals to freedom of speech.[100]

Given the weight of legal precedent, it is worth contemplating why Sean Hannity, for example, a self-proclaimed Roman Catholic with his heart perhaps set on someday seeing his heavenly home, would insist that citizens recite the Pledge as though they were mindless captives of some authoritatian régime. What's more, why is the recitation of such an oath really such an issue for a man who has claimed, at least implicitly in his public persona, to have taken up his cross and followed after Him?[101]

As a powerful media personality, Mr. Hannity, like Father Coughlin once was, is well positioned to couch a host of

---

[100] For more details on this fascinating piece of Americana, visit http://www.loc.gov/exhibits/treasures/trr006.html
Another more recent example of dissent has emerged in Arkansas where ten-year-old Will Phillips of West Fork School District in Washington County, Arkansas, has refused to stand during his class' recitation of the Pledge. Undeterred by the social backlash his resistance has created, Will maintains that he doesn't believe there is freedom and justice for all and, thus, will continue his symbolic protest until everyone realizes freedom and justice. For details, see http://www.youtube.com/watch?=MOcAWn7Rp9s

[101] A reference to Mark 8:34 where details describe denying one's ego to create communion with the Christ.

hollow questions in purely black-and-white terms. In Hannity's estimation, those who would refuse to recite the Pledge either "detest their country or are ignorant of its greatness."[102] His attempt here, like his others we have parsed, is clearly to filter the premises to two and, thus, the boundaries of the argument: (1) hatred for country or (2) ignorance of its greatness. But, is Hannity actually framing what he sees as the problem in honest terms, or is he merely cynically calling attention to an entirely meaningless issue? For a more enlightened perspective, we recall the words of Hannity's master who had observed during His ministry

> ... swear not an oath; neither by heaven ... nor by the earth ... nor by your head, because you cannot make one hair white or black. But let your 'Yes' be 'Yes,' and your 'No,' 'No.' (Mat. 5:34-7)

Although Hannity cannot turn his hair one shade or another in this Biblical sense, he *can* turn a purportedly sacred theme into a strictly "white or black" political dichotomy. For what reasons, though, would anyone refuse to pledge allegiance to a flag? There must be more than two, it seems reasonable to conclude. Yet, Hannity's overconfidence in hastily dismissing motives that may fall between the two extremes is surprising. What begs for a fuller response is Hannity's propensity to connect the intrinsic power of temporal institutions and ideologies to patriotism and to some supposed G-d-ordained duty to venerate them.

Whenever he seems to sense that a reasoned debate of topics that touch on patriotism will ensue, but which

[102] Borrowed from a *Hannity & Colmes* broadcast of June 12, 2003

call for thoughtful qualifiers, his rhetorical methods tend to devolve into fallacious thinking, hasty generalizations, and black-and-white reasoning: "Is it you hate this president or that you hate America?" (2003). Of all the other pundits whose words we have examined for this study, Hannity remains the most consistent spelunker who delves the depths of black-and-white reasoning.

One wonders, though, from what font Hannity draws his spiritual inspiration — beyond what appears to be a near-neuortic adulation for the state. Given the great number of other nations, peoples, and cultures that call Earth home in light of Hannity's proclaimed Christian worldview, one cannot help but be thoroughly mystified by his thought processes, and by his conceited confidence that the "U.S. is the greatest, best country God has ever given man on the face of the earth."[103]

Perhaps Mr. Hannity was reminded of Hillary Clinton and, not wanting to be outdone by the former First Lady who had observed that America's charity is what makes it "the strongest and best nation in the history of the world,"[104] he felt compelled to go a step farther by tying the nation's greatness to divine providence. Yet, nowhere in the Biblical canon he claims moral guidance from could we isolate a single reference to citizens of the United States of America being "given" this nation. Nonetheless, we must resist the impulse to hastily dismiss those who hold such views as deluded by their own subjective experiences. These supposedly patriotic public calls

---

[103] Borrowed from a *Hannity's America* broadcast of June 6, 2008.

[104] Michael Janofsky writes in "Delegates Hope to Prolong Volunteer Spirit" that Hillary Clinton was likely recounting the impressions that Alexis de Tocqueville had of Americans and their "habits of the heart," to be charitable toward others.

to recite pledges are grounded in a genuine spirit of exceptionalism. Each generation evidently has its share of noteworthy jingoists who wrap themselves in the patriotic passions of the moment and who attempt to compel others to align with their personal conceptions of normal behavior.

A clergyman and protestant cohort of Father Coughlin's, Gerald L. K. Smith confirms connections still very much alive and swirling around ideas of patriotism, ideology, and the promise of political power. Of his public oratory in concert with Father Coughlin and his affinity for receiving praise, Gerald Smith, Schlesinger wrote, was

> [d]runk with the shrieks of the crowd, [and] perceived no limit to his power. Gerald Smith observed that "Religion and patriotism, keep going on that. It's the only way you can get them really 'het up.'" Once "het up," they would follow a strong man anywhere. "Certain nerve centers in the population will begin to twitch — and the people will start fomenting, fermenting, and then a fellow like myself, someone with courage enough to capture the people, will get on the radio and have the people with him, hook, line, and sinker. I'll teach 'em to hate. The people are beginning to trust leadership." (Schlesinger, 2003 p. 627)

Since the 1940s, the filters fear and hate in America remain widely appealing to xenophobes and jingoists. Perhaps former-VP Dick Cheney's rude retort, "go f--k yourself," to Senator Patrick Leahy[105] has come to serve as a cue for

---

[105] In citing rules of civility, transcribed by George Washington from the work of Jesuit priests, Sheryl Stolberg notes that Rule 49 (Use no reproachful language against any one; neither curse nor revile) was apparently forgotten by VP Dick Cheney when he launched a verbal salvo against Senator Leahy, evidently incensed by the Senator's earlier

Hannity and his fellow Neo-conservative commentators in recent years. Whether Hannity is telling his audience, for example, "who should be tortured and killed at Guantanamo — every filthy Democrat in the U.S. Congress,"[106] stirring passions for state secession,[107] or contemplating revolution,[108] we wonder if the patriotic USP he turns to so often doesn't conflict with his call for pledging allegiance to the flag.

Hannity's ideological ally, Bill O'Reilly, seems on the surface to take a more even-handed approach to the Pledge. Despite his feelings that children are no longer "being taught the basic disciplines of life," O'Reilly believes that the Pledge of

---

persistent criticisms of Cheney's close ties to Halliburton (2004).

[106] Borrowed from http://www.hannity.com. It is worth noting that this concentration of venom injected into public discourse isn't part of a new strain of invective or a new communication practice. In his book, *The Eliminationists*, David Neiwert cites the words of Mussolini who, during his "climb to power in Italy in 1920, ... " replied to " ... a Leftwing critic: 'The democrats of *Il Mondo* want to know our program? It is to break the bones of the democrats of *Il Mondo*'" (2009, p. 139). "This fist-shaking style of political discourse," Neiwert goes on to note, "in fact, was one of the real hallmarks of Fascism. It signaled, above all else, the rightness of power by virtue of it being used to intimidate and silence dissenters. To the fascist leader, diplomacy is a parlor game for the weak; what counts is the raw will of the man of action" (p. 139). Is it any wonder that all of the Neo-conservative pundigandists both embrace decisive military action and employ PM filters that frame current events in appeals to fear and patriotism?

[107] Borrowed from Youtube at http://www.youtube.com/watch?v=jN8cV5SxCVA

[108] Sean Hannity's website provides a forum for the discussion of a poll posing possible approaches to revolution. He limits approaches to the overthrow of the government to only three: (a) Military Coup; (b) Armed Rebellion; or (c) War for Secession. Perhaps, because of public pressure for their removal, details of the poll were once offered at http://forums.hannity.com/showthread.php?t=1326121. The details remain preserved at other sites featuring criticism of Hannity's radical views such as http://www.dailykos.com/story/2009/2/26/171533/093/468/702281

Allegiance should not be compulsory " ... because of [his] respect for dissent [although, he adds,] all students would have to rise while the Pledge [is being] recited out of respect for the country that is educating them."[109] As earlier noted, though, O'Reilly's conception of dissent tends to be acceptable only when it squares with his conception of reality. Challenging him, therefore, over details about the authenticity of his brave service in combat produces a vigorous, negative response.

Today, while the spirit of dissent remains alive and well, it continues to meet strident opposition. In choosing either to ignore or to remain ignorant of a previous Supreme Court ruling on the Pledge of Allegiance and its marginalized place in the culture, pundigandists who insist that this oath remain compulsory argue through the filter of patriotism. Thus, unsuspecting audience members are duped into choosing between one of two false alternatives: being patriotic or not being patriotic. Perhaps more important, though, is the illusion created by this patriotic USP.

The emotional bridges these commentators build to patriotic feelings create the false impression that free speech is a privilege to be vigorously challenged by everyone rather than a right to be preserved or even practiced. Pundigandists who practice playing on the relative ignorance of their audience, thus, create the illusion that those citizens who apply their rights, whether speaking freely or choosing not to speak at all, are no more than dangerous radicals to be marginalized. Hannity's attempts in marginalizing Obama, for example, have

---

[109] Borrowed from Fox News at http://www.foxnews.com/story/0,2933,53633,00.html

become like pseudo-events [110] — "dramatic productions," according to Chris Hedges, "orchestrated by publicists, political machines, television, Hollywood or advertisers" (2009). Although he critiques America's largely uncritical acceptance of the Obama brand of executive governance, at least early on in Obama's administration, Hedges notes that the president brings no more of a threat than George W. Bush did to effectively disrupting the status quo and dismantling the military-industrial-corporate nexus.

Whether he is being handled in a positive light by his campaign managers or in a negative light by his detractors, Obama — like Bush — remains a mass media object in the production of pseudo events. Whereas the "war president" George W. Bush had famously landed on the deck of an aircraft carrier to signal "Mission Accomplished," Barack Hussein Obama has landed in Neo-conservative headlines with creative fabrications about his repugnance of reciting the Pledge of Allegiance.[111] Notwithstanding the evidence that

---

[110] "Because they can evoke a powerful emotional response," Hedges observes, pseudo-events can overwhelm " ... reality and [replace] reality with a fictional narrative that often becomes accepted truth. The unmasking of a stereotype damages and often destroys its credibility. But pseudo-events, whether they show the president in an auto plant or a soup kitchen or addressing troops in Iraq, are immune to this deflation. The exposure of the elaborate mechanisms behind the pseudo-event only adds to its fascination and its power. This is the basis of the convoluted television reporting on how effectively political campaigns and politicians have been stage-managed. Reporters, especially those on television, no longer ask if the message is true but if the pseudo-event worked or did not work as political theater" (Hedges, 2009).

[111] The non-partisan Factcheck.org destroys recent myths circulating in media, yet the distortions persist. Among his supposed aversion to citing the Pledge, one distortion claims "Obama is 'certainly a racist' by virtue of belonging to Chicago's Trinity United Church of Christ, which it says 'will accept only black parishioners' and espouses a

clearly repudiates fantastic claims that Obama is some foreign-born Muslim radical, pundigandists such as Hannity and Limbaugh carry on the jihad and continue, unceasingly, to employ the PM filters of fear and patriotism to frame Obama as a fearsome invader from the fringes of society.

---

commitment to Africa." Researchers at Factcheck state that actually, "a white theology professor says he's been 'welcomed enthusiastically' at the church, as have other non-blacks." They also note that other fabrications abound: i.e. "Another e-mail claims that Obama 'is a Muslim,' attended a 'Wahabi' school in Indonesia, took his Senate oath on the Koran, refuses to recite the Pledge of Allegiance and is part of an Islamic plot to take over the U.S. Each of these statements is false. These false appeals to bigotry and fear remind us of the infamous whispering campaign of eight years ago, when anonymous messages just before the South Carolina primary falsely accused Republican candidate John McCain of fathering an illegitimate child by a black woman."

"An idea is something you have;
an ideology is something that has you."
—*Morris Berman*

AMERICAN EXCEPTIONALISM

Sean Hannity suggests in his book, *Deliver Us from Evil*, that the problem with the Left is twofold: Liberals both fail to see history and ignore the lessons of it (if it's possible, that is, to ignore what one cannot see). He, nonetheless, briefly wonders why this is so before offering a fairly mystifying rationale: "Because their approach toward world events is based on ideology, not on logic — on politics, stalling, hair-splitting, not on moral judgment" (2004, p. 113).

In this line of reasoning, a few extra problems are, on the surface, immediately self-apparent. Implied in his use of "ideology" is a seemingly unintended irony. Our sense is that he had allowed his routine tendency to use hyperbole to cloud what seems his already challenged sense of judiciousness.

Aren't ideologies, after all, a way of seeing the world? Do they not color, so to speak, the ways in which we see other peoples and cultures and, thus, influence whether or not we choose to interact with them? To suggest that the members of your clan or political party or that of your enemies embrace no ideology suggests that we are all but a collection of androids with no shared or competing vision of reality or direction in which to pursue and shape that reality.

Hannity's conflation of ideology, a lens through which we observe the world, and logic, a process of reasoning, are simply not parallel. We may choose to change the lens if we, after having discovered fallacious logic at work in us, possess the inner strength to be reflective, humble, and willing to change.

Beyond his hasty combining of discordant concepts, Hannity's use of the expression "hair-splitting" represents merely an alternative way of saying "thoughtful," "circumspect," "prudent," "unwilling to launch an invasion of another nation that posed no harm," or "hesitant to exacerbate tensions with our enemies."[112] In claiming ownership of the alternative and utterly counter-productive approach to international relations, the vaunted Bush Doctrine, [113] Hannity and his Neo-

---

[112] Glenn Kessler and Peter Baker of the *Washington Post* suggest that the famous "Axis of evil" speech, one component of the Bush Doctrine, served to isolate Iran and North Korea even further but also noted served to encourage these nations to hasten their nuclear ambitions.

[113] According to *Washington Post* columnist, Dan Froomkin, "Preemption has in fact been a staple of our foreign policy for ages — and other countries' as well. The twist Bush put on it was embracing 'preventive' war: Taking action well before an attack was imminent — invading a country that was simply perceived as threatening. Froomkin continues by pointing out that the Bush Doctrine, centered around pre-emptive action, is actually many doctrines which are "utterly inoperative."

conservative colleagues' uncritical glorification of American exceptionalism must also live with the consequences of reasoning that divide the world into false dichotomies — *it's us against them, folks* (according to Rush Limbaugh). Martin Sellevold speculates on America's perceived need to

> ... constantly glorify itself, to make itself out to be special, set apart, almost holy, in relation to all other nations[.] At first glance it might seem like something of a paradox. If we disregard the comparatively minute number of Native Americans, the US is entirely made up of the historically recent descendants of European and Asian immigrants, the descendants of African slaves, and, even more recent, immigrants from Central America and the Caribbean. One would think, then, that if there were one nation on the planet devoid of national prejudice, the United States would be it. Clearly, this is not the case. But the paradox is only apparent, for it is indeed from this very multicultural nature that the aggressive American patriotism arises. (Sellevold, 2003)

Whether or not our ideological frames are unconsciously assembled through socialization at the community level, or linguistically constructed, we all come to develop a particular view of the world, that is to say under normal circumstances. Perhaps the better issue to be raised here is not that we hold this or that *Weltanschauung* but, rather, how did we come to develop a particular harmful worldview so that its spread can be contained or treated.

We suggest that the narratives created in the corporate media, and branded by whatever ideology we are fed from cradle to grave, give substantial shape to our perspectives. Hannity pretends that his party lives in some hermetically sealed plain of existence beyond the reach of corporate influence. But, Christopher Lasch argues in *The Revolt of the Elites and the Betrayal of Democracy* that due to the

> ... decay of civic institutions ranging from political parties to public parks and informal meeting places, conversation has become almost as specialized as the production of knowledge. Social classes speak to themselves in a dialect of their own, inaccessible to outsiders .... (1996, p. 117)

In a society of great wealth distilled in the hands of a few privileged mainstream storytellers (e.g., Fox News, CNN, MSNBC, The New York Times), those stories that mostly serve the agendas of the corporate elite reach the mass public in print or broadcast form.[114] Prevailing business models that tend to drive media corporations, namely profit-driven "news" (dominated so often today by spectacles of celebrity and sensationalism), illustrate the level of attention given to the bottom line.[115] In keeping with the entertainment value of public

---

[114] Even while alternative media, such as blogs, continue to "grow in size and influence," according to a 2008 Technorati study of the blogosphere, "the lines between what is a blog and what is a mainstream media site become less clear." Indeed, "95% of the top 100 US newspapers have reporter blogs." The concentration of wealth is accelerating to levels unheard of since The Great Depression. As of 2004, during the last Census, the wealthiest 1% of Americans controlled approximately 35% of the nation's wealth (Domhoff, 2009; Johnston, 2005). Johnston further observes that "... some of the wealthiest Americans, including Warren E. Buffett, George Soros and Ted Turner, have warned that such a concentration of wealth can turn a meritocracy into an aristocracy and ultimately stifle economic growth by putting too much of the nation's capital in the hands of inheritors rather than strivers and innovators."

[115] The current modus operandi of cable news, which has 24 hours of

spectacle are the discourse practices of Sean Hannity and his apostles. When they incessantly praise him as a "great American" or when Rush Limbaugh says he "hope[s] Obama fails," we suspect that expressions of contempt such as these come with special connotations whose precise meanings elude those outside the Neo-conservative inner circle.

Returning to Hannity's charge that Liberals operate exclusively in an ideological vacuum, we wonder what sort of worldview Neo-conservatives presently abide by. What ideology colors their perspectives? The same USP implied in Hannity's sense of patriotism and O'Reilly's proposition discussed earlier appears in another Neo-conservative claim. It is, it seems, an appealing proposition to those who invest in the *follower-leader* ideology.

To those who do, US is not merely an abbreviation for the name of a North American nation, but also a word. The word appears to be much like the objective *us*, which oddly can create a conceptual demarcation between ourselves and "them." Like *in and out*, *up and down*, or *on and off*, *us and them* resides in distinctly different cognitive categories that the mind, through its developmental course, uses to apprehend conflicting or diverging concepts or phenomena.

It is not immediately necessary to know who "them" is at this point, but to recognize that mass media tend to frame "them" as invaders or as common criminals by definition rather than as immigrants desperate to provide for their families, just as our own immigrant ancestors were. We tend to buy these

---

airtime to fill, is to take, say, a celebrity death or an octuple birth and stretch this "news" item, which is, in fact, devoid of practical value to the viewer, so that every possible angle of a banal "event" can be explicated in minute detail until all 24 hours are filled with "substance."

definitions, too, since positive alternatives are rarely offered. Given the prevailing tendency to measure the worth of those outside the so-called tribe, of what value is this sort of critical self-reflection? Put simply, a more reasoned, empathetic, and realistic view of the world and our place in it is always more helpful and healthful for the development of a just society whose members are free to pursue happiness.

Nevertheless, every society has had to contend with its narrow-minded influential ideologues. Today, it has become increasingly easy to put demagoguery into perspective and apprehend the historical influence that intolerant agitators appear to have had when they wield large media megaphones. Rush Limbaugh, as earlier noted, reaches 20 million listeners per week and scarcely ever fails to remind his audience of his extremely narrow views.[116] His principal USP (i.e. the promotion of American exceptionalism) has come to represent a powerful sign of how deeply pride resonates with some people.

The proposition, persistently reinforced over the decades, appeals to his listeners two-fold: (a) racial pride (even if his audience is unaware of it) and (b) patriotic pride. As a consequence, the more the nation's economic and military prestige sinks relative to China's, Iran's, or North Korea's the more receptive that chauvinistic consumers become to

---

[116] The following quotes illustrate Limbaugh's incendiary racial views. To an African American female caller, he remarked, "Take that bone out of your nose and call me back." In his attempt to degrade then-Presidential candidate Obama, Limbaugh called the Senator a "Halfrican American" and repeatedly aired a song entitled "Barack the Magic Negro." Limbaugh is clearly attempting to exploit white working-class anger felt by some white working-class folks who cannot believe that Obama, an 'uppity' black guy with his Ivy League Hah-vard education and his foreign-sounding name, could possibly be in the White House.

Limbaugh's jingoistic and ethno-centric narratives.

Limbaugh's show creates public space that legitimates a latent desire to preserve or recreate white privilege. His work seems to address a nostalgia that some whites still feel for an era when there were whites-only bathrooms or water fountains and when "The White House" tended to be the residence of exclusively white occupants.

When listeners, likely almost exclusively white males,[117] hear Barack Obama referred to as the "Magic Negro," or the late-Senator Strom Thurmond[118] lauded as a voice of reason, they may be more apt to feel their increasingly diminishing "racial superiority" as whites revitalized.[119]

---

[117] We infer from Limbaugh's own comments about blacks, "They're 12% of the population. Who the hell cares?" that he perceives his audience to be largely non-African American. He surely has some black listeners but has certainly gone out of his way to alienate African Americans in his quest to entertain his intended demographic. A 2009 Pew Research poll reveals that 72% are male. Other related Limbaugh observations can be found at http://www.fair.org/index.php?page=2549.

[118] In 1993, Limbaugh praised former segregationist Sen. Strom Thurmond for calling a gay soldier 'not normal', saying "He's not encumbered by being politically correct .... If you want to know what America used to be — and a lot of people wish it still were — then you listen to Strom Thurmond." (TV show, 9/1/93, transcript archived on Nexis) But, in the America that 'used to be,' Thurmond was one of the country's leading racists, running for president in 1948 on the Dixiecrat ticket, with a platform that opposed federal anti-lynching laws and boasted the slogan, 'Segregation Forever!'" Race baiting, another part of Limbaugh's repertoire, may also appeal predominantly to white males with latent prejudices: "... let me put it to you this way. The NFL all too often looks like a game between the Bloods and the Crips without any weapons. There, I said it" (October 14, 2009).

[119] Recent socio-demographic trends indicate that by 2050, whites will be in the minority due to non-white immigration and higher birthrates. For more information, see http://pewsocialtrends.org/pubs/703/ population-projections-united-states

Paradoxically, this feeling may explain both Limbaugh's cult-like popularity with his 20-million dittoheads and why his appeal can never grow beyond this particular unreflective herd. In addition to his racist appeals, Limbaugh also appeals to national chauvinism.

The other appeals that he makes are to national identity and prestige, the notion that America sits alone at the top of the heap of all other nations. How is Limbaugh able to manufacture such an appealing USP? Creating a clique is a way of binding ourselves with like-minded members of our community, a way of expressing a group's uniqueness in terms of how its members think or act and as a way of contrasting these features with others we may feel don't quite fit in. It is a form of tribalism that, thanks to mass media's national and global reach, can brainwash a multitude of people into embracing a harmful ideology.

The Neo-conservative conception of America's clique centers on America's purported self-evident exclusivity. Lakoff (2009) illustrates this point in his argument that Rightwing radicals have created a range of mythical narratives governed by radical Conservative values that they want to go "back" to. Among them is the prevailing narrative that

> ... America is inherently good and has an evangelistic duty to spread its way of life — and when it fails or harms people, it is because it was betrayed from within by 'defeatists,' by cowards who would 'cut and run,' by 'leftist extremists,' and so on.' (2009, p. 69)

A recurring theme espoused by Limbaugh is the belief that Liberals are simply a collection of "defeatists" who would rather "cut and run" from obligations, such as preventive war, and sit around singing kumbaya — hardly characteristic of America's exceptional military might. Even the occasional listener of Limbaugh will likely find it difficult to change the channel before hearing some implicit or explicit reference to America's unique and vaunted status among the planet's many other nations.[120] In his article *A Look at American Exceptionalism*, Martin Sellevold, a Norwegian writer working in London, discusses why this may be so and provides some perspective beyond America's borders:

> It seems the idea of American exceptionalism is not so much manifested in an actual difference between the US and other countries in terms of outward behaviour, but more in terms of a 'truth' about the mental and moral superiority of Americans being actively reiterated by American culture to the American public via movies, television and political rhetoric. To generalise, all Americans are told every day in the media that only they know how the world really works, and only they know how it should be worked. In this way, the myth is kept alive. It is in this that the United States of America truly is unique and set apart from other Western nations. (p. 48)

---

[120] In a July 23, 2009 interview with Greta Van Susteren, Limbaugh was pontificating about the preeminence of America's healthcare system and American exceptionalism, asking how any other system in the world could compare to ours: "I mean nobody leaves this country for health coverage ..." Yet ironically, Limbaugh could not be more wrong in claiming that Americans' healthcare is preeminent in the world. In fact, the citizens of most western democracies, on average, outlive Americans (e.g., the Japanese live 5-6 years longer than Americans do and even Cubans, who spend about 1/18 per person what the U.S. spends on healthcare, nonetheless, have about the same longevity). Yet because Limbaugh has activated a latent cognitive frame in his listeners' minds, he need not offer evidence for his outlandish claims; after all, America is the greatest country in the world!

While Sellevold interprets this exceptionalism purely on a national level, Limbaugh, as noted earlier, extends it to a racial level as well. One could say that Limbaugh imbues his appeals with an additional sense of mental and moral superiority: that of whites over blacks.

Critics may wonder whether Limbaugh is simply some crude chauvinist to be ignored. Clearly, he isn't and isn't the loquacious hillbilly he feigns to be. Limbaugh is also a shrewd polemicist, and his daily theater figures prominently in the public discourse and the mindset of listeners tickled by his black-and-white criticisms of the Left suffused with dogmatic paeons to Conservative leaders.[121]

Consider the following paradox: The more *un*exceptional America and its working class become, the more

---

[121] Writes Kathryn Jean Lopez of *National Review Online*, "Rush Limbaugh has spent 20 years reminding us what a wonderful country we live in..." (2008). Also, observes Andrew McCarthy, "Rush is only the most influential conservative of his generation. ... Through the ups and downs of two decades, his message — always delivered with optimism, civility, and good humor — has been faithful to two core convictions: the power of freedom and the power of American exceptionalism." What follows are some characteristic patterns of optimism and civility: Arguing during the 2008 campaign that no one is permitted to criticize Barack Obama: "You can't criticize the little black man-child. You just can't do it, 'cause it's just not right. It's not fair. He's such a victim." (Radio, 8/20/08); Reacting to a report of black students assaulting a white student on a bus (an incident that police determined was not racially motivated), Limbaugh brought in Barack Obama: "In Obama's America, the white kids now get beat up with the black kids cheering, 'Right on, right on, right on'" (9/15/09); Upon learning from a caller to his show that St. Louis was extending a light rail system into East St. Louis — a community of some 40,000 residents, almost all of whom are black (radio, 6/27/94): "They got a light rail system to East St. Louis where nobody goes?" http://www.fair.org/index.php?page=3928

receptive working-class Americans become to exceptionalist messages from pundits such as Limbaugh and Hannity. That is, a country whose working-class standards were once the envy of the world now finds it can scarcely make ends meet. Jobs are tough to come by; salaries are stagnant; consumers continue sinking deeper into debt. Internationally, America now owes increasingly more capital to its competitors and financiers who are sometimes not so sociable, i.e., Saudi Arabia and China. Once accustomed to decisive military victories over superpowers like Germany and Japan, the United States now struggles to impose military solutions on even small nations such as Iraq and Afghanistan.

In light of these hard times, what working-class folks are most yearning for, we suspect, is not the *segregation* of the '50s and '60s, but the burgeoning economic growth of that era. At that time, the nation didn't need a Ronald Reagan to tell us it was morning in America or a Rush Limbaugh to tell us what an exceptional country we live in. We already maintained a healthy self-esteem. A working man holding a high school diploma could earn a relatively stable, respectable, and considerable income. In this day and age, even college graduates face shrinking wages with meager fringe benefits and little job security.

Yet, the solutions to these problems are much too complex to be explained by Neo-conservative knee-jerk objects of ridicule. To add real substance to the public discourse over these issues, Limbaugh *could be* talking about the seismic changes that have occurred in our economy, namely economic polarization, the outsourcing of labor, the fact that we are no longer building things but simply dreaming up intangible "products" like fancy financial derivatives and clever methods in trading on margin. These "business" practices enrich a few bankers and enable devious scam artists (i.e. Michael Milken, Bernie Ebbers, Bernie Madoff, etc.) but do nothing for the long-term fundamental health of the economy, thereby undermining the honest endeavors of working class America.

Limbaugh's listeners seem to yearn for a time when America actually built products (cars, televisions, refrigerators, etc.) rather than blowing huge investment banking and housing bubbles — which have driven America's economic growth for the past ten or so years. Limbaugh *could* argue for more vigorous government investment in, say, alternative energies so that America could once again ground its economics in tangible products. Limbaugh *could also* call attention to how much our living standards are based on borrowed money, even though doing so would require facing problems that don't lend themselves to easy solutions (e.g., paying down our debt will mean either raising taxes or enduring a lower standard of living; investing in alternative energies would also mean higher taxes). So, he shrewdly lets those sleeping dogs lie and focuses, with black-and-white precision, on convenient scapegoats: if only we eliminated welfare (which accounts for only a minute fraction of the Federal budget[122]) and affirmative action (which has barely affected the most powerful if secluded sectors, corporate boardrooms,[123] and the Senate[124]), then society

[122] According to McLaughlin (1997), 1% of the national budget and 2% of state budgets are devoted to welfare. The widespread misperceptions about the extent of welfare exacerbate the problems of poverty. The actual cost of welfare programs is about 1% of the federal budget and 2% of state budgets (McLaughlin, 1997)

[123] Although the US population as a whole continues to rapidly diversify, 85.1% of corporate board seats remain occupied by whites. The

would be back on track and, as Lakoff observed, moving toward the values we really need to get "back to."

Thus far, we have sketched out *how it is* that Limbaugh creates his USP, but *what is it* that really motivates him to do so? Since he seems so ever content to arouse white's emotions (their fears about minorities taking over) rather than challenge their intellects, it's worth exploring some of his possible motivations.

Exceptional Purposes

Limbaugh's philosophy of how American society ought to run seems fed by a strong, if misconstrued, understanding of the work of Alex de Tocqueville who had surveyed the young nation and its people well before corporations, as we understand them today, co-opted institutions held, traditionally, in the public trust. Tocqueville observed in his seminal work, *Democracy in America*, that the

> ... American position is ... entirely exceptional, and it is quite possible that no democratic nation will ever be similarly placed. Their strictly puritanical origin, their exclusively commercial habits, even the country they inhabit, which seems to divert their minds from the pursuit of science, literature, and the arts, the nearness of Europe, which allows them to neglect such study without relapsing into barbarism, a thousand such reasons of which I have been able to signal only the main ones, have singularly concurred

---

remaining 14.9% are occupied by minorities. (2005). For more details, visit http://www.catalyst.org/press-release/116/launch-of-alliance-for-board-diversity-calls-for-fair-representation-on-corporate-boards

[124] Presently, there is only one African American, Barack Obama's replacement, and he has pledged not to run election in 2010.

> to fix the mind of the American upon purely practical objects. His passions, his wants, his education, and everything about him seem to unite in drawing the native of the United States earthward; his religion alone bids him turn, from time to time, a transient and distracted glance to heaven. Let us cease, then, to view all democratic nations under the example of the American people (2003, pp. 525-6).

Tocqueville analyzed the largely commercial sensibilities that characterize citizens' daily routines, the chiefly pragmatic pursuit of material wealth that had developed in society only a bit more than a generation after the nation's inception. What is, perhaps, most exceptional about his assessment of America then is what it means for us now. A hundred and fifty or so years since, we can see Tocqueville's observations as a signpost of both how little, in some ways, and how much, in other ways, America has changed.

In one sense, we still seem principally driven by material goals, clinging self-destructively to lavish lifestyles that hasten what we can now foresee as the destruction of delicate eco-systems, the accumulation of dangerous national or personal debt, and the depletion of petroleum reserves. In his essay, *Two Minds*, author Wendell Berry (2002) referred to these pursuits as part of the work of the "Rational Mind," objecting, as it were, to its withdraw from all of human life that involves feeling, affection, familiarity, reverence, faith and loyalty. Favoring, in its place, the exclusive pursuit of money, the Rational Mind fails to prevent massive damage to nature and to human economy and, to confess its complicity in the equation: knowledge=power=money=damage (p. 22).

In another sense, the vast oceans that once insulated

America from other countries, and therefore, from the temptation to wage wars, no longer inhibits us, as our military maintains garrisons in nearly 130 countries[125] and we are embroiled in two wars, both, as Tocqueville would have predicted if he'd lived to see an oil-based economy, probably related to our unquenchable thirst for oil.

Tocqueville's description of America, then, signals how far and fast the Republic drifted from its truly revolutionary past, a period presently romanticized by pundigandists who still maintain that the Revolution was more about the realization of lofty abstractions, like liberty and freedom from tyranny, than about concrete issues of economics and taxation.

The irony of Limbaugh's capitalist spin on America's past ethos of exclusivity is that it elevates the self-congratulatory version of America as the benevolent protector of oppressed peoples (say, Iraqi or Afghani) that invades and occupies sovereign territories not because of petroleum reserves or proximity to Caspian Sea oil, but only out of its concern for the beleaguered masses.

Somewhat like the exclusively commercial habits that Tocqueville disparaged, Limbaugh's values embrace at once the romantic, Hemingway-esque nostalgia that today's so-called patriotic pundits hold for war and the pseudo-humanitarian impulse of those fighting and dying to "protect" others from "oppression" — as opposed to, say, protecting the profits of oil companies and defense contractors who want to appropriate foreign oil rights or who have a financial stake in prolonging a

---

[125] According to the nonpartisan website GlobalSecurity.org as of 2005, the U.S. maintains troops in nearly 130 nations. For more details, see http://www. Globalsecurity.org/military/ops/global-de ployments.htm

costly war indefinitely.[126]

This may explain why Limbaugh's popularity has been growing since the wars of Iraq and Afghanistan began.[127] The collective feeling that seemed to permeate the American psyche just after the attacks of 9/11 was one of emasculation when 20 ordinary psychopaths with box cutters nearly brought the world's sole superpower to its knees — at least emotionally and, perhaps, economically, — so Limbaugh has cleverly and successfully tapped into that desire for masculine revenge, whether against an actual perpetrator or simply a convenient scapegoat like Iraq.[128] It should be noted, too, that any

---

[126] We should acknowledge, incidentally, that in the hierarchy of motives, those who engage in war for war's sake — those warriors motivated by an atavistic desire to prove their manhood — are certainly less admirable than those who engage in war in the belief, however misguided, that their efforts will improve the lives of the people they're fighting for. Finally, we consider those who profit financially from war — defense contractors who actually have an interest in prolonging a war as long as possible and who may see a foreign war as a chance to gouge American taxpayers since there may be little oversight on how contracts are fulfilled and how many cost overruns are justified — to be the least admirable, indeed, to be worthy of contempt.

[127] It must be also be noted that the recent spike in the popularity of angry Neo-conservative pundigandists can be correlated with a spike in the level of uncertainty about the market, about jobs, about the budget deficit, and about the nation's future economic growth. In a metaphorical sense, Limbaugh — like Hannity and O'Reilly and perhaps Olbermann and Schultz on the left — are peaking in popularity right now because they are collectively the anti-Obama: Their stentorian, unequivocal pronouncements about how Obama should act on foreign and domestic policy starkly contrast with the incremental, bring-all-sides-to-the-table approach of Obama. In economic hard times, the public increasingly prefers powerful, even dictatorial leaders who propose clear and easy solutions and paint both the problem and the enemy in black-and-white terms (Coughlin and Huey Long in the Depression, e.g.). (Murray Edelman, Politics of the Spectacle).

[128] Instead of directly addressing a caller's question about America facing defeat in Iraq and perpetuating feelings of hatred toward the US,

opposition to the call for vengeance generally and to the Bush-Cheney project for Iraq specifically has met total relegation to the fringe — especially in the case of Cindy Sheehan[129] who, according Rush Limbaugh, was just another

> ... Bill Burkett.[130] Her story is nothing more than forged documents. There's nothing about it that's real, including the mainstream media's glomming onto it. It's not real. It's nothing more than an attempt. It's the latest effort made by the coordinated Left.[131]

While that purported attempt by "the coordinated left" was largely one grieving mother's call to bring an end to an unjust war, Limbaugh's framing of the Crawford, Texas, protests cast Sheehan as a mere cog in the Democrat political machinery.

Limbaugh also appeals to those who construe America's role in the world as the planet's sole policeman, punishing unjust countries and rescuing the oppressed even if it means invading sovereign nations and replacing their leaders. So, it behooves Limbaugh to overlook the possibility that there

---

Limbaugh castigates his caller by accusing him of being an imposter, i.e. a skilled Liberal operative. Unable to answer the question, Limbaugh demonizes those who would even question the possibility of America's ill-conceived military venture. A detailed recording of the exchange can be found at http://www.youtube.com
/watch?v=WGlsyuivCYA

[129] Cindy Sheehan is "a mother whose oldest child, Casey, was killed in Iraq, and [she] has been on a crusade to end the wars and hold George Bush accountable...." Sheehan's blog can be found at http://cindysheehanssoapbox.blogspot.com/

[130] Bill Burkett is the self-confessed liar who produced forged documents from an as-of-yet unknown Lucy Ramirez allegedly detailing the reasons behind George W. Bush's questionable service record during Vietnam. (Wikipedia entry)

[131] Borrowed from http://mediamatters.org/mmtv/200508160009

may be baser economic motives working beneath the hallowed abstractions "freedom" and "liberty" so often carelessly tossed around today.[132]

While Tocqueville's portrait of America describes a time when business practices centered largely around the activities of tradesmen and their apprentices, his depiction throws into sharp relief the seismic shifts that have since taken place in the social and political economy: the massive influence that corporations have come to wield in nearly all facets of contemporary American society.[133]

Property As Persons

---

[132] The following quotation from "Politics and the English Language" illustrates how the tactics of demagogues have hardly changed since Orwell's time: "The words democracy, socialism, freedom, patriotic, realistic, justice have each of them several different meanings which cannot be reconciled with one another. In the case of a word like democracy, not only is there no agreed definition, but the attempt to make one is resisted from all sides. It is almost universally felt that when we call a country democratic we are praising it: consequently the defenders of every kind of régime claim that it is a democracy, and fear that they might have to stop using that word if it were tied down to any one meaning. Words of this kind are often used in a consciously dishonest way. That is, the person who uses them has his own private definition, but allows his hearer to think he means something quite different. Statements like 'Marshal Pétain was a true patriot,' 'The Soviet press is the freest in the world,' 'The Catholic Church is opposed to persecution,' are almost always made with intent to deceive. Other words used in variable meanings, in most cases more or less dishonestly, are: class, totalitarian, science, progressive, reactionary, bourgeois, equality."

[133] *The Truman Show* is an interesting satire of current realities and a wry commentary on the extent to which even our private lives have become salable. For example, we watch movies with product placement; we wear logos for products; and we have even become products. We allow cliché-laden Hallmark cards to express our feelings for us on intimate occasions for our loved ones.

Where America, or the American judiciary, has become exceptional today is in its understanding and treatment of corporations as persons who have brought about " ... our current political predicament whereby corporate agents exercise [the] government-backed right to undermine the will of citizens ... " (Ritz, 2007, p. 196). A recent Supreme Court ruling (5-4) on January 21, 2010, illustrates the desire to carry on this creative tale. Adam Liptak[134] reports that the financial backing that corporations engage in, in political campaigns, cannot be limited as such limitations would violate a company's First Amendment protections. Such a ruling may not seem, on the surface, to be so strikingly odd. Juxtaposed to the following observation, though, the ruling takes on new meaning.

In a personal communication, William P. Meyers (January, 2001) noted that "Slavery is the legal fiction that a person is property. Corporate personhood is the legal fiction that property is a person." The very fact that corporations continue to enjoy the unique rights of personhood and, thus, a range of Constitutional protections underscores the kind of double-standard that Limbaugh finds appealing.

On the one hand, corporations receive all the rights and privileges of private citizens; on the other, corporations, like say, R. J. Reynolds,[135] cannot be held liable for the crimes they

---

[134] See also Holland & Kuhnhenn (2010)

[135]For example, studies funded by tobacco companies themselves reveal that addicting young people to nicotine is the most effective way of creating a lifetime smoker; thus, the tobacco companies have a vested interest in targeting young people, *á la* the wildly popular Joe the Camel brand image. Yet when those young people age, later becoming susceptible to emphysema, lung cancer and a host of other illnesses

commit against real people.[136] However, to Limbaugh, free market Capitalism and the corporate entities that exist and operate within it can always fix what ails us, no matter how exploitative they can be. This argument has been extended to the present fight over healthcare overhaul.

According to Limbaugh, "Nobody has the right to good health. *Nobody* has the right to good health [his emphasis]," [137] except — he deftly fails to note — for the insurance corporations who have been found at times to

---

influenced by smoking, the tobacco companies deny any responsibility.

[136] As Molly Morgan and Jan Edwards observed in their paper "Abolish Corporate Personhood" (2003), "[i]t is important to remember what a corporation is to understand the implications of corporate personhood for democracy. A corporation is not a real thing; it's a legal fiction, an abstraction. You can't see or hear or touch or smell a corporation — it's just an idea that people agree to and put into writing. Because legal personhood has been conferred upon an abstraction that can be redefined at will under the law, corporations have become super-humans in our world. A corporation can live forever. It can change its identity in a day. It can cut off parts of itself — even its head — and actually function better than before. It can also cut off parts of itself and from those parts grow new selves. It can own others of its own kind and it can merge with others of its own kind. It doesn't need fresh air to breathe or clean water to drink or safe food to eat. It doesn't fear illness or death. It can have simultaneous residence in many different nations. It's not male, female, or even transgendered. Without giving birth it can create children and even parents. If it's found guilty of a crime, it cannot go to prison."

[137] Borrowed from RushLimbaugh.com on September 23, 2009, at http://www.rushlimbaugh.com/home/daily/site_08290 9/content/01125110.guest.html. It is necessary to call attention to Limbaugh's denial of the Jeffersonian logic — "that all men are endowed ... with alienable rights ... [to] life, liberty and the pursuit of happiness" — that effectively challenged one form of tyranny. That 'health' is tied to 'life' itself and the ability to pursue 'happiness' appears beyond the powers of Limbaugh's reasoning. Although sound health is not premised upon any Constitutional right, it is fundamental to our right to life.

fraudulently deny certain other citizens their due coverage in order to maximize, no doubt, the company's financial well-being.[138] Of course, taking action legal against corporate "persons" like those who consistently and legally exploit others means damaging the health of the corporation itself. While we can agree — in this day and age — that, like the right to wealth,[139] nobody has the right to health, the political systems that grant corporate "persons" exceptional rights to exploit authentic persons born of human mothers must be challenged.

Limbaugh's concept of American exceptionalism seems tied directly to some tacit belief in America's corporate manifest destiny: to be not only regulation-free and exploitative for the short-term bottom line, but to be proactive in the long term in the search for new geographic regions or peoples deemed ripe for capitalist exploitation.[140] Corporations have, effectively, come to supplant the early frontiersmen as primary explorers and exploiters of uncharted territories. That is, while "the frontier experience [has been] the principal theme of American national life," we have come to "identify [our] liberty

---

[138] Even in these lean times when so many companies are struggling to survive, the industry continues to enjoy record profits as insurance premiums continue two and three times the rate of inflation.

[139] This reference to wealth neither embraces nor rejects the U.S. Senate's 2003 vote to "supply major aid to the rich in their pursuit of event greater wealth" (Buffet, 2003). Warren Buffet's full commentary appears at http://www.washingtonpost.com/

[140] It's worth noting the similarity of exceptionalism to a lecture Woodrow Wilson had given at Columbia in 1907: "Since trade ignores national boundaries and the manufacturer insists on having the world as a market, the flag of his nation must follow him, and the doors of the nations which are closed against him must be battered down. Concessions obtained by financiers must be safeguarded by ministers of state, even if the sovereignty of unwilling nations be outraged in the process."

with [our] free movement to new and uncharted frontiers."[141] Nearly thirty years since he made this observation, Kim Young Hum would likely not be so surprised by the frontier mentality that still prevails.

In a speech at a recent conference celebrating the 100th anniversary of *The Progressive*, Naomi Klein references the types of exceptionalism that Limbaugh's new political protégé, Sarah Palin, also embraces. Just two weeks before Lehman Brothers' implosion, believed by many economists to have precipitated the present global financial meltdown, Palin was extolling the wealth of Alaska's vast natural resources — still open to potential development. In Klein's view, nonetheless, Palin's scarcely-veiled open invitation to plunder the untamed wealth of Alaska emerges naturally from an uncritical faith in the raw unchecked powers of Capitalism and of deregulated markets where unlimited investment can flow freely to new ventures because, of course, a new frontier will always lie just beyond the next tundra.

Yet, as America has painfully learned in the lengthy occupations[142] of both Iraq and Afghanistan, "exploring" these new frontiers often comes at a steep price. The Iraq War has cost nearly a trillion dollars and over 4000 American lives,[143]

---

[141] Young Hum Kim observes in the Preface of his book *American Frontier Activities in Asia* (1981).

[142] Or, fights for "freedom" and "liberty" as Neo-conservatives would term the two wars. Yet, it is worth noting that if the U. S. military were to abandon the "Green Zones" in Kabul and Baghdad, the two governments would probably collapse like a house of cards.

[143] Other reported monetary losses appear as follows: (a) U.S. 2009 Monthly Spending in Iraq - $7.3 billion as of Oct 2009; (b) U.S. 2008 Monthly Spending in Iraq - $12 billion; (c) U.S. Spending per Second - $5,000 in 2008 (per Senate Majority Leader Harry Reid on May 5, 2008); (c) Cost of deploying one U.S. soldier for one year in Iraq -

and the access to cheap oil we were implicitly promised has not significantly materialized. And, in the meantime, countries such as Germany and China (who are indirectly financing these military ventures) are now moving away from oil altogether and investing heavily in greener technologies like wind and solar power that can inhibit global warming and preserve the planet's more finite resources.[144]

Klein sees this sort of exceptionalist USP of perpetual exploitation as a comforting but dangerous lie — ridiculing the very notion that the planet can offer developers an unending supply of commodities and products.[145] But, how, one must ask,

---

$390,000 (Congressional Research Service) (d) Lost & Unaccounted for in Iraq - $9 billion of US taxpayers' money and $549.7 million in spare parts shipped in 2004 to US contractors. Also, per ABC News, 190,000 guns, including 110,000 AK-47 rifles; (e) Missing - $1 billion in tractor trailers, tank recovery vehicles, machine guns, rocket-propelled grenades and other equipment and services provided to the Iraqi security forces. (Per CBS News on Dec 6, 2007.); (f) Mismanaged & Wasted in Iraq - $10 billion, per Feb 2007 Congressional hearings; (g) Halliburton Overcharges Classified by the Pentagon as Unreasonable and Unsupported - $1.4 billion; (h) Amount paid to KBR, a former Halliburton division, to supply U.S. military in Iraq with food, fuel, housing and other items - $20 billion; (i) Portion of the $20 billion paid to KBR that Pentagon auditors deem "questionable or supportable" - $3.2 billion. Details about human costs may also be found at http://usliberals.about.com/od/homelandsecurit1/a/IraqNumbers.htm

[144] Ironically, the largest solar company in America just moved to China where they can enjoy more generous tax incentives (Friedman, 2009 September 27). Clearly, China and Germany are not acting in exceptionalist ways, but are addressing the global realities of climate change and finite natural resources and of the need to cooperate with other nations.

[145] Worth noting is the level of political attention paid to the destruction of ecosystems throughout Appalachia where mining corporations have been practicing mountaintop removal techniques that alter natural topography, contaminate water tables with toxic compounds, bury streams, and threaten communities with potential floods and

can we reconcile the unrelenting corporate quest for higher profits and the pervasive disregard for the planet's limited natural resources with a proactive position on reversing trends in global climate change?[146] And, from where, it's worth asking, does this belief emerge? The contemporary concept of modern

---

mudslides. According to sources at the non-profit OMB Watch, "No industry other than oil has benefited more from the attack on environmental and safety regulations over the last 6 years by the Bush Administration and the congressional leadership. From weakening mercury rules and attempts to weaken the Clean Air Act (in the form of the Orwellian "Clear Skies Act"), to weakening the Clean Water Act by allowing mining waste to be dumped indiscriminately in our nation's waterways, the massive investments by the coal industry to buy the favor of Congress and the White House has never seen a better return on investment." Other source material can be found at http://www.ombwatch.org/files/bush legacy.pdf

[146] Despite Limbaugh's repeated protests that global climate change is a hoax, that it is "just part and parcel of the divide we face, the Universe of Lies, the Universe of Reality and what is really intended for this country and the world at the hands of both domestic and international leftists and Marxists" (2009, December 7), he offers no evidence that the members of every national science academy are, in fact, "leftists and Marxists" engaged in some elaborate global conspiracy. In Limbaugh's world of discourse, ad hominem hasty generalizations serve as necessary and sufficient proofs. Since concerns voiced by researchers around the globe about the environment in general and the climate in particular don't square with the interests of Capitalism, it is necessary, therefore, to marginalize any perspective that does not support the essential, inherent aims of capitalist expansion. While it is true that the recent scandal involving the emails of researchers at the University of East Anglia may have damaged the credibility of those researchers, Limbaugh *et al.* fail to note that there are four main places where climate data are collected, so that even if the data at one of the institutions is compromised, the data at the other three are not. Furthermore, it should be noted that every major scientific organization — from the National Academy of Sciences to the Intergovernmental Panel on Climate Change to George Bush's own EPA — avers that global warming is largely caused by man and can only be slowed by man.

capitalism, Klein observes,

> … was born with the so-called discovery of the Americas. It was the pillage of the incredible natural resources of the Americas that generated the excess capital that made the Industrial Revolution possible. Early explorers spoke of this land as a New Jerusalem, a land of such bottomless abundance, there for the taking, so vast that the pillage would never have to end. (2009)

As it springs from Biblical stories describing both earthly and human devastation, regeneration and redemption, the exceptionalist philosophy of limitless supply strikes a chord in certain Christian communities wedded to the bogus belief that corporate and personal power gained through pure Capitalism is G-d-ordained and, so, entirely justified. Limbaugh's concept of America is "exceptional" for what it appears to take from these core narratives, of catastrophic "floods and fresh starts, of raptures and rescues" (Klein), and how it turns them into an ideology that fits Neo-conservative beliefs in Capitalism's "divine rights."

Limbaugh's view of American exceptionalism is a relic of times past before corporations were granted the full rights of personhood and consumers saw themselves as citizens who tended to be more aware of their civic responsibilities and in the affairs of government.[147] He and his fellow commentators

---

[147] The argument began with former solicitor general Theodore Olson challenging the precedents as stifling expression "that is at the very core of the First Amendment," namely debate about candidates for office. Olson was representing Citizens United, a nonprofit corporation whose documentary critical of Hillary Clinton (Hillary: The Movie) last year was found by the FEC to violate the ban on corporate expenditures for electioneering communication. Justice Ruth Bader

certainly have grounds to eulogize the spirit of pragmatism that once turned the early settlers into pioneers who turned prairielands into cities and subdivisions.[148] But, Neo-con pundits are misguided in clinging to conceptual understandings of the past that don't square with contemporary America where political institutions have ceded control over much of America's vast wealth to private interests.[149] In her book, *Living with the Fluid Genome*, geneticist and ethicist Mae Wan Ho describes the effects of corporate personhood and its unregulated power. She argues that

> ... under the banner of the 'free market' and 'free choice' we are losing our right to self-determination and self-sufficiency in every aspect of our daily lives: our food,

---

Ginsburg quickly jumped in, asking Olson whether individuals and corporations have the same First Amendment rights. "A corporation, after all, is not endowed by its creator with inalienable rights." Olson invoked the 1964 case New York Times Co. v. Sullivan and the 1936 decision Grosjean v. American Press for the proposition that "corporations are persons entitled to protection under the First Amendment." For the full article, please visit http://www.firstamendmentcenter.org/analysis.aspx?id=22052

[148] Giovanni Arrighi observes in his book, *The Long Twentieth Century*, that " ... as soon as the Revolution ... freed the settlers' hands, they set out to conquer as much of North American continent as was profitable and to recognize its space in a thoroughly capitalistic manner. Among other things this meant 'removing the Natives' to make room for an ever-expanding immigrant population ... " (1996, p. 60).

[149] In his incisive attack on free market globalization, Christopher Hedges argues the "corporate forces that are looting the Treasury and have plunged us into a depression will not be contained by the two main political parties. The Democratic and Republican parties have become little more than squalid clubs of privilege and wealth, whores to money and corporate interests, hostage to a massive arms industry, and so adept at deception and self-delusion they no longer know truth from lies" (2008).

> health, social mores, the way we choose to live and most seriously of all, our right to think differently from the corporate establishment. (2003, p. 26)

Like other pre-emptive Neo-conservative attacks on social programs proposed to benefit the people, Limbaugh's discontent springs largely from his 'strict-father' perspective. As he easily consents to corporate persons who can make the most of the very free market Capitalism that precipitated the present global financial meltdown, he conversely advocates for the "tough love" approach to helping human persons on the socio-economic fringe.

"Nothing is easier than leading the people on a leash.
I just hold up a dazzling campaign poster,
and they jump through it."
—*Joseph Goebbels*

A Rhetoric of Color

Colors comprise a fairly significant part of our understanding the world around us, as well as our making supposedly informed choices about how we should best interact with the world, its various natural phenomena and other humans with whom we share the planet. Color is like an instant messenger. Of all the non-verbal forms of communication, Leatrice Eiseman notes, color is the most immediate means of communicating messages and meanings (2000, p. 6). J. H. Kleynhans notes that " ... colour stimulates and works synergistically with all of the senses, symbolizes abstract concepts and thoughts, expresses fantasy or wish fulfillment, recalls another time or place and produces an aesthetic or emotional response" (2007, p. 46).

Strangely enough, outside the mind, color does not exist. In physical terms, objects can be said to have the color of the light reflected off their surfaces, which depends on the spectrum of that light, the viewing perspective, and the angles of illumination. So, what do these aspects of physics mean for us all as consumers of mass media? That is, how do these qualities of the physical world play into the practice of propagandizing? We can conclude that recognizing colors and deriving from them meaningful emotional responses is part of the human process of perception (Mayer, et al. 1990). Our very ability to derive meaning at this basic level of perception is fundamental to understanding why brainwashing works as well as it does.

One group of meticulous professionals who make a study of color, its emotional weight and meanings, is artists. To acknowledge first the patently obvious, artists have long recognized the role that color and light play in human perception. Michael Douma, for example, recalls the words of Jacques Riviere who observed that "the true purpose of painting is to represent objects as they really are, that is to say differently from the way we see them. It tends always to give us their sensible essence, their presence, this is why the image it forms does not resemble their appearance ..., " because the appearance changes from moment to moment (2008, ¶4).

One notable explicit effort in giving color " ... greater emotional and expressive power" was undertaken by the Fauvists in the early part of the 20th century (Douma, 2008). Their desire to imbue color with this greater emotive power forced Fauvist painters to implement an unusual approach to portraying what they perceived. Douma observes that the " ...

impossibility of liberating [color] from form on a two-dimensional canvas led the Fauvists to adopt the only physiologically viable solution: painting common objects and scenes in the 'wrong' colors" (2008).

Beyond what artists have sensed about the effects of color and luminance on perception, some researchers, too, have come to theorize another effect that color and light produce on the human psyche. Though most psychologists question the value of color therapy as an area of fruitful inquiry, color as a universal language, nonetheless, leaps cultural boundaries "in our electronically- technologically- satellite-linked 'Global Village'" (Kleynhans, 2007, p. 47). For example, hues in the red area of the spectrum are known as "warm" colors and include orange and yellow which evoke emotions ranging from feelings of comfort to anger and hostility. These intriguing insights into the physical properties of light and the mind's ability to perceive color have still encouraged the development of new approaches to helping people contend more easily with the effects of various mental disorders.

Kleynhans notes that "culture conditions the colours that we see" (p. 52.) "Colour is therefore intimately bound up with language because it supplies a system of arbitrary signs" (Gage, 1995, p. 79). In relying on certain culturally-based connections among colors and the emotional states of individuals, some psychologists have endeavored to enhance their therapeutic approaches with meaningful colors that evoke positive responses to various stimuli. Some professional advocates of color therapy have observed, for example, that combative patients in manic states have responded to pale pink or soft blue walls of psychiatric wards in positive and calculable ways. Conversely, patients in depressive states appear to respond more favorably to brighter colors (Bradley & Zeiss, 2006).

Other researchers have suggested that the colors green and blue may reduce anxiety. Orange and yellow are thought to produce higher heart rates and, perhaps, higher measures of tension. Even the absence of light, which means the absence of color and knowledge, can have profound effects on our social and intellectual development. From these anecdotal examples of color's various effects on us, we can conclude that appreciating the significance of color as meaningful is not only part of our cognitive processes and socialization, but also a behavioral trait — part of the practice of attending to personal tastes.

Beyond these clinical considerations, social psychologists have recently gained extraordinary new awareness of the role that colors can play in decision-making processes and, thus, partisan politics. Caruso et al. (2009) have demonstrated, for example, that political biases directly "influence people's visual representations of a bi-racial political candidate's skin tone" (p. 20168). Subjects who took part in the study were shown various images of a candidate whose skin tone had been re-enhanced to reflect both lighter and darker shades. Unaware of the changes in the photos, participants consistently rated the lightened photos as more representative of the candidate whose political ideology aligned with theirs.

These ways of perceiving meaning in color, or the shade of a person's skin, say much about group membership, such as in a political institution, as well as the extent to which an express connection to group power "affects conscious and unconscious reactions toward members of the in-group[150] and those of the out-group."[151] Perhaps most intriguing was the discovery that group membership correlates both with our social judgments of others and our visual perception of their physical features.[152] Caruso and his team observed that "political partisanship is a form of group membership that may bias interpretations of a bi-racial candidate's skin color so that visual representations of the candidate fit coherently with the desire to see one's own group members positively (p. 20168).

With this understanding, we can, thus, argue that certain colors can serve as useful political tools as well. Given the psychosocial qualities they carry, carefully chosen colors in media can help flesh out the desires and intentions of political partisans. The Fascists during Hitler's régime relied heavily on the semiotic import of color. With an understanding of the potential power of color on the formation of consent and its influence on the mind, Dr. Joseph Goebbels, Reichsminister of Propaganda, recognized the emotive effects of colors on the formation of meaning in the thoughts of the individual. It has been observed, for example, that Goebbels could play on the will and emotions of the masses as though he were playing a musical instrument. Hues in the red spectrum tended to predominate visual propaganda designed to appeal to and stir patriotic feelings while darker shades, such as black and gray,

---

[150] Whereas an "in-group" is a social group toward which a member feels loyalty and respect, an "out-group" is a social group toward which an individual feels contempt, opposition, or a desire to compete. (Wiki)

[151] Fiske S. T. (1998) cited in Caruso, E. M. (2009)

[152] Darley J. M. (1983) and Pauker, K., Rule N. O. & Ambady N. (in press) cited in Caruso, E. M. (2009)

tended to prevail in propaganda designed to activate anti-Semitic emotions. But, this apparent public talent for leading people where he wished was belied, as history shows, by a more deliberate plan to carry out the designs of the fascist régime he had been serving. According to the German historian, author and critic Joachim Fest, Goebbels could drive "his listeners into ecstasy, ... not through the passionate inspiration of the moment, but as the result of sober psychological calculation" (1970).

Like the perception of meaning in rhetorical locutions, the perception of meaning in colors is, on the subjective level, part of a complex cognitive process of selecting, organizing, and interpreting sense data. In terms of our ability as consumers of media to assess the strength of truth claims, though, these processes only further complicate our efforts in negotiating the maze of media filters through which the political narratives stream into public space for mass consumption. That is to say, colors when used as rhetorical devices can disrupt our critical focus on core issues and complicate our efforts in separating an abiding truth from 'truthiness.'

The Color of Patriotism

Color in American public discourse has, since 9/11/01, become increasingly useful to the formation of widespread consent to questionable political endeavors such as the Patriot Act or the pre-emptive war launched by former President George W. Bush and his colleagues. When new policies devised on spurious grounds are set in motion, the media ideologically and financially wedded to those policies must devise discourse practices that aim to create the necessary popular assent while filtering out of their organizations those employees who would dare communicate their opposition.

Little beyond the continued consolidation of power[153] in American corporate media appears to have changed since General Smedley Butler's incisive post-WWI treatise on the contemptible interconnectedness of companies that profited from the war. Then it was DuPont, during WWI, that largely felt the rhetorical fury of General Butler while today it is Halliburton in the crosshairs of ethically responsible cultural critics. Although readers may agree with General Butler that "war is [indeed] a racket" (2003, p. 1), war remains in the eyes of would-be warmongers a very lucrative and legal one at that. Today, while News Corps (the parent company of Fox) operates in over 70 countries across the globe, General Electric is both

---

[153] In recent years, Australian-born billionaire Rupert Murdoch has used the U.S. government's increasingly lax media regulations to consolidate his hold over the media and wider political debate in America. Consider Murdoch's empire: According to *Business Week*, "his satellites deliver TV programs in five continents, all but dominating Britain, Italy, and wide swaths of Asia and the Middle East. He publishes 175 newspapers, including the *New York Post* and *The Times of London*. In the U.S., he owns the Twentieth Century Fox Studio, Fox Network, and 35 TV stations that reach more than 40% of the country ... His cable channels include fast-growing Fox News, and 19 regional sports channels. In all, as many as one in five American homes at any given time will be tuned into a show News Corp. either produced or delivered." (Center for American Progress, 2004) More recently, Kathleen Jamieson and Joseph Cappella note that "Rupert Murdoch ... has built a media empire on the realization that there is commercial value in creating media outlets that tilt to the right. In late June 2007, Murdoch secured a deal with the Bancroft family, owners of Dow Jones and Company, purchase that company and with it the *Wall Street Journal* ... " (2008).

a major weapons manufacturer and an owner of many prominent news outlets, such as MSNBC and NBC.[154] In terms of selling stories, points of view, and the vital military hardware, both multinational corporations stand to gain immensely by framing and promoting certain dubious wars and police actions in just the "right colors" — an expression to be elaborated on shortly.[155]

Alternatively, those employed in the corporate media machines, such as Phil Donahue, Jon Dupre and Clara Frenk, who had remained critical of corporate news policies at the top, who didn't fall in line with certain patriotic promotions of

---

[154] Norman Solomon notes also that when "the long-running PBS panel show *Washington Week* announced Boeing as a new underwriter in 2006, it caused no stir. Boeing's decision to plunk down money for the influential program was understandable; sales of the firm's military aircraft and weaponry have always depended on favorable action in political Washington — exactly the landscape covered each week by the half-hour telecast. That none of the journalists around the table would go negative on the 'military-industrial-complex' was a safe bet, made perhaps a little safer by the influx of cash from Boeing. For good measure, *Washington Week* soon added Chevron as another underwriter. It would have been hard to find two companies with more at stake in the nation's capital" (2007, p. 157).

[155] Another way of gaining added an perspective on methods of manufacturing consent, as noted earlier, comes from Christopher Hedges' dissection of recent pseudo-events: "When opinions cannot be distinguished from facts, when there is no universal standard to determine truth in law, in science, in scholarship, or in reporting the events of the day, when the most valued skill is the ability to entertain, the world becomes a place where lies become true, where people can believe what they want to believe. This is the real danger of pseudo-events and why pseudo-events are far more pernicious than stereotypes. They do not explain reality, as stereotypes attempt to, but replace reality. Pseudo-events redefine reality by the parameters set by their creators. These creators, who make massive profits peddling these illusions, have a vested interest in maintaining the power structures they control" (2009).

warfare, tend to fall out of work.[156] As regards the role of informing and instilling the right values, the PM throws light on the consequences that "right-minded media personnel" endure if they themselves publicly voice private dissent on ethical grounds. Imbuing the issues and points of view with the right colors, therefore, becomes much more than a figurative process. The following discussion of how certain pundits tend to frame issues in ways most beneficial to the corporate line rests on a study of the overt uses of color as rhetorical signs as well as the political issues made of color as emblematic of patriotism.

Lapel Pins & Power Ties

In her book, *Philosophy in a New Key* (1979), Susanne Langer observed that the interpretation of signs forms

> ... the basis of animal intelligence. Animals presumably do not distinguish between natural signs or artificial [ones]; but they use both kinds to guide their practical activities. We do the same all day long. We answer bells, watch the clock, obey warning signals, follow arrows, take off the kettle when it whistles, come at the baby's cry, and close the windows when we hear thunder. (p. 59)

Fashions and accessories are signs as well, the interpretations of which are wide open to both fallacies and facts. The old

---

[156] Donahue asserts that before his firing he was pressured to present only pro-war segments on his talk show after he insisted on a two-to-one ratio of pro-war to anti-war commentators be given time to talk.

adage, for example, that "clothing makes the man" (and/or woman) has been greatly abused since its inception, especially so in recent years. Even the casual observer can feel fairly confident that more than a handful of women have also been critiqued for mixing, say, a hot-pink Versace handbag with a pair of gold-framed Gucci sunshades.[157] Current feelings connected to this old saying are that what color coordinates we wear or don't wear amount to who we are or who we are not. These sorts of interpretations, though, when offered by certain political pundits, appear even more dreadful, an issue which is, in the words of Riva Gold, "part of a broader illness affecting our society" (2009).

These common efforts in conflating dress with behavior and seeking to derive meaning from the result follows the customary lines of black and white reasoning, i.e., He chose to wear a bow tie to his job interview, so he's either an apprentice to a circus clown or a social misfit. In terms of judging fairly the person's character, rather few competing explanations to these conclusions tend to be entertained by pundits in Neo-conservative circles. Yet, isn't an individual's dress inconsequential to an individual's behavior or moral sense? After all, dress is often no indication of these traits and sometimes signals the opposite of what can be discerned on the surface.

Langer's observations decades ago still challenge current conventions regarding political dress codes,

---

[157] Though not a fashionista per say, "Michelle Obama," Riva Gold notes, " ... did wear a cape-like contraption that apparently had a violent collision with Big Bird. Who cares? Why is it that when an intelligent, articulate, and accomplished woman is put into the spotlight, all we talk about this what she's wearing?" (2009)

suggesting that the logical source of our interpretations, "the mere correlation of trivial events with important ones, is really very simple and common; so much so that there is no limit to what a sign may mean" (p. 59). Today, it is the sign, or absence of a sign, on the lapel of a politician's jacket that tends to receive some of the most myopic and vitriolic assessments. Though the hot topic of color as a political tool has cooled somewhat since the last general election that put Obama into power, the methods of propagandizing with colors remain an issue worth exploring.

Not long after the catastrophic attacks were carried out in New York City and Washington DC in September 2001 did officials of most political persuasions appear in public with a conspicuous new look to their attire. Power neckties in colors approximating traditional partisan differences, Republican red and Democrat blue, were exchanged for a new sign of bipartisan unity. Red, white and blue lapel pins suddenly became en vogue. Evidently, this new sign was meant to communicate the message that these were the sorts of people who knew who they were, and the rest of us should darn well know the same.

From pantsuits to sport jackets, blazers to suit coats, the American flag lapel pin has since become nearly ubiquitous in political circles.[158] Fair or not, the $1.[29] accessory has come to embody a range of emotional associations: patriotism, unity,

---

[158] Not since the culture wars of the late '60s and early '70s has the flag lapel pin seen such widespread use. "Then came 9/11," observes Gilbert Cruz, "Taking a page from the Nixon Administration, George W. Bush and his aides donned the pins [and] so did anchors on Fox News ... " (2008).

honor, responsibility, a sense of duty, allegiance, freedom, liberty, etc. With its widespread use, though, has come an irrational widespread belief and expectation that only those who love the homeland, who are actually true patriots, wear the thing.

Whether the size or the number worn, the pin has become, for some commentators, a sort of strange quantitative measure of that sublime feeling of affection that Americans have for their country and countrymen. It appears neither to matter nor to occur to political pundits, especially of the Neo-conservative camp, that such a simple pin cannot adequately symbolize those sorts of warm feelings citizens reserve for their country. And so, because of these recycled meanings of duty and patriotism that pundits heap upon a simple badge, an uncritical audience is often unready to assess, neutrally, those who would choose not to fall in line with the arbitrary politicizing of color and fashion.

A Literary Response to Propaganda

As a way of illustrating the power of symbols and the danger of voluntary subordination to arbitrary norms, Shirley Jackson responded critically, in her short story *The Lottery* (1948), to the ghastly details of Nazi gas chambers and firing squads that had emerged from the Nuremberg Trials. Unwavering compliance to the authority of a town's traditions, typified in people's unconscious inhumanity toward one another, finds parallels in the sort of ritualistic conformity certain pundits exhibit to political influence. Jackson's tale reveals details of a community's participation in the stoning of one person singled out for sacrifice while Hannity's tale of Obama reveals designs for a political stoning. In both instances there appears the filter for fear — the dread of consequences for not abiding by traditions and the dread of consequences for not following traditional protocols of fully white presidents.

Like the setting of *The Lottery* with its theme of uncritical obedience to authority, the period that shortly followed the 9/11 attacks was a time marked by anxiety, anger, fear and uncertainty, and a call to align with the traditions of political power. Who, in Jackson's short story, would be the victim of tradition? Who would experience the condemnation of an entire community bent on abiding by certain odd traditions, or policies? In similar ways, the subtext to public criticism leveled at certain real-life members of the community who challenge tradition today by periodically foregoing, say, the lapel pin is that these leaders are resisting the very conventions that bespeak blind obedience to some temporal authority. In other words, if the color of your badge, button or pin doesn't square with the political fashion norms of the day, you risk having your fashion sense questioned publicly in the most unreasonable and extreme way. Of course, other sensibilities are construed as fair game and thrown onto the heap of absurd critiques as well, such as a citizen's sense of patriotism.

For example, one notable effort in imbuing color with " ... greater emotional and expressive power" in the political discourse, indeed, of "painting common objects ... in the 'wrong' colors" (2008) was Sean Hannity's incessant critiques of then-Senator Barack Obama and his apparent inability, or unwillingness, to observe the new arbitrary norms. Although a somewhat dated example of color propaganda, it remains a rather useful model for study of how colors can serve to underscore the political preferences of pundigandists and how, even fashion, can become emblematic of perverted analysis pretending to be part of a serious critical discourse.

A 'HANNATIZING' OF COLORS

Borrowed from an October 2007 Sean Hannity broadcast, the following quote on offer at Media Matters serves to frame the following deconstruction of Hannity's efforts. Mr. Hannity begins his critique with a reference to a reporter's question put to Obama about the senator's choice of attire. The curious Iowan journalist wonders whether Obama's lapel shouldn't also be adorned like everyone else's with that omnipresent pin. In assuming the position of self-appointed fashion constable, Hannity can politicize the exchange by suggesting that the standard political reply from Obama to the reporter should have been something like, "My patriotism speaks for itself." [159] The false disappointment offered from the "fair-and-balanced" talking head, thus, paved the way for a lengthy negative criticism of Obama's sense of patriotism. Instead of answering the reporter's question in the only way Hannity sees as valid,

> ... the senator answered the question at length, explaining that he no longer wears such a pin at least in part because of the Iraq war. He said, quote, 'You know, the truth is, is that right after 9/11, I had a pin. Shortly after 9/11,

---

[159] The full transcript can be found at http://www.mediamatters.org /items/200710060001?f=s_search

> particularly because as we were talking about the Iraq war, that became a substitute for I think true patriotism, which is speaking out on issues that are of importance to our national security, I decided I won't wear that pin on my chest.' 'Instead,' he said, 'I'm going to tell the American people what I believe will make this country great, and hopefully that will be a testimony to my patriotism.' (2007)

The issue that Hannity had wanted to make of the pin, or lack of pin, on Obama's chest is a standard black-and-white oversimplification of then-Senator Obama's process of reasoning. It is unreasoned and, arguably, akin to the kind of conclusion an irritated member of the Crips might hastily draw about a member of the Bloods passing through their turf — or vice-versa. The colors blue and red evidently precipitate highly emotional responses in some individuals. Nevertheless, the Fox commentator's initial reflex is, like a stereotypical gang member's, to assault now and ask questions later. One wonders whether Hannity would have changed course and, rather, kowtowed to Barack Obama had he espied the then-Senator in public wearing a sandwich board painted up in the American flag design.

Having developed relatively equal cognitive skills in processing new ideas, impressions, beliefs and sense data, all humans — one could confidently conclude — are not mere machines. In other words, humans are complex creatures intellectually endowed enough to think in non-linear terms, socially, advanced enough to communicate complex thoughts about, say, an unjust war beyond the narrow patriotic emotions and thoughts embodied in the colors of a mere lapel pin.

As Hannity's apparent personal understanding of patriotism represents simply an overt fashionable display of the symbolic colors red, white, and blue, one could argue that patriotic feelings may be expressed in alternative ways. What Mr. Hannity's ire for Mr. Obama amounts to is merely the same sort of observation that former President G. W. Bush had made in his '01 address to the US Congress, not long after the attacks.[160] Directly proportional in its rhetorical symmetry to the former President's proclamation is Hannity's implied intent: You are either with us and our lapel pin or against us and our lapel pin. The Neo-conservative commentator in this case leaves no middle ground for thoughtful reflection or reasoned discussion of why lapel pins of any color are entirely meaningless.

Perhaps even more significant are some of the other reasons that Hannity sites for his public displeasure. In the transcript, we learn that the Obama campaign had declined to expound the import of the Senator's words at the time. The stunned and disgusted Hannity responds by asking his audience

> ... why do we wear pins? Because our country was under attack. And to politicize once again the war to this extent. Well, who cares about the war? Are you proud of your country? Do you believe in America? Do you believe that America has been, continues to be the greatest force for good in this world? I think the answer, if you ask that question of any, you know, [L]iberal today, I think they doubt that America is a force for good in the world, that America

---

[160] "You're either with us or against us in the fight against terror." (Bush, 2001, November 6)

> has been, continues to be a force for good in the world. And I think it's, you know, the greatest gift God gave us and continues to be a force for good. (2007)

It is best, for now, to let Hannity's non sequiturs about America as a force for continued good in the world hang in the air to let readers answer for themselves his wholly irrelevant questions. What begs for rebuttal is Hannity's implicit conclusion that his political foes fail to recognize a key difference between the war and how our feelings about the war are expressed.

He asks his audience to contemplate briefly the question of who cares about the war, as if to imply that no one really does care anymore, only that we continue to "stay the course" despite where that path takes us – a hauntingly similar sort of response to the one expected of the townsfolk in "The Lottery." Disengage from critical reflection and discussion; then, abide unquestionably by the expectations of the norm.

We are not suggesting here, as Fest had noted about Goebbels, that Hannity is in the same way attempting to whip "his listeners into [an] ecstasy, ... through the passionate inspiration of the moment," but Hannity does appear to be contemplating the possible "result of [his] sober psychological calculation" (1970) on the masses. That is to say, his approach appears to be, as Jacques Ellul affirms, in keeping with the techniques of modern propaganda derived from analyses of modern psychology and sociology (1973, p. 4).

Just beyond the notion that colors carry potentially significant psychological and emotional weight, the flag pin itself has become a conventional symbol, a widely recognized marker of abstract feelings for a nation and its people. We are reminded, here, of the words of Walter Lippmann, former journalist, media critic, philosopher, and presidential advisor, who suggested that symbols have been used by men to both liberate minds and enslave them.

In his book, *Public Opinion*, Lippmann argues that if we view ourselves as thoughtful, reasoned people, sensible and pragmatic, that we must also recognize other features of our personalities that are not nearly as flattering, such as our voluntary subordination to symbols. Lippmann acknowledges that it is

> ... impossible to conclude that symbols are altogether instruments of the devil. ... But in the world of action they may be beneficent, and ... sometimes a necessity. The necessity is often imagined, the peril manufactured. But when quick results are imperative, the manipulation of masses through symbols may be the only quick way of having a critical thing done. It is often more important to act than to understand. It is sometimes true that the action would fail if everyone understood it. There are many affairs which cannot wait for a referendum or endure publicity, and there are times, during war for example, when a nation, an army, and even its commanders must trust strategy to a very few minds; when two conflicting opinions, though one happens to be right, are more perilous than one opinion which is wrong. The wrong opinion may have bad results, but the two opinions may entail disaster by dissolving unity. (1997, p. 151)

Lippmann's words ring especially loud and clear today as the resolve of a once fairly unified nation, just after the Twin Towers and Pentagon attacks, has since dissolved into two predominantly warring political factions holding onto sharp disagreements. As Rush Limbaugh routinely reminds his listeners, "It's us against them, folks," we are reminded of a desperate Adolf Hitler stirring the passions of a German people fearing a loss of social and economic power at the hands of some citizens whom they came to believe were undermining the nation.

Today in the US, obvious fractures in the once-shared rock-solid resolve to destroy the "evil doers" have since formed, and it seems for virtually self-evident reasons — the Bush Doctrine,[161] its collision with Iraq, and the blind acceptance of this doctrine by some commentators who have politicized aggression and killing as a patriotic duty. As a way of attempting to rationalize the now-open divisions between opponents and proponents of the Bush Doctrine, media commentators of the Neo-conservative variety have tirelessly attempted to explain away the dissent by appealing to our sense of pathos.

Playing to our emotions has helped partially reframe the unjust invasion of Iraq as part of some patriotic duty to pulverize the "evil doers" wherever we might suspect they hide and no matter what kinds of facts are presented to the contrary. Given the natural emotional responses to certain colors, already discussed, and their suggested connections to good and evil, a pundit can successfully

> ... adopt the template and language of Manichean moralism as a tool for persuading citizens of the necessity and justifiability of certain actions. Controversial actions

---

[161] The Bush Doctrine has been formulated as a collection of strategy principles, practical policy decisions, and a set of rationales and ideas for guiding United States foreign policy. Two main pillars are identified for the doctrine: pre-emptive strikes against potential enemies and promoting democratic regime change. (Wikipedia entry)

> that, in fact, have little ... to do with the concern of good and evil ... can nonetheless be rhetorically justified via a dualistic appeal – that the action in question is necessary to fight for Good and defend against Evil. Thus, issues can be framed in Manichean terms by insincere leaders [or pundits] to manipulate public opinion, to cast morally neutral or even immoral policies as necessary for the defense of the Good and to thereby generate support for actions they wish to undertake. (Greenwald, 2007, p. 49)

Beyond the stockpiles of certain mysterious weapons of mass-destruction, the Bush-Cheney-manufactured link between Al Qaeda and Saddam Hussein still stands as one notable example of 'truthiness' cast in Manichean terms. Since human emotions represent fertile ground for patriotism to find roots, appealing to those feelings can engender fear and mistrust and, thus, a powerful urge to act with aggression in the face of evidence that would ordinarily call for a more reasoned response, such as diplomacy.

In effect, one could argue that pundits invested in a particular political ideology would like the public to see the fractures in resolve as having developed for reasons related more exclusively to our sense of patriotism. In the minds of certain Neo-conservative pundits, dissenting or even questioning the morality of the war is confused for disloyalty. Conversely, commentators of the opposing political camp have attempted to cast the issue of Iraq as an ethical and moral dilemma. Having reflected on the faults in the major premise used to warrant a pre-emptive defense of freedom on foreign shores, those Liberals who oppose the Doctrine have endeavored to recast the issue of pre-emptive war as logically, ethically and morally vacant. The powerful voices in both parties appear to be caught in a sort of pitched battle of painting and repainting the pre-emptive war issue in colors that best represent their stance. Thus, if you endorse the Doctrine, it is best to be the first, it seems, to wrap yourself in the colors red, white and blue and hope that no one notices you've been attempting to co-opt the conventional signs of patriotism for your own political purposes.

At last, it's worth recalling once more the efforts put forth by the early Fauvists. Like them, one could argue that practitioners of this approach to painting the issues are using the wrong colors, albeit for different reasons, even as the medium has moved to contemporary Neo-conservative mass media and the subject-matter shifted from still-lifes to Barack Obama. Hannity *et al* have attempted to render this new political subject in shades of what Obama appeared to be to them rather than what he is. The effect they have achieved is remarkable in terms of the sheer pull on emotions.[162] In terms of honesty and clarity, though, the effects are grossly distorted, if not unfair and unbalanced.

If one were to uncritically accept the premises upon which talk "entertainment" is laid today, that the so-called entertainers already know "the imperatives of large-market talk radio," that it's not their "job to be responsible, or nuanced" but, simply, to "be stimulating" (Wallace, 2005, ¶13), then — perhaps — a new definition of "news" is necessary. That is to say, if "news" is defined as previously unknown information, should the definition also be further qualified with "not

---

[162] The fiery sermons and prayers of Pastor Steven Anderson that call down from the heavens fatal afflictions such as brain cancer illustrate the overly emotional reactions to Barack Obama.

necessarily true" information? Until the meanings of today's key terms reflect "concepts and facts known to be true" (American Dialect Society, 2006), public challenges to meaningless political fashion norms must move beyond panic-stricken appeals to emotions like those stirred up by Sean Hannity. The 'truthiness' manufactured by these "entertainers" about war and about associated symbolic expressions condemning it must be stripped of emotional adornments for lasting truths to emerge.

"Either you are with us, or you are with the terrorists."

—George W. Bush (2001 Address to Congress)

"George Bush deserves a Nobel Peace Prize."

—Sean Hannity (October, 9, 2009)

DIVISIONS OF BLACK AND WHITE

Since the attacks of September 11 on American soil, the minds of otherwise reasonable men have been effectively split in two — creating a veritable intellectual corpus callosotomy.[163] George W. Bush himself, having already developed an Orwellian taste for representing truth, noted during the manufacturing process for the public's consent to war that " ... when we talk about war, we're really talking about peace."[164] Among the long-term psychological effects of this rhetoric on the

---

[163] A surgical procedure that disconnects the cerebral hemispheres

[164] These were Remarks by the President on Homeownership at the Department of Housing and Urban Development. For more information see, http://www.hud.gov/news/speeches/pressremarks.cfm

punditocracy have been schizophrenic suggestions[165] that George W. Bush is owed some sort of international recognition for creating peace.[166] On the surface, Hannity's suggestion may seem simply absurd. To the concerned clinician, though, these sorts of remarks may suggest the presence of some serious dissociative abnormality. Why more people aren't thoroughly perplexed by Hannity's split-brain observation, especially in light of his media prominence, at the least, says something about the sheer power of radio to anesthetize the mind, or prime it for creative interpretations of the truth. Indeed, "Radio is the theater of the mind," observes Larry King, "It is anything you want to make it; all you have to do is use your imagination" (1984, p. 262).

Analogously, when people are anxious about their safety and protecting their interests, pundigandists attempt to use mass media to fool the imagination and justify a president's jingoism. Too many people hastily develop a perspective that pits themselves as members of the in-group against others of the out-group. And we apparently regress into this worldview for a variety of reasons " ... including extreme nationalism (manifested as a belief that one's own

---

[165] Schizophrenia is a "disturbance [whose] positive symptoms include distortions or exaggerations of inferential thinking (delusions), perception (hallucinations), language and communication (disorganized speech) .... Delusions ... are erroneous beliefs that usually involve a misinterpretation of perceptions or experiences. Their content may include a variety of themes (e.g., persecutory, referential, somatic, religious, or grandiose" (American Psychiatric Association, DSM-IV, 1994, pp. 274-5).

[166] It must also be noted that the current president Barack Obama, speaking at the Nobel Peace Prize awards ceremony in Oslo, used similarly Orwellian remarks in defending war as a means of establishing peace.

country is intrinsically good and anyone who opposes it is pure Evil); ideological, racial, or ethnic supremacy; or even unrestrained fear (causing one to adopt a view of themselves as the good victim with the sole priority being 'protection' from the threat posed by forces of Evil)" (Greenwald, 2007).

Olbermann's April 2007 commentary, for example, called attention to Rudolph Giuliani's attempt to use fear as a filter for garnering support for an exclusive Republican approach to maintaining the public's safety. In adopting the *follower-leader* template, Giuliani was able to clear the groundwork of his argument, stating that Republicans are strong and have the resolve to be offensive[167] while implying that Democrats are weak and are happy to be defensive. Perhaps because of his own willingness to regularly use black-and-white reasoning to frame the "Worst Person of the Week," Olbermann deftly picked up on and picked apart the Giuliani ploy: "But the question is how long will it take and how many causalities will we have. If we are on defense, will have more losses and it will go on longer."

To this, Olbermann called attention to the supremely ironic yet often ignored, or forgotten, point that the attacks of 9/11 had actually occurred during the Republicans' watch — both in Washington and in Gotham City. Part of Giuliani's ploy, though, is that people hastily accept the terms he uses to define the issue over how best to maintain America's long-term security. Like the "Strict-Father" who can impart with authority some profitable life lessons, such as telling his son to forgo

[167] That is, 'offensive' in the sense of remaining in a perpetually offensive wartime posture against enemies, but not necessarily insulting, unpleasant, nasty, provocative, abusive, or odious.

alcohol if he's going to drive the car, Giuliani also assumes the position of the infallible father himself. Indeed, he steps across the strict father role into the position of prophet, telling anyone who will listen with such certainty what the future holds if his words are not heeded. Free from any sensible modal qualifiers,[168] such as *may*, *possibly*, *potentially*, or *probably*, the structure of Giuliani's claim — like those made by the Neo-conservative pundits we have discussed — works on our psyche by calling forth images of dread.

If his framing of the argument for who is best to lead the nation is not accepted, he can intensify the fear and tension by pushing into the future tense the very likely outcomes of more attacks. Since the prophet can foresee future events *and* since so many Americans understand, at least implicitly, what sort of power prophets wield in the Biblical canon, Giuliani can further legitimize and thus sell his USP. Pundigandist discourse practices are awash with future tense constructions that frame debatable propositions yet which free prophets, like Giuliani, from the fairly difficult task of supplying the necessary evidence.

Some Shades of Gray

Of course, things aren't always as black-and-white as they seem. One proposition we had wished to validate was that

---

[168] Some claims include qualifiers such as "probably," "likely," or "certainly," which indicate the strength in the connection between the warrant and the data (evidence). The strength of a claim is signaled when we hear, say, a meteorologist predict that the chances of precipitation are ninety percent. Modal qualifiers answer the unspoken question, "How certain are we of arriving at our destination?"

pundits, despite their propensity to wax dogmatic, do periodically display modest abilities to be reasonable. Having given a fairly wide-ranging analysis of our subjects, their methods, and their possible motives, we suggest now that rather than the rare occasion of reasonableness, it is, more importantly, that rare pundit who is brave and yet modest enough to treat pressing issues with a modicum of balance that deserves some higher regard.

A September 14, 2009, call to Alan Colmes' radio show represents a first-rate illustration of the sort of ideal discourse practices one should expect to find, or perhaps demand, in talk radio — approaches to discussion that further critical thinking rather than curb it. Colmes has come to develop (a) the most open and democratic method of stimulating discussion — encouraging Conservatives and Liberals to contribute to the show — and (b) the most cognitively complex [169] method of arguing his cases — considering both sides in his argument, though ultimately advancing his Liberal side as the most reasonable.[170]

This fairly recent example clarifies our point. Approximately three minutes into the show's opening, Colmes received a call from a listener "concerned about some comments" she'd heard Colmes "say on a previous show regarding Van Jones" (author, attorney, and clean energy

---

[169] When pundits reasonably consider both sides of a given issue before arguing their side, they are exhibiting cognitive complexity.

[170] Colmes is not without fault, though, losing his cool on occasion after dealing with a slew of combative conservative callers. He periodically snaps, screaming out *ad hominems* at the last caller he has cut off and insisting to his producer that he never accept conservative callers. Yet, the next day the same pattern of receiving conservatives repeats itself, suggesting that Colmes' order was more tongue-in-cheek than literal.

advocate). According to her, Colmes had concluded that those "people who were upset about Van Jones were just doing it to attack Obama."

She admits that the reason for her apprehension is different, that it is not to attack Mr. Obama but to express a growing concern about "the proliferation of people with Communist views that they have expressed very clearly in the past." When Colmes challenges her to clarify what she means, she suggests that there are a number of them, namely Mark Lloyd, recent appointee to the newly created post, Associate General Counsel, at the FCC.

When Colmes playfully responds by asking his "crack team" of researchers to substantiate whether or not Mark Lloyd is "another commie we have to look out for," his caller slips reflexively into a black-and-white view of the world. She infers from Colmes' mildly sardonic response that he doesn't care about the country since, from her slippery slope vantage point, it is being overrun with Communists.[171]

According to her, "Mark Lloyd sung the praises of (Hugo) Chávez" [*sic*] — an act that apparently transforms anyone, involuntarily, into a dreaded Communist. Unsatisfied with the unrepresentative cases of Van Jones and Mark Lloyd [172] as support for the position that there is a

---

[171] This sort of hyperbolic observation about the nation being overrun, infiltrated, or invaded by a foreign people or ideology has the same structure and emotional force referenced earlier in J. David Cisneros' paper wherein "wetbacks" are described as pollutants infecting the nation.

[172] Mark Lloyd is a senior fellow at the Center for American Progress focusing on communications policy issues, including universal service, advanced telecommunications deployment, media concentration and diversity. Lloyd's full bio can be found at http://www.netcaucus.org/biography/mark-lloyd.shtml

"proliferation" of Communists in the current Administration, Colmes pushes his caller further to offer more reasonable examples. While his insistent prodding forces her to finally abandon the dialogue with the annoyed talk show host, his approach, however, forces his listeners to contemplate critically the rhetorical abuses of hastily labeling people without warrant.

By vigorously challenging his caller with a series of such terse questions, Colmes helps his queries to linger unanswered even longer in the air with much greater effect, thus teasing out the absurdities of the caller's position. The ensuing dead airspace implies more about the vacuous arguments than the caller's emotive language can. The effect creates a kind of caution to all listeners to reflect on the irrational alternative discourses offered in other talk radio shows widely known already for their propagandizing. What's more, although Colmes displays clear annoyance and challenges his caller to submit the names of supposed "Commies," he forces his audience to fit the caller's concerns into a broader historical context, namely the dark era of Communist witch hunting made fashionable by then-Senator Joe McCarthy.

We ask our readers to consider momentarily the stark distinction between Colmes' nuanced approach here and Hannity's black-and-white reasoning offered in a September 17 monologue.[173] Hannity first plays a sound bite in which Jimmy

---

[173] We realize it may seem an apples-and-oranges comparison to juxtapose Colmes' dialogue with Hannity's monologue, but consider that Colmes almost exclusively creates discussion whereas Hannity almost exclusively stifles any dialectical exchange. That is, Hannity's approach is largely linear featuring few callers with fewer dissenting perspectives as

Carter warns that there are racist undertones to the current attacks against President Obama.

Hannity responds to this by arguing *ad hominem* that Carter is just a bitter old man and that this bitterness is his motive for calling the attacks against Obama racially motivated; then, he adds that Carter is the worst president of all time and, what's more, the "worst ex-president of all time." Hannity does reason that Carter's alleged bitterness is due to his loss to Ronald Reagan in 1980. Yet, Hannity fails to acknowledge that Carter, hardly content to retire, went on to found a peace institute and broker peace treaties and, indeed, was recognized for his efforts by winning the Nobel Peace Prize — is this evidence of a bitter old man or "the worst ex-president of all time"? If it were, what would second worst ex-president do, win the Peace Prize for founding a war institute? Rather than refute such counterevidence, Hannity simply begs the question, assuming, perhaps, that his audience already agrees with him wholesale and thus needs no evidence of his claims.

Returning to Colmes' encounter with the "concerned" caller about a proliferation of so-called Communists in the current Administration, Colmes observes:

> This is McCarthyism; we have a list; there's a proliferation of communists; they're in the administration; we gotta find out who they are! This is McCarthyism — modern day McCarthyism.

Colmes continues the rant but justifiably so, assuming not the role of prophet but pundit who serves the public by advancing

---

Colmes' is largely transactional featuring many callers with at least two strongly divergent perspectives.

critical reflection on the potentially momentous issue over "Communists" in the White House cabinet (see Appendix H for full commentary). While Colmes is not necessarily taking the "gray path" of ideologically balanced discussion, he does use the Socratic Method deftly, encouraging callers to think critically. What's more, Colmes seems to strive more than the other pundits we've discussed to acknowledge and sometimes credit the other side.

In keeping with his claim that he is, " ... a true Liberal, someone who considers both sides," he often features Conservative guests whose views he doesn't share as well as debates between opposing camps, and one of his book's chapters is titled "Where Right is Right," a clear nod to the other side of the political spectrum that would be difficult to imagine being given by, say, Limbaugh or Olbermann.

Yet paradoxically, he is independent in another sense as well: taking positions well to the left of the Democratic Party. Whereas Hannity's book, *Let Freedom Ring*, is full of arguments that could have come directly from Republican National Committee talking points, Colmes often stakes out positions well to the left of many of the Democratic Party's leaders on issues from the Iraq War to drugs to welfare. True, readers may wonder whether Colmes is just a faux Liberal who only looks Progressive on a network of Right-wingers, given his early support for the Iraq invasion and his flimsy attempts to rationalize his employment at Fox News (he claims that Fox News anchors are entirely unbiased). Yet in the hundred or so shows we have critically listened to, Colmes has consistently and vigorously sought to rebut the many Conservative callers who seem to dominate his time.

Every gun that is made, every warship launched, every rocket fired signifies, in the final sense, a theft from those who hunger and are not fed, those who are cold and are not clothed. This world in arms is not spending money alone. It is spending the sweat of its laborers, the genius of its scientists, the hopes of its children. The cost of one modern heavy bomber is this: a modern brick school in more than 30 cities. It is two electric power plants, each serving a town of 60,000 population. It is two fine, fully equipped hospitals. It is some 50 miles of concrete highway. We pay for a single fighter with a half million bushels of wheat. We pay for a single destroyer with new homes that could have housed more than 8,000 people. This, I repeat, is the best way of life to be found on the road the world has been taking. This is not a way of life at all, in any true sense. Under the cloud of threatening war, it is humanity hanging from a cross of iron.

Parting Words

Neither Castro, Gandhi, nor even Marx was inspired to string together the insightful, predictive, but socially attuned (some might say Socialistic) thoughts in the above epigraph. The heavy words here, uttered more than fifty years ago, well portrayed the concerns and tensions of the time. Yet, the mere audacity of a nation's new leader to so consider the needs of his people, indeed the needs of people across the globe, as well as to throw into question the excessive aims of the military establishment would, nowadays, precipitate certain political suicide. As former Supreme Commander of Allied Expeditionary Forces during WWII, President Dwight Eisenhower observed, in part, that human success was tied to peace and to the collective human potential and concern for the welfare of individuals (see Appendix I for the full transcript). That "the world in arms"[174] amounts to a grave sort of thievery from the people may come as a major revelation to those in the current-day punditocracy who continue conflating patriotism with military might and action. Eisenhower's first public address as President was, ironically, to the nation's mass media "editors ... [who were,] in such a vital way, both representatives of and responsible to the people of [the] country [who depend] in great part upon [the media's] intelligence, ... integrity, [and] ... devotion to the ideals of freedom and justice."

Having long witnessed what the media's "intelligence" and "integrity" really mean and what these can do for the manufacture of consent, especially for fascist régimes, Edward Bernays observed in the opening chapter of *Propaganda* that the

> ... conscious and intelligent manipulation of the organized habits and opinions of the masses is an important element in democratic society. Those who manipulate this unseen mechanism of society constitute an invisible government, which is the true ruling power of our country." (2005, p. 1)

Bernays' rather cynical view of democratic societies and his apparent conviction that their citizens ought to be propagandized, so as to develop the "right" opinions for the sake of

---

[174] Frida Berrigan (2009) observes that these words — that military spending is a material, intellectual and spiritual theft — are more true today than when uttered 48 years ago: there is more spending, and thus more theft. Today, the nations of the world devote an estimated $1.464 trillion dollars to their military budgets. The United States of America alone accounts for almost half of global military spending. This year's military budget is $534 billion dollars, a 4% increase over President George W. Bush's last military budget.

social order, says much about the perceived dangers of pure Democracy itself. Recall Orwell's observation that the " ... defenders of every kind of régime claim that it is a democracy, and fear that they might have to stop using the word if it were tied down to any one meaning." The Democratic People's Republic of Korea, for example, is neither necessarily democratic nor a republic in the classical sense. Thus, is it even possible for the key players in America's current punditocracy to put forward a coherent definition of Democracy? Or, would they even dare try?

Since the original publication of *Propaganda* in 1928, Democracy still appears to be an idea too powerful and dangerous for totally 'free' citizens, especially so for those with rights to bear arms. With the aid of Herman and Chomsky's propaganda model, we have shown that, at least, the postmodern version of American Democracy is managed and contained within parameters set by the powerful players of the corporate economy.

We had intended to extend the PM into contemporary public discourse, to confirm that mass consent to political policies remains largely a matter of framing issues in just the 'right' ways, as the interlocking concerns of government and corporations are reinforced at the expense of the public interest. We have shown that the conscious manipulation of the habits and opinions of the masses, as referenced by Bernays, appears today in the fairly widespread mass media usage of the following filters: color, fear, patriotism, and American exceptionalism.

That society's powerful elites get to define and control the meanings of key terms as well as set the boundaries of debate is not as surprising, though, as the idea that in Democracy a certain level of mind-control is believed to be useful, even necessary, for social order. Brainwashing as a mind-control technique used on military prisoners of war has been a handy tactic for turning enemies into friends, or at least apathetic collaborators. The word itself that describes this action is also a useful metaphor that vividly suggests the level of mental cleansing that must take place were the brainwasher, or re-programmer, to succeed on his or her subject. As we have shown, history records plenty of examples of social engineering, the most chronicled of which appeared in Nazi Germany.

As historian Joachim Fest records of Goebbels, "He openly acknowledged that he was exploiting the lowest instincts of the German people, racism, xenophobia, class envy and insecurity." Regarding the pundigandists whose work we have parsed throughout these pages, perhaps more outrageous than their reluctance to openly acknowledge their biases is their apparent desire to maintain the pretense of being "fair and balanced," of upholding "broadcast excellence," or offering "straight talk from the heartland." Fashionable slogans of chicanery, such as these, beget significant social and political consequences, not the least of which is a deeply felt and pernicious mistrust of others.

Fear's Effects

Bound to popular notions of Democracy in America are the desire for and the presumption of equality. Social and economic inequalities endure, in part, because of the underlying fear we may harbor toward members of the out-group — the invading hoards from wherever they may come. Perhaps resistance to or a tacit contempt for true equality appears from unspoken fears of relinquishing too much control over things and events in the world. Some of us, for example, may fear handing over control to an insurance company chartered to care more for its bottom line than for patients while others may fear handing over control to a government that may care more about its re-election than about fairly determining who can receive what treatments and when.

But, various levels and sorts of fear permeate all societies, especially, it seems, the pluralistic kinds. The United States, for instance, has certainly seen its fair share of the effects of fear — Y2K Apocalypse, National Threat Levels, Illegal Immigration, Africanized Honey Bees, Sleeper Cells. Each of these social and natural phenomena were, and arguably still are, subject to the tensions of society's underlying fears. Fear has, effectively, forced fundamental changes in our attitudes as well as the words we select to express our attitudes. As Jeffery Klaehn (2009) reminds his readers, fear is still a principal filter used for sifting news and ideas fit to print, and, we should add, fit to discuss over the airwaves. As we have tried to show, fear has become a principal frame used almost reflexively to contextualize vital issues that should be free from emotional weight. But, is this frame the only one available to us to challenge current practices of public discourse? Or, are we necessarily doomed in these days of uproar, of waging a perpetual war on abstractions such as terrorism to live out our days in fear?

Trust, the converse of fear, though, begets peace. Is it

any wonder that more peaceful and productive societies have used equality as the cornerstone of their social order? If the pundits whose work we have parsed really mean to profess trust in their G-d, their words should then reveal some minute hint of trust in people, G-d's creation, some taste of a desire to create a truly equal society where the best ideas surface through an open, democratic dialogue.

To assertions like these, a few natural responses might appear: But, aren't men's mouths full of deceit anyway? Who can really trust his neighbor, let alone the neighbor whose name he can't pronounce? What does it profit any one of us in power to share it, to even try to create a community, or a greater society, that engenders fairness and equality over the interests of the individual? After all, equality for all erodes my personal freedom and autonomy to rise above the dregs of society. Doesn't it?

Yet, despite its appeal to those who value hard work and personal initiative, this level of reasoning presupposes that men are but wild beasts fighting for survival against all the other beasts and against the forces of nature itself. Why do I hold on so tightly to ideologies and institutions that further social inequities and environmental degradation? To survive and feel secure, I must take advantage of each opportunity to exercise my relative power and freedom over others and, even, over the natural world.

We would argue, though, that one man's material gain in equality is really not, in any way, another man's loss. The concrete benefits of more equal societies appear in the overwhelming evidence uncovered by Wilkinson and Pickett (2009). The evidence shows that the reverse, in fact, holds true:

> The quality of social relations is worse in less equal societies. Evidence on inequality in relation to trust, community life and violence ... all tell the same story. Inequality divides people by increasing the social distances between us and widening differences in living standards and lifestyles. By increasing residential segregation of rich and poor, it also increases physical distances. Governments and policy makers are increasingly interested in 'social capital' or social cohesion, trust, and involvement in community life. Everyone knows these are an important part of the quality of life and make a difference to what a society feels like to live in, but there has been little recognition that greater equality is an important pre-condition for strengthening community life. People trust each other most in the Scandinavian countries and the Netherlands; just within the rich market democracies there are at least five-fold differences in levels of trust, and researchers have shown repeatedly that high levels of trust are linked to low levels of inequality, both internationally and among the 50 US states, and that trust is linked to health and well-being. (2005)

As we have attempted to illustrate all along, discourse practices can be used to undermine democratic ideals, and actions, influencing society to either condone or participate in a wide range of questionable, indeed corrupted, ideas, beliefs and acts.[175] As Orwell so perceptively observed " ... if thought corrupts language, language can also corrupt thought" (1949). This peculiar kind of interplay of intention and meaning was

---

[175] Even in that most democratic era of American democracy, the New Deal years, FDR prodded by the xenophobic cries of demagogues like Father Coughlin felt compelled to incarcerate many patriotic Americans of Japanese descent. For more see, H. W. Brands' *Traitor to His Class: The Privileged Life and Radical Presidency of Franklin Delano Roosevelt* (2008, pp. 655-9).

recounted by academic, author, and critic Raymond Williams who, after his release from active duty during WWII, returned to Cambridge and one day happened upon a former fellow artilleryman. Too preoccupied with trying to understand the "strange new world" of academia to stop and recount war stories, they both agreed, almost simultaneously, that "they [academics and artillerymen] just don't speak the same language" (1976, p. 11).

Largely lacking in current political discourse are the real intentions of powerful people to mean what they say before sending out the artillerymen into harm's way. What is missing are details about the destructive nature of discord and distrust sewn in large part by pundits who represent the views of these powerful people, who are engaged in elevating — over all other pressing societal concerns — their party's agenda.

Though we don't all speak the same language and nurse the same fears, these differences should not prevent us all from, at least, trying to be understood. In our increasingly interconnected global community, the deceptive ways of representing truth forestall the honest efforts of people across the globe attempting to preserve mutual understandings and trust. Are efforts such as these no more than part of a naïve and idealistic hope?

Not according to Robert Wright, who argued that the world is already "full of non-zero-sum relationships," such as the current relationship between the Japanese, who help US consumers by making affordable, reliable cars, and such consumers, who help the Japanese economy by buying such cars. Alternatively, we might consider our own military's insistence that if the U.S. can win the "hearts and minds" of

Muslims — can convince the many hundreds of millions of nonviolent Muslims that peaceful co-existence and trade relations can benefit both sides by raising the living standards of both sides — "it will have drained the swamp in which terrorists thrive," that is, the swamp of discontentedness among Muslims.

Wright warns that many people don't really see these relationships as non-zero-sum or don't really see the opportunities for such relationships. Crucially, he says that influential clerics and other Westerners [think Limbaugh, Hannity, *et al.*] have tended to act rather irresponsibly by preaching to Americans that Muslims "... don't worship the same god as Christians and Jews do and that Islam is a 'very evil and wicked religion.'" That's no way to treat people you're in a non-zero-sum relationship with! And Franklin Graham is not alone. Plenty of western evangelicals view Muslims with suspicion, and view relations between the West and the Muslim world as a "clash of civilizations," or as a zero-sum game.

Wright further argues that much of this suspicion stems from the fact that Americans largely receive their news about Muslims from mass media, particularly the electronic media, and TV generally accentuates those who are upsetting the status quo (by bombing, marching, or otherwise rebelling), rather than the majority who are not; thus, Americans tend to have a distorted perspective about and heightened antipathy toward Muslims. And this antipathy hurts the US in two ways: (a) It causes us to "retaliate rhetorically in ... broad brush" strokes and generalize negatively about all Muslims, *á la* Rev. Graham's pejorative statements (e.g., his claim that Islam is "a very evil and wicked religion"). Generalizations like these only alienate the Muslims who are *not* burning flags or protesting or providing safe haven for terrorists — the very Muslims whose hearts and minds our generals tell us we need to win; and (b) such stereotypes make it impossible to empathize with Muslims, and thus to create policies that dissuade moderate Muslims from joining the ranks of the terrorists.

Wright argues that "... antipathy can impede comprehension" by "cramping our moral imagination, our capacity to put ourselves in the shoes of another person." He adds that this cramping is "built into our brains [and is] part of the [mental] machinery that leads us to grant tolerance and understanding to people we consign to the non-zero sum category." He explains that we are good at empathizing with friends and relatives, who have non-zero-sum links with us, and bad at empathizing with rivals and enemies with whom we perceive to be in a zero-sum relationship.

For example, the Saudi Arabian régime, though undeniably undemocratic and brutal toward many of its own people, is our "friend" — it jawbones the other members of OPEC to keep oil prices low for Americans. So, we tend not to empathize with the many Saudis who resent their unelected régime; we see these "radicals" as undermining our friend. Conversely, Iran is our enemy — so we are quick to empathize with the iconic Iranian victim Neda Soltan[176] and the many other students (note that we don't see them as radicals,

---

[176] Now honored as a martyr for the cause of political freedom in Iran, Neda Soltan was the young woman who, while looking on at the gathering protests against the outcome of the election, was gunned down reportedly by a member of the government's paramilitary forces in the streets of Tehran.

even though they are calling for precisely the sorts of sweeping changes the "radical" Saudi protestors are seeking) who protested our enemy in the name of a fairer election and more political freedom.

Nevertheless, it is important to empathize not only with the freedom-loving Iranians, but also with the freedom-loving Saudis. Doing so will enable us to win more hearts and minds and drain that swamp in which terrorist support festers. Indeed, rarely is it mentioned in the media that Bin Laden and Al Qaida used to be our friend — the CIA helped train and equip Al Qaida to fight the Russians in Afghanistan. But after the Persian Gulf War, the U.S. stationed U.S. troops in Saudi Arabia, close to the second holiest of Muslim lands, Mecca, partly in order to protect an undemocratic Saudi régime that was loathed by many Saudi Arabians. This act enraged Bin Laden and others deeply resentful of their leaders. It is, thus, not entirely coincidental that fifteen of the nineteen hijackers on 9/11, not including Bin Laden, carried Saudi passports. What's more, Al Qaida received financial support from wealthy Saudis and Saudi banks. Perhaps this is why, not long after 9/11, President Bush, belying his famous dictum — "You're either with us or with the terrorists" — quietly pulled the U.S. troops out of Saudi Arabia.

He certainly deserves praise for having done so, but if America had pulled the troops out years earlier and called for the kinds of democratic reforms in Saudi Arabia that we now seem to be seeking in Iran — but not Saudi Arabia — perhaps the Saudi extremism would have dissipated and 9/11 never would have occurred.

Wright further argues that the world has reached a

point where

> ... the movement toward moral truth has become globally momentous. Technology has made the planet too small, too finely interdependent, for enmity between large blocs to be in their enduring interest. The negative-sum side of the world's non-zero-sum-ness is too explosively big to be compatible with social salvation. In particular: in any envisioned "clash of civilizations" between Islam and the West, neither side can realistically hope for conquest. (2009, pp. 434-7)

This is why it is so important that pundigandists, given their extraordinary social influence, preach tolerance and advance non-zero-sum dialogues and policies that everyone can benefit from. After all, when fifteen or so countries finally develop nuclear weapons and radical groups like Al Qaida are desperately trying to acquire such doomsday weapons, the planet literally hangs in the balance. The more that extremists foment hatred and succeed in dividing humanity — into Christian vs. Muslim or immigrant vs. native or Communist vs. Capitalist — the more motivated each side will be to attack the other side in hot wars (*á la* Iraq and Afghanistan) or cold wars (*á la* North Korea and Iran, both of whom apparently intensified their nuclear weapons programs *after* being publicly placed on George W. Bush's Axis of Evil "enemies list").

Pundits who tout a strong US Constitution as being in everyone's interest — not just the terrorists'[177] — are proposing

[177] The word "terrorist" can be misleading, in that many of the detainees at Guantanamo Bay were ultimately released — by the Bush Administration, no less — precisely because they turned out not to be a threat to the U.S. Many had simply been in the wrong place at the wrong time during their capture. This is why it is so important that the remaining detainees be given fair trials.

a zero-sum solution in that they are invoking rights that protect *everyone* (from the falsely accused "illegal combatant" to the concerned American who doesn't want Military Tribunals to be construed as Kangaroo Courts in the Muslim world and used as recruiting tools for Al Qaida). They are presenting America to the world as a model of the rule of law and thus encouraging other countries to act in kind.

So, following Wright's non-zero-sum emphasis, we argue that talk show hosts, given their power as opinion leaders, need to engage in the following: (a) push for policies that take advantage of non-zero-sum opportunities; (b) emphasize to their audience that most of those belonging to a given ethnic group or religion are not typified by the extremists whose actions dramatically fill our TV screens; and (c) continually stress our commonalities with other countries and religions over our differences, including the survival of the planet, the mutually beneficial consequences of free trade (as we've found with Communist China, without whose financial support our economy would be in catastrophic shape right now).

As we earlier noted, in a zero-sum, hotly contested decision a week or so from this writing, the Supreme Court overturned 100 years of precedence and ruled that corporations can be considered persons in the political arena as well — that is, free to contribute whatever amount they choose to parties and candidates.[178] Representative Alan

---

[178] It should be acknowledged that the Court's decision applied not only to corporations but to labor unions, but since unions, whose numbers and wages have been diminishing for many years, now have relatively little power compared to corporate America, the decision empowers corporations considerably more than it does unions. For example, a

Grayson said that this decision

> ... basically institutionalizes and legalizes bribery on the largest scale. Corporations will now be able to reward politicians that play ball with them — and beat to death the politicians that don't. ... You won't even hear anymore about the Senator from Kansas. It'll be the Senator from General Electric or the Senator from Microsoft. (qtd. In Hari, 2010)

So, at a time when the voice of the public is becoming increasingly muted, we argue that talk radio and broadcast television can better serve as a megaphone to amplify that voice and counteract the increasing corporatization of American politics and discourse. That is, we call for shows, like Colmes', that encourage more callers to participate and voice a greater diversity of opinion — particularly those so moved to "speak truth to power" and cause more discomfort to powerful interests.

This is one critical component absent from the current public discussion: open debate about big ideas.[179] A counter-terrorism expert who has advised President Obama's Homeland Security Council on homegrown terror, Mohamed Elibiary, suggests as much and argues convincingly that suppressing discussion is dangerous. Since everyone doesn't embrace the non-violent approach to expressing grievances and challenging power, discourse practices perceived by the public to serve the exclusive interests of the powerful alienate

---

multi-billion dollar corporation who contributes, say, $50,000,000 to Candidate X will likely have greater influence than the UAW, which is barely staying afloat, and certainly greater influence than the average citizen who might send in, say, 100 hard-earned dollars.

[179] such as national security, healthcare reform, or deficit reduction

news consumers, creating discord, distrust, and, ultimately, danger. But can this kind of danger recreated each day by society's elite storytellers be diffused?

We take some inspiration from the words of the late Howard Zinn who noted that this growing oligarchy can only be challenged " ...from the bottom up, from the people themselves." Isn't this, at least, the sort of Democracy we'd like to imagine we have?

Appendices

Appendix A

Sean Hannity

9/14/09 To everyone who says he only tell half the truth... who in this day and age ever tells the truth, period?? and to everyone who says he is one-minded, arent you, in leaving these comments?? this is a person who strongly believes in what he believes in. why are you so hateful, toward someone who is willing to stand up for that, if your trying to be the good guy? it doesnt make sense. yeah maybe on FOX he is a little rude or whatever, but its a dog eat dog world, and it looks like he is going home with the bacon. not them and not you. Conservative has its meaning for a reason.

8/25/09 Seems he spends more time talking about his view rather than explaining exactly what's it is that's happening or why people are against or for the issue. He never seems to let anyone complete a thought no matter who they are.

5/29/09 Racist, pro hate speech, coward, liar, guilty of treason, bully. A true embarrassment to the right. He and O'Neill and Limbaugh are destroying the credibility of the right and making the republican party a sad caricature of what it once proudly stood for. Reagan would be so ashamed that they were considered spokespeople for his party.

4/16/09 Dear god, deliver us from another crazy conservative, who's simple-minded enough to claim that liberals are plain evil! Burn them! To think that morons like that make a fortune selling books...And are seen as heroes to some...

2/25/09 Terrible is high praise for this talk show. I think Hannity had a major, negitive effect on the outcome of the 08 election for the GOP. This is nothing but "hate" radio at best and he is NOT a great American.

10/26/08 Hannity is making a fortune by dividing the country with lies and distortions. He constantly interupts the Democratic guests and then pretends he wins the argument. He is pandering to Rush Limbaugh's flock of sheep, the 'Ditto-Heads'. He tells them what they want to hear and they walk away feeling that all their biases are justified.

Appendix B

Alan Colmes

10/23/2008 Original inspiration for Stephen King's Thinner

10/02/2008 CONSTANTLY TALKS OVER PEOPLE!! NEVER LETS A PERSON FINISH A SENTENCE IF IT DISAGREES WITH HIS VIEW OF THINGS!

6/17/2008 A former stand-up comic, brother-in-law of Neo-con zealot Monica Crowley, his was the name Rupert Murdoch used to bring up constantly to demonstrate just how "fair and balanced" Fox News (or "Noise" as Keith Olbermann so aptly puts it) truly was. Murdoch doesn't mention him so much anymore, as only the most obtuse or cultish bring up the "fair and balanced" label now without laughing out loud. Of course, as Al Franken once said, they could have billed the show, "HANNITY AND...oh, yeah...colmes..." It might seem superficial but it also doesn't help that Hannity, whatever his numerous other flaws, is a handsome, well-groomed guy while Colmes looks like he just slithered out of the alien space-craft. And, as Loerke points out, liberals tend to have the facts on their side..."you'd have to be a complete coward to bow to the conservative attack machine." Even with facts, Colmes came across as lame. I've occasionally heard him as a solo act on late night radio. He's certainly not stupid, and does seem to be showing some spine lately, but it's probably too little spine too late. I can't imagine anybody ever taking him seriously at this point. He's the Garrett Morris of talk-radio/TV.

8/18/2007 Not as stupid as his TV counterpart Sean Hannity is -although I do remember a show where Alan Colmes said that human beings have only been on Earth for about 2000 years or so, which I guess makes him an Intelligent Design Follower - but Colmes comes off like a guy who really hates doing his radio show, and is annoyed with every single caller.

Seriously. He has this beligerent attitude toward everybody, no matter who or what they're talking about, as if he has someplace else he'd rather be, and is annoyed by being there

2/20/2006 Alan is alright. He's ugly as hell; that's a given. And yes, I do believe he was kicked in the family jewels every day from the time he was 11 until he turned 23. But the points he makes are valid, and he doesn't resort to screaming. He's also not one for blowhard repetition, which is great. That Alan Colmes; he's alright.

Appendix C

Rush Limbaugh

8/13/09 It is hard to keep up with all the lies and misinformation that this man tells his poor misguided listeners.

5/30/09 Rush inspires his listeners to have integrity, to think for themselves and to do what they want to do, to pursue the American Dream. We are to analyze and think about things, not just base our actions and opinions on feelings. Rush demonstrates why capitalism works and why socialism doesn't. He points out the bias of mainstream media. He explains how liberals are trying to control our lives. You think that's a conspiracy contrived by Rush? He puts the facts out there and it's clear to see what's happening. The man makes perfect sense. You liberals think Rush has brainwashed millions. The truth is, Rush speaks the truth in an age when a major political force is out to brainwash the masses. Rush's audience is comprised of thinkers who challenge the status quo and challenge the direction our nation is headed in. We will not sit idly by and watch socialism take over our way of life.

3/10/09 Rush is not talk show host . . . . . he's a thug! He runs a protection racket for corporate America called the Rush Limbaugh Show.

11/23/08 Rush Limbaugh dropped put of college? After 1 semester to pursue a career as a radio DJ. He has no credentials, education, or background in journalism. When Limbaugh is confronted by a well-informed and educated opponent who is well armed with the facts ... he is exposed for what he is every single time ... a windbag with a microphone with an equally ignorant, uneducated audience .... wake up, open your mind, think for yourself, and try reading a newspaper once in a while .... and there you have it ....

8/15/07 I can't believe this show still has listeners. Rush relies on hate speech and the black and white reasoning of his listeners (in more ways than one).

Appendix D

Keith Olbermann

9/23/2009 Olbermann is the most obnoxious, arrogant, egotistical, pompous, conceited, lousy excuse for a reporter or commentator I have ever seen besides Rachel Maddow. They both should be fired. Neither of them have a clue about good journalism. Charles Miller Haslet, Texas

4/18/2008 Tried it, really tried it - couldn't do it. He's just another nasty-mouth bashing the other side. If I wanted to hear Bill O'Reilly's opinions, I'd watch Fox. After hearing all this praise about his intelligence and "wit", I'm disappointed. He reminds me of a middle school girl: nastyness, drama and putdowns passing for commentary and popularity.

2/18/2008 tomall Just a little to the left of Karl Marx. OK except he seems to believe he's being impartial. Get a grip Keith.

08/24/2007 Desert Chief, He's intelligent, he's funny, he's honest, he's real and he's nobody's shill. He's not afraid to stand up to right-wing lies and smear tactics and he's not afraid to call out Democrats when they act like a bunch of wimps. Finally a voice for reasonable, thinking people that makes us feel like we aren't alone in the world!

05/11/2007 SchadenfreudianSlip Let's face it. The numbers don't lie, unless of course you're a data analyst in the Bush Administration, where THEY DAMNED BETTER or you're out of a job. Olbermann consistently–to paraphrase the prez after his rare moment of doubt pursuant to the 2006 elections–WHUMPS O'Reilly. I'm a little tired of his poking at Bill, which is about as fun as burning ants through a magnifying glass...fun at first, but it gets old.

Keith's going to be, and is, on the road to "great future" while O'Reilly will be dressing down his guests and squeezing little girls' "nalgas." Putting O'Reilly ahead of Olbermann means one of about four things:

1. You cannot abide by anyone who doesn't do the GOP lemming dance ("Helmy, you're doin' a heckuva job"); 2. You don't "get" Olbermann, which leads to; 3. You need to have a sardonic wit to appreciate Olbermann's; 4 You have perfected psychological projection, which implies that all of the issues you find fault with (on O'Reilly and others), you misdirect and place onto the portrait of Olbermann. Who knows? You and I will always disagree about Keith. Tell me your opinion, Gary, of Chris Matthews; maybe we can agree on something.

Oh, and Gary, women are always perfect little adorable truth-tellers, aren't they? They have nothing to gain by lying, do they? [Thinking of

Tawanna Brawley, the Duke Lacrosse fiasco, Runaway Bride, the list goes on and on...] Despite his low ratings in bed, he's obviously doing something right on TV? I wonder if Ms. Brown-Haired beauty would be so kind to "do" O'Reilly so we could further perpetuate the feud. [Now feels like an idiot himself, a la O'Reilly, after realizing he just responded to a participant with a (0) behind the user name...]

Appendix E

Ed Schultz

3/24/08 he has completely lost the plot. I stopped listening. I like Obama but Schultz has drank so much Obama Kook-aid it is boring. Whatever happened to critical thinking? Obama is great but I don't think he is the second coming. All shultz does is give a show 100 % pro-obama and 100 % anti-clinton. No perspective whatsoever.

9/9/07 Informative however very abrasive even to his fans. Does not take criticism well even when constructive.

6/27/07 Nothing more than a liberal cheerleader, avoids issues and ignores problems with the left. Limbaugh wannabe but ain't. just another loser.

6/10/07 It's pretty easy to see why Ed "Big Eddie" Schultz is blowing Rush and the righties out of the water. His show absolutely ROCKS! If you're lucky enough to get on (the one downside is the wait) you'll enjoy chatting with him. If you're unable to get through, just listening to him is a pure pleasure. Big Ed also takes the time to chat with his listeners once in a while on the forum at his website. There's a reason he was rated #5 in the nation in the April 07 "Talkers Magazine" and #1 in the "progressive talk" area – he is AWESOME! One thing listeners love about the redhead from Fargo, is that he accepts calls from people of all political persuasions. Can't say that about some radio hosts we know. Keep it up Eddie!!

Appendix F

Bill O'Reilly

11/1/08 I have heard this show which is on in the afternoons here where I live. I've got to say it offers nothing but a forum for O'Reilly to talk about himself. I believe he calculates his positions to appear in the "center." His recent rant about the right wing talk show hosts lying to us was the deal breaker for me. I'm sure it was done to generate ratings, but he shouldn't pee down my back to make me listen to him. I'm sure he feels that this makes him an independent when in fact, he's a rudderless goofball with a mediocre show. I'd rather listen to sports or gardening. Bye bye Bill.

9/30/08 Bill has no understanding of politics or economics. He offers no analysis or insight just shoots from the hip and incites class warfare. Oh those evil corporations.

9/25/08 Cuts through the party lines and tells us the truth, even if we may not want to hear it.

3/22/07 The guy is a mish-mash of rambling, incoherent logic combined with a misguided belief that he's the only one who's right. He is right - a right wingut blow-hole who merely spouts whichever talking point the conservatives want put out over the air. His show in most markets is sinking faster than the Titanic.

2/26/07 Who can believe this guy? I have never heard such rudeness and lies on the air. How can you call this debate when he never has anyone with an opposing view. It's all 1-sided!

12/13/06 Best analyst of news on the radio.

10/12/06 Takes himself too seriously. Comes across as arrogant, abrasive and self-righteous. Too much of a GOP shill.

6/23/06 He is fair and states his views.

6/21/06 sickening, bullying liar

Appendix G

Let it not be said that people in the United States did nothing when their government declared a war without limit and instituted stark new measures of repression. The signers of this statement call on the people of the US to resist the policies and overall political direction that have emerged since September 11, 2001, and which pose grave dangers to the people of the world. We believe that peoples and nations have the right to determine their own destiny, free from military coercion by great powers. We believe that all persons detained or prosecuted by the US government should have the same rights of due process. We believe that questioning, criticism, and dissent must be valued and protected. We understand that such rights and values are always contested and must be fought for. We believe that people of conscience must take responsibility for what their own governments do - we must first of all oppose the injustice that is done in our own name. Thus we call on all Americans to resist the war and repression that has been loosed on the world by the Bush administration. It is unjust, immoral, and illegitimate. We choose to make common cause with the people of the world. We too watched with shock the horrific events of September 11. We too mourned the thousands of innocent dead and shook our heads at the terrible scenes of carnage - even as we recalled similar scenes in Baghdad, Panama City, and, a generation ago, Vietnam. We too joined the anguished questioning of millions of Americans who asked why such a thing could happen. But the mourning had barely begun, when the highest leaders of the land unleashed a spirit of revenge. They put out a simplistic script of "good v evil" that was taken up by a pliant and intimidated media. They told us that asking why these terrible events had happened verged on treason. There was to be no debate. There were by definition no valid political or moral questions. The only possible answer was to be war abroad and repression at home. In our name, the Bush administration, with near unanimity from Congress, not only attacked Afghanistan but arrogated to itself and its allies the right to rain down military force anywhere and anytime. The brutal repercussions have been felt from the Philippines to Palestine, where Israeli tanks and bulldozers have left a terrible trail of death and destruction. The government now openly prepares to wage all-out war on Iraq - a country which has no connection to the horror of September 11. What kind of world will this become if the US government has a blank check to drop commandos, assassins, and bombs wherever it wants?

In our name, within the US, the government has created two classes of people: those to whom the basic rights of the US legal system are at least promised, and those who now seem to have no rights at all. The government rounded up over 1,000 immigrants and detained them in secret and indefinitely. Hundreds have been deported and hundreds of others still languish today in prison. This smacks of the infamous concentration camps for Japanese-Americans in the Second World War. For the first time in decades, immigration procedures single out certain nationalities for unequal treatment. In our name, the government has brought down a pall of repression over society. The President's spokesperson warns people to "watch what they say". Dissident artists, intellectuals, and professors find their views distorted, attacked, and suppressed. The so-called Patriot Act - along with a host of similar measures on the state level - gives police sweeping new powers of search and seizure, supervised if at all, by secret proceedings before secret courts. In our name, the executive has steadily usurped the roles and functions of the other branches of government. Military tribunals with lax rules of evidence and no right to appeal to the regular courts are put in place by executive order. Groups are declared "terrorist" at the stroke of a presidential pen. We must take the highest officers of the land seriously when they talk of a war that will last a generation and when they speak of a new domestic order. We are confronting a new openly imperial policy toward the world and a domestic policy that manufactures and manipulates fear to curtail rights. There is a deadly trajectory to the events of the past months that must be seen for what it is and resisted. Too many times in history people have waited until it was too late to resist. President Bush has declared: "You're either with us or against us." Here is our answer: We refuse to allow you to speak for all the American people. We will not give up our right to question. We will not hand over our consciences in return for a hollow promise of safety. We say not in our name. We refuse to be party to these wars and we repudiate any inference that they are being waged in our name or for our welfare. We extend a hand to those around the world suffering from these policies; we will show our solidarity in word and deed. We who sign this statement call on all Americans to join together to rise to this challenge. We applaud and support the questioning and protest now going on, even as we recognise the need for much, much more to actually stop this juggernaut. We draw inspiration from the Israeli reservists who, at great personal risk, declare "there is a limit" and refuse to serve in the occupation of the West Bank and Gaza. We also draw on the many examples of resistance and conscience from the past of the US: from those who fought slavery with rebellions and the underground railroad, to those who defied the Vietnam war by refusing orders, resisting the draft, and standing in solidarity with resisters. Let us not allow the watching world today to despair of our silence and our failure to act. Instead, let the world hear our pledge: we will resist the machinery of war and repression and rally others to do everything possible to stop it.

From: Michael Albert; Laurie Anderson; Edward Asner, actor; Russell Banks, writer; Rosalyn Baxandall, historian; Jessica Blank, actor/playwright; Medea Benjamin, Global Exchange; William Blum, author; Theresa Bonpane, executive director, Office Blase Bonpane, director, Office of the Americas; Fr Bob Bossie, SC; Leslie Cagan; Henry Chalfant, author/filmmaker; Bell Chevigny, writer; Paul Chevigny, professor of law, NYU; Noam Chomsky; Stephanie Coontz, historian, Evergreen State College; Kia Corthron, playwright; Kevin Danaher, Global Exchange; Ossie Davis; Mos Def; Carol Downer, board of directors, Chico (CA) Feminist Women's Health Centre; Roxanne Dunbar-Ortiz, professor, California State University, Hayward; Eve Ensler; Leo Estrada, UCLA professor, Urban Planning John Gillis, writer, professor of history, Rutgers; Jeremy Matthew Glick, editor of Another World Is Possible; Suheir Hammad, writer; David Harvey, distinguished professor of anthropology, CUNY Graduate Centre; Rakaa Iriscience, hip hop artist; Erik Jensen, actor/playwright; Casey Kasem; Robin DG Kelly; Martin Luther King III, president, Southern Christian Leadership Conference; Barbara Kingsolver; C Clark Kissinger, Refuse & Resist!; Jodie Kliman, psychologist; Yuri Kochiyama, activist; Annisette & Thomas Koppel, singers/composers; Tony Kushner; James Lafferty, executive director, National Lawyers Guild/LA; Ray Laforest, Haiti Support Network; Rabbi Michael Lerner, editor, Tikkun magazine; Barbara Lubin, Middle East Children's Alliance; Staughton Lynd; Anuradha Mittal, co-director, Institute for Food and Development Policy/Food First; Robert Nichols, writer; Rev E Randall Osburn, executive vice president, Southern Christian Leadership Conference; Grace Paley; Jeremy Pikser, screenwriter; Jerry Quickley, poet; Juan Gumez Quiones, historian, UCLA; Michael Ratner, president, Centre for Constitutional Rights; David Riker, filmmaker; Boots Riley, hip hop artist, The Coup; Edward Said; John J Simon, writer, editor Starhawk; Michael Steven Smith, National Lawyers Guild/NY; Bob Stein, publisher; Gloria Steinem; Alice Walker; Naomi Wallace, playwright; Rev George Webber, president emeritus, NY Theological Seminary; Leonard Weinglass, attorney; John Edgar Wideman; Saul Williams, spoken word artist; Howard Zinn, historian

(http://www.guardian.co.uk/world/2002/jun/14/usa.internationaleducationnews1)

Appendix H

This is not arguing about different political philosophies; this is smearing. So what if someone was a communist? Communism is a philosophy; ... a political philosophy, and if you want to talk about from each according to his ability to each according to his needs, ... clearly that's not the kind of government we have in the United States; we have a representative form of government that is not in any way being threatened, but if you have somebody who is really good at a job, as Van Jones was, who wrote a best-seller on green jobs, that was his specialty, and let's say he believed from each according to his ability to each according to his needs, do you think he should not be allowed anywhere near the portholes of Washington D.C. because he has a *philosophy* [speaker's emphasis], that doesn't mean you're a totalitarian; that doesn't mean you agree with the former Soviet Union; it doesn't mean you want to have gulags and pogroms; it means you may have an economic theory that is different than capitalism. ... Because you happen to have a socialist or communist economic theory does not make you fascist totalitarian. (Alan Colmes, September 14, 2009)

Appendix I

The Chance for Peace
by Dwight D. Eisenhower
April 16, 1953
Washington, D.C.

President Bryan, distinguished guests of this Association, and ladies and gentlemen: I am happy to be here. I say this and I mean it very sincerely for a number of reasons. Not the least of these is the number of friends I am honored to count among you. Over the years we have seen, tanked, agreed, and argued with one another on a vast variety of subjects, under circumstances no less varied. We have met at home and in distant lands. We have been together at times when war seemed endless, at times when peace seemed near, at times when peace seemed to have eluded us again. We have met in times of battle, both military and electoral, and all these occasions mean to me memories of enduring friendships. I am happy to be here for another reason. This occasion calls for my first formal address to the American people since assuming the office of the presidency just twelve weeks ago. It is fitting, I think, that I speak to you the editors of America. You are, in such a vital way, both representatives of and responsible to the people of our country. In great part upon you - upon your intelligence, your integrity, your devotion to the ideals of freedom and justice themselves - depend the understanding and the knowledge with which our people must meet the facts of twentieth-century life. Without such understanding and knowledge our people would be incapable of promoting justice; without them, they would be incapable of defending freedom. Finally, I am happy to be here at this time before this audience because I must speak of that issue that comes first of all in the hearts and minds of all of us - that issue which most urgently challenges and summons the wisdom and the courage of our whole people. This issue is peace. In this spring of 1953 the free world weighs one question above all others: the chances for a just peace for all peoples. To weigh this chance is to summon instantly to mind another recent moment of great decision. It came with that yet more hopeful spring of 1945, bright with the promise of victory and of freedom. The hopes of all just men in that moment too was a just and lasting peace. The 8 years that have passed have seen that hope waver, grow dim, and almost die. And the shadow of fear again has darkly lengthened across the world. Today the hope of free men remains stubborn and brave, but it is sternly disciplined by experience. It shuns not only all crude counsel of despair but also the self-deceit of easy illusion. It weighs the chances for peace with sure, clear knowledge of what happened to the vain hopes of 1945. In that spring of victory the soldiers of the Western Allies met the soldiers of Russia in the center of Europe. They were triumphant comrades in arms. Their peoples shared the joyous prospect of building, in honor of their dead, the only fitting monument - an age of just peace. All these war-weary peoples shared too this concrete, decent purpose: to guard vigilantly against the domination ever again of any part of the world by a single, unbridled aggressive power. This common purpose lasted an instant and perished. The nations of the world divided to follow two distinct roads. The United States and our valued friends, the other free nations, chose one road. The leaders of the Soviet Union chose another. *The way chosen by the United States was plainly marked by a few clear precepts, which govern its conduct in world affairs. First: No people on earth can be held, as a people, to be an enemy, for all humanity shares the common hunger for peace and fellowship and justice. Second: No nation's security and well-being can be lastingly achieved in isolation but only in effective cooperation with fellow-nations. Third: Every nation's right to a form of government and an economic system of its own choosing is inalienable. Fourth: Any nation's attempt to dictate to other nations their form of government is indefensible. And fifth: A nation's hope of lasting peace cannot be firmly based upon any race in armaments but rather upon just relations and honest understanding with all other nations.* In the light of these principles the citizens of the United States defined the way they proposed to follow, through the aftermath of war, toward true peace. This way was faithful to the spirit that inspired the United Nations: to prohibit strife, to relieve tensions, to banish fears. This way was to control and to reduce armaments. This way was to allow all nations to devote their energies and resources to the great and good tasks of healing the war's wounds, of clothing and feeding and housing the needy, of perfecting a just political life, of enjoying the fruits of their own toil. The Soviet government held a vastly different vision of the future. In the world of its design, security was to be found, not in mutual trust and mutual aid but in force: huge armies, subversion, rule of neighbor nations. The goal was power superiority at all cost. Security was to be sought by denying it to all others. The result has been tragic for the world and, for the Soviet Union, it has also been ironic. The amassing of Soviet power alerted free nations to a new danger of aggression. It compelled them in self-defense to spend unprecedented money and energy for armaments. It forced them to develop weapons of war now capable of inflicting instant and terrible punishment upon any aggressor. It instilled in the free nations - and let none doubt this - the unshakable conviction that, as long as there persists a threat to freedom, they must, at any cost, remain armed, strong, and ready for the risk of war. It inspired them - and let none doubt this - to attain a unity of purpose and will beyond the power of propaganda or pressure to break, now or ever. There remained, however, one thing essentially unchanged and unaffected by Soviet conduct. This unchanged thing was the readiness of the free world to welcome sincerely any genuine evidence of peaceful purpose enabling all peoples again to resume their common quest of just peace. And the free world still holds to that purpose. The free nations, most solemnly and repeatedly, have assured the Soviet Union that their firm association has never had any aggressive purpose whatsoever. Soviet leaders, however, have seemed to persuade themselves, or tried to persuade their people, otherwise. And so it has come to pass that the Soviet Union itself has shared and suffered the very fears it has fostered in the rest of the world. This has been the way of life forged by 8 years of fear and force. What can the world, or any nation in it, hope for if no turning is found on this dread road? The worst to be feared and the best to be expected can be simply stated. The worst is atomic war. The best would be this: a life of perpetual fear and tension; a burden of arms draining the wealth and the labor of all peoples; a wasting of strength that defies the American system or the Soviet system or any system to achieve true abundance and happiness for the peoples of this earth. Every gun that is made, every warship launched, every rocket fired signifies, in the final sense, a theft from those who hunger and are not fed, those who are cold and are not clothed. This world in arms is not spending money alone. It is spending the sweat of its laborers, the genius of its scientists, the hopes of its children. The cost of one modern heavy bomber is this: a modern brick school in more than 30 cities. It is two electric power plants, each serving a town of 60,000 population. It is two fine, fully equipped hospitals. It is some fifty miles of concrete pavement. We pay for a single fighter plane with a half million bushels of wheat. We pay for a single destroyer with new homes that could have housed more than 8,000 people. This is, I repeat, the best way of life to be found on the road the world has been taking. This is not a way of life at all, in any true sense. Under the cloud of threatening war, it is humanity hanging from a cross of iron. These plain and cruel truths define the peril and point the hope that come with this spring of 1953. This is one of those times in the affairs of nations when the gravest choices must be made, if there is to be a turning toward a just and lasting peace. It is a moment that calls upon the governments of the world to speak their intentions with simplicity and with honesty. It calls upon them to answer the question that stirs the hearts of all sane men: is there no other way the world may live? The world knows that an era ended with the death of Joseph Stalin. The extraordinary 30-year span of his rule saw the Soviet Empire expand to reach from the Baltic Sea to the Sea of Japan, finally to dominate 800 million souls. The Soviet system shaped by Stalin and his predecessors was born of one World War. It survived with stubborn and often amazing courage a second World War. It has lived to threaten a third. Now a new leadership has assumed power in the Soviet Union. Its links to the past, however strong, cannot bind it completely. Its future is, in great part, its own to make. This new leadership confronts a free world aroused, as rarely in its history, by the will to stay free. The free world knows, out of the bitter wisdom of experience, that vigilance and sacrifice are the price of liberty. It knows that the peace and defense of Western Europe imperatively demands the unity of purpose and action made possible by the North Atlantic Treaty Organization, embracing a European Defense Community. It knows that Western Germany deserves to be a free and equal partner in this community and that this, for Germany, is the only safe way to full, final unity. It knows that aggression in Korea and in southeast Asia are threats to the whole free community to be met only through united action. This is the kind of free world which the new Soviet leadership confronts. It is a world that demands and expects the fullest respect of its rights and interests. It is a world that will always accord the same respect to all others. So the new Soviet leadership now has a precious opportunity to awaken, with the rest of the world, to the point of peril reached and to help turn the tide of history. Will it do this? We do not yet know. Recent statements and gestures of Soviet leaders give some evidence that they may recognize this critical moment. We welcome every honest act of peace. We care nothing for mere rhetoric. We care only for sincerity of peaceful purpose attested by deeds. The opportunities for such deeds are many. The performance of a great number of them waits upon no complex protocol but only upon the simple will to do them. Even a few such clear and specific acts, such as Soviet Union's signature upon an Austrian treaty or its release of thousands of prisoners still held from World War II, would be impressive signs of sincere intent. They would carry a power of persuasion not to be matched by any amount of oratory. This we do know: a world that begins to witness the rebirth of trust among nations can find its way to a peace that is neither partial nor punitive. With all who will work in good faith toward such a peace, we are ready, with renewed resolve, to strive to redeem the near-lost hopes of our day. The first great step along this way must be the conclusion of an honorable armistice in Korea. This means the immediate cessation of hostilities and the prompt initiation of political discussions leading to the holding of free elections in a united Korea. It should mean, no less importantly, an end to the direct and indirect attacks upon the security of Indochina and Malaya. For any armistice in Korea that merely released aggressive armies to attack elsewhere would be a fraud. We seek, throughout Asia as throughout the world, a peace that is true and total. Out of this can grow a still wider task - the achieving of just political settlements for the other serious and specific issues between the free world and the Soviet Union. None of these issues, great or small, is insoluble - given only the will to respect the rights of all nations. Again we say: the United States is ready to assume its just part. We have already done all within our power to speed conclusion of a treaty with Austria, which will free that country from economic exploitation and from occupation by foreign troops. We are ready not only to press forward with the present plans for closer unity of the nations of Western Europe but also, upon that foundation, to strive to foster a broader European community, conducive to the free movement of persons, of trade, and of ideas. This community would include a free and united Germany, with a government based upon free and secret ballot. This free community and the full independence of the East European nations could mean the end of the present unnatural division of Europe. As progress in all these areas strengthens world trust, we could proceed concurrently with the next great work - the reduction of the burden of armaments now weighing upon the world. To this end we would welcome and enter into the most solemn agreements. These could properly include: 1. The limitation, by absolute numbers or by an agreed international ratio, of the sizes of the military and security forces of all nations. 2. A commitment by all nations to set an agreed limit upon that proportion of total production of certain strategic materials to be devoted to military purposes. 3. International control of atomic energy to promote its use for peaceful purposes only and to insure the prohibition of atomic weapons. 4. A limitation or prohibition of other categories of weapons of great destructiveness. 5. The enforcement of all these agreed limitations and prohibitions by adequate safeguards, including a practical system of inspection under the United Nations. The details of such disarmament programs are manifestly critical and complex. Neither the United States nor any other nation can properly claim to possess a perfect, immutable formula. But the formula matters less than the faith - the good faith without which no formula can work justly and effectively. The fruit of success in all these tasks would present the world with the greatest task, and the greatest opportunity, of all. It is this: the dedication of the energies, the resources, and the imaginations of all peaceful nations to a new kind of war. This would be a declared total war, not upon any human enemy but upon the brute forces of poverty and need. The peace we seek, founded upon decent trust and cooperative effort among nations, can be fortified, not by weapons of war but by wheat and by cotton, by milk and by wool, by meat and timber and rice. These are words that translate into every language on earth. These are the needs that challenge this world in arms. This idea of a just and peaceful world is not new or strange to us. It inspired the people of the United States to initiate the European Recovery Program in 1947. That program was prepared to treat, with equal concern, the needs of Eastern and Western Europe. We are prepared to reaffirm, with the most concrete evidence, our readiness to help build a world in which all peoples can be productive and prosperous. This Government is ready to ask its people to join with all nations in devoting a substantial percentage of any savings achieved by real disarmament to a fund for world aid and reconstruction. The purposes of this great work would be to help other peoples to develop the undeveloped areas of the world, to stimulate profitable and fair world trade, to assist all peoples to know the blessings of productive freedom. The monuments to this new war would be roads and schools, hospitals and homes, food and health. We are ready, in short, to dedicate our strength to serving the needs, rather than the fears, of the world. I know of nothing I can add to make plainer the sincere purposes of the United States. I know of no course, other than that marked by these and similar actions, that can be called the highway of peace. I know of only one question upon which progress waits. It is this: What is the Soviet Union ready to do? Whatever the answer is, let it be plainly spoken. Again we say: the hunger for peace is too great, the hour in history too late, for any government to mock men's hopes with mere words and promises and gestures. Is the new leadership of the Soviet Union prepared to use its decisive influence in the Communist world, including control of the flow of arms, to bring not merely an expedient truce in Korea but genuine peace in Asia? Is it prepared to allow other nations, including those in Eastern Europe, the free choice of their own form of government? Is it prepared to act in concert with others upon serious disarmament proposals? If not, where then is the concrete evidence of the Soviet Union's concern for peace? There is, before all peoples, a precarious chance to turn the black tide of events. If we failed to strive to seize this chance, the judgment of future ages will be harsh and just. If we strive but fail and the world remains armed against itself, it at least would need be divided no longer in its clear knowledge of who has condemned humankind to this fate. The purpose of the United States, in stating these proposals, is simple. These proposals spring, without ulterior motive or political passion, from our calm conviction that the hunger for peace is in the hearts of all people - those of Russia and of China no less than of our own country. They conform to our firm faith that God created man to enjoy, not destroy, the fruits of the earth and of their own toil. They aspire to this: the lifting, from the backs and from the hearts of men, of their burden of arms and of fears, so that they may find before them a golden age of freedom and of peace. Thank you.

Transcript borrowed from the Miller Center of Public Affairs, The University of Virginia

Cited Works

American Dialect Society. (2006, January 6). Truthiness voted 2005 Word of the Year by American Dialect Society. Press release. Retrieved October 2, 2009 From http://www.americandialect.org/Words_of_the_Year_2005.pdf

American Psychiatric Association. (1994). *Diagnostic and statistical manual of mental for mental disorders* (4th ed.). Washington, DC: Author

Amnesty International (2008, June 15). Iraq: Rhetoric and Reality: The Iraqi Refugee Crisis. Retrieved June 25, 2010, from http://www.amnesty.org/en/library/asset/MDE14/011/2008/en/43d5f798-3637-11dd-9db5-cb00b5aed8dc/mde140112008eng.html

Arak, J. (2003, August 23). W. House molded EPA's 9/11 reports. *CBC News*. Retrieved November 20, 2009. From http://www.cbsnews.com/stories/2003/08/09/national/main56749.shtml

Arrighi, G. (1996). *The long twentieth century: Money, power, and the origins of our times*. New York: Verso.

Ayers, B. (2001, September 23). Letter to the editor, *Chicago Tribune*, retrieved June 8, 2008

Ayer, H. B. (2009, September 13). Scary people, scared people. *The Anniston Star*. Retrieved Octover 31, 2009. From http://www.annistonstar.com/pages/full_story/push?article-H-+Brandt+Ayers-+Scary+times-+scared+people%20&id=3590607&instance=columnistsPageAyers2

Bai, M. (2005, July 17). The framing wars. *New York Times*. Retrieved November 30, 2009 From http://www.nytimes.com/2005/07/17/magazine/17DEMOCRATS.html?_r=1&pagewanted=1&ei=5070&en=e3e686efd4fa97c5&ex=1183608000

Barstow, D. (2008, April 20). Behind TV analysts, Pentagon's hidden hand. *New York Times*. Retrieved November 25, 2009 From http://www.nytimes.com/2008/04/20/us/20generals.html?_r=1&pagewanted=print

Burnham, G., Lafta, R., Doocy, S. & Roberts, L. (2006, October 11). Mortality after the 2003 invasion of Iraq: A cross-sectional cluster sample survey. *The Lancet*. Retrieved June 25, 2010, from http://citeseerx.ist.psu.edu/viewdoc/summary?doi=10.1.1.88.4036

Berrigan, F. (2009, September). Fact sheet on US military budget. *New America Foundation*. Retrieved January 7, 2010 From http://www.ipb.org/i/pdf-files/Berrigan-Milspending-Fact-sheet-0909.pdf

Bernays, E. (2005). *Propaganda*. New York: Ig Publishing. (Original work published in 1928).

Berry, W. (2002, November 14). Two minds. *The Progressive*, 66(11), 21-29.

Bourdieu, P., & Passeron, J. C. (1977). *Reproduction in education, society and culture* (L. J. D. Wacquant, Trans.). London: Sage Publications.

Bradley, K. E., & Zeiss, R. A. (2006, October). Environmental and therapeutic issues in psychiatric hospital design: Toward best practices. Psychiatric Services, (57) 1376-1378

Brock, D. (2003). *Blinded by the Right: The Conscience of an Ex-Conservative*. New York: Three Rivers Press.

Buffet, W. (2003, May 20). Dividend voodoo. Washington Post. Retrieved September 26, 2009 From http://www.washingtonpost.com/ac2/wp-dyn?pagename=article&node=&contentId=A13113-2003May19

Butler, S. D. (2003). War is a racket. Los Angeles: Feral House (Original work published in 1935)

Cameron, D. (1995). Verbal hygiene. London: Routledge.

Carr, D. & Arango, T. (2010, January 9). A Fox chief at pinnacle of media and politics. *New York Times*, Retrieved January 11, 2010 From http://www.nytimes.com/2010/01/10/business/media/10ailes.html?emc=eta1

Cartledge, P. (2009). *Ancient Greek political thought in practice*. Cambridge: Cambridge University Press.

Caruso, E. M., Mead, N. L., & Balcetis, E. (2009). Political partisanship influences perception of biracial candidates' skin tone. *Proceedings of the National Academy of Sciences of the United States*. 106 (48) pp. 20168-20173

Casten, L. (2005). The media can lie. *Censored 2005: The top 25 censored stories*. (Ed. Peter Phillips). New York: Seven Stories Press.

Chomsky, N. (1989). *Necessary illusions*. Boston: South End Press.

Chomsky, N. & Barsamian, D., (2001). *Propaganda and the public mind*. Cambridge: South End Press.

Center for American Progress. (2004, July 16). Who is Rupert Murdoch? Retrieved October 2, 2009 From http://www.americanprogress.org/issues/2004/07/b12

2948.html

Cialdini, R. B. (2001). *Influence: Science and practice.* Boston: Allyn and Bacon.

Cisneros, J. D. (2008). Contaminated communities: The metaphor of 'Immigration as pollutant' in media representations of immigration. *Rhetoric & public affairs, 11*(4), 569-602.

Clark, I. L. (1996). *Taking a stand.* New York: Harper Collins.

Colbert, S. (Host). (2005, October 17). The Colbert Report [Television broadcast]. New York City: Comedy Central.

Crichton, T. (2004, July 11). The weakness of the approach is not to appreciate the need for real hard power. Bush went to the opposite extreme. *Glasgow Sunday Herald,* p. A1. Retrieved June 25, 2010, from http://www.ufppc.org/us-a-world-news-mainmenu-35/1039-news-fukuyama-publishes-new-book-denounces-bush-a-rumsfeld.html

Danesi, M. & Perron, P., (1999). *Analyzing Cultures: An Introduction and Handbook.* Bloomington, IN: Indiana University Press.

Darley, J. M., & Gross P. H. (1983). A hypothesis–confirming bias in labeling effects. *Journal of Personality and Social Psychology.* (44) 20-33.

Domhoff, W. G. (2009). *Who rules America?* New York: McGraw-Hill

Douma, M., curator. (2008). Microconsciousness. In Cause of Color. Retrieved September 11, 2008 From http://www.webexhibit.org/causeofcolor/3.html.

Eiseman, L. (2000). Pantone guide to communicating with color. Sarasota: Grafix Press Ltd.

Eisenhower, D. D. (1953, April 16). The chance for peace. (Speech). http://www.edchange.org/multicultural/speeches/ike_chance_for_peace.html

Ellul, J. (1973). *Propaganda: The formation of men's attitudes.* (Trans. K. Kellen & J. Lerner). New York: Vintage Books.

Fairclough, N. L. (1995). *Critical Discourse Analysis. The Critical Study of Language.* London: Longman Group.

Fairclough, N. L. (1998). Political discourse in the media: An analytical framework. In A. Bell & P. Garrett (Eds.) *Approaches to Media Discourse* (pp. 142-161). Oxford: Blackwell Publishers Ltd.

Fairclough, N. L. (2001). *Language and power.* London: Pearson Longman.

Fest, J. C. (1970). *The face of the Third Reich*, London: Weidenfeld & Nicolson.

Fiske, S. T. (1998). *The Handbook of Social Psychology.* (Eds. Gilbert d. T. Fiske, S. T. & Lindsey, G.) Boston: McGraw-Hill. pp. 357-411

Fraser, G. (2004, December 24). Empires prefer a baby and the cross to the adult Jesus: From Constantine to Bush, power has needed to stifle a revolutionary message. *The Guardian.*

Friedman, T. (2009, September 27) The new Sputnik. *New York Times.* Retrieved September 28, 2009 From http://www.nytimes.com/2009/09/27/opinion/27friedman.html

Fritz, B. (2003, November 12). Colmes alone. *The American Prospect.* Retrieved September 30, 2009 From http://www.prospect.org/cs/articles?article=colmes_alone

Froomkin, D. (2008, September 12). What is the Bush Doctrine, anyway? *Washington Post.* Retrieved November 30, 2009 From http://www.washingtonpost.com/wp-dyn/content/blog/2008/09/12/B2008091201471.html

Frum, D. (2009, March 2). Why Limbaugh is Wrong. *Newsweek.* Retrieved September 15, 2009 From http://www.newsweek.com/id/188279

Gabler, N. (2010, April 24). Screaming extremism: Vying for attention in a high-decibel world. *The Boston Globe.*

Gage, J. (1995). Colour and culture: Practice and meaning from antiquity to abstraction. London: Thames and Hudson.

Gold, R. (2009). Judging people by the colour of their clothes. The McGill Tribune. Retrieved November 26, 2009, From http://www.mcgilltribune.com/media/storage/paper234/news/2009/01.27/Opinion/Count.Her.Feet.Judging.People.The.Colour.Of.Their.Clothes-3598595.shtml

Gore, A. (2007). *The assault on reason.* New York: Penguin.

Goldhagen, D. J. (1997). *Hitler's willing executioners: Ordinary Germans and the Holocaust.* New York: Vintage Books.

Graber, D. A. (2010). Mass media and American politics. (8th ed.), Washington, D.C.: CQ Press.

Greenwald, G. (2007). *A tragic legacy: How a good vs. evil mentality destroyed the Bush presidency.* New York: Crown Publishers.

Guthmann, E. (2003, December 2). An outbreak of partisan warfare on the best-seller list is encouraging authors to stoke the fires of readers hungry for political squabbles – and the Bay Area is fertile ground for Bush-whackers. *San Francisco Chronicle*. Pg D-1

Hari, J (2010, January 28). This corruption in Washington is smother America's future. The Huffington Post. Retrieved February 10, 2010 From http://www.huffingtonpost.com/johann-hari/this-corruption-in-washin_b_441308.html

Hannity, S. (2007, October 5). Where is Hannity's flag lapel pin? Media Matters for America. Retrieved July 20, 2009 From http//mediamatters.org/research/200710050012

Hedges, C (2008, December 29). Why I am a Socialist. *Truthdig*. Retrieved December 13, 2009 From http://www.truthdig.com/report/item/20081229_why_i_am_a_socialist/

Hedges, C. (2009, May 4). Buying brand Obama. *Truthdig*. Retrieved October 2, 2009 From http://www.truthdig.com/report/item/20090503_buying_brand_obama

Hiestand, M. (2005, June 13). Despite scorched bridges, Olbermann rejoins ESPN. *USA Today*. Retrieved October 30, 2008 From http://www.usatoday.com/sports/2005-06-13-olbermann-espn_x.htm

Herman E., & Chomsky, N. (1988). *Manufacturing consent: The political economy of the mass media*. New York: Pantheon.

Hightower, J. (2009, December 30). Should a local business be 'local'? Jimhightower.com. Retrieved December 31, 2009 From http://jimhightower.com/node/7020

Ho, M. W. (2003). *Living with the fluid genome*. London: Third World Network.

Holland, J., & Kuhnhenn, J. (2010, January 21). Justices block key part of campaign law. *New York Times*. Retrieved January 22, 2010 From http://www.nytimes.com/aponline/2010/01/21/us/AP-US-Supreme-Court-Campaign-Finance.html

Jamieson, K. H. & Cappella, J. N. (2008). Echo chamber: Rush Limbaugh and the conservative media establishment. New York: Oxford University Press.

Janofsky, M. (1997, April 30). Delegates hope to prolong volunteer spirit. *New York Times*. Retrieved May 5, 2009 From http://www.nytimes.com/

Jensen, R. (2003, March 3). Bush's contempt for democracy: Bribing the government of Turkey. Counter Punch. Retrieved May 5, 2009, From http://www.counterpunch.org/jensen03032003.html

Jensen, R. (2005). *The heart of whiteness: Confronting race, racism, and white privilege*. San Francisco: City Lights Publishers.

Johnston, D. C. (2005, June 5). Richest are leaving even the rich far behind. Retrieved July 27, 2009, from http://www.nytimes.com/2005/06/05/national/class/HYPER-FINAL.html?_r=1&scp=1&sq=johnston%202005%20some%20of%20the%20wealthiest%20Americans,%20including%20Warren%20E.%20Buffett,%20George%20Soros%20and%20Ted%20Turner&st=cse

Kessler, G., & Baker, P. (2006, October 10). Bush's 'Axis of Evil' comes back to haunt United States.

Washington Post. Retrieved November 30, 2009, From http://www.washingtonpost.com/wp-dyn/content/article/2006/10/09/AR2006100901 3.html

Kim, Y. H. (1981). *American frontier activities in Asia: U.S.-Asian relations in the twentieth century*. Chicago: Nelson-Hall.

King, L. (1984). Radio talk shows: Where the real America speaks up. In R. Atwan, B. Orton & W. Vesterman (Eds.) *American mass media: Industries and issues* (pp. 261-4). New York: Random House.

Klaehn, J. (2002). A critical review of Herman and Chomsky's 'Propaganda Model'. *European Journal of Communication*. 17(2) 147-182.

Klaehn, J. (2003). Behind the invisible curtain of scholarly criticism: Revisiting the Propaganda Model. *Journalism Studies*. 4(3). 359-369.

Klaehn, J. (2009). The Propaganda Model: Theoretical and methodological considerations. *Westminster Papers in Communication and Culture*. 6(2) 43-58.

Klaehn, J. & A. Mullen. (2010). The Politics of the Herman-Chomsky Propaganda Model: Understanding the media and society. *Synaesthesia: Communication across cultures*. 1(1) 10-7.

Kleynhans, J. H. (2007). The use of colour as a tool for propaganda. *Interim: Interdisciplinary journal*. 6(1) 46-53.

Klien, N. (2009, July 25). Capitalism, Sarah Palin-style. Common Dreams.org Retrieved August 20, 2009 From http://www.commondreams.org/view/2009 /07/25-3

Krugman, P (2009, April 12). Tea parties forever, New York Times. Retrieved August 12, 2009 From http://www.nytimes.com/2009/04/13/opinion/13krugman.html

Krugman, P. (2009, August 14) Republican death trip. Common Dreams.org. Retrieved August 15, 2009 From http://www.commondreams.org/view/2009/08/14-0

Krugman, P. (2007). *The conscience of a liberal.* New York: W. W. Norton & Co.

Krugman, P. (2007, June 24). Trust and betrayal. *New York Times.* Retrieved June 25, 2009 From http://select.nytimes.com/2007/05/28/opinion/8krugman.html?_r=1

Krugman, P. (2005, June 24). War president. *New York Times.* Retrieved June 24, 2009 From http://www.nytimes.com/2005/06/24/opinion/24krugman.html?_r=1&scp=2&sq=bush%20war%20president&st=cse

Lakoff, G. (2009). *The political mind: A cognitive scientist's guide to your brain and its politics.* New York: Penguin Books.

Lakoff, G. (2006). *Whose freedom? The battle over America's most important idea.* New York: Picador

Lakoff, G. & Turner, M. (1989). *More than Cool reason: A field guide to poetic metaphor.* Chicago: The University of Chicago Press.

Langer, S. K. (1979). *Philosophy in a new key: A study in the symbolism of reason, rite and art.* Cambridge: Harvard University Press.

Lippmann, W. (1997). *Public opinion*. New York: Free Press. (Original work published in 1922)

Liptak, A. (2010, January 21). Ruling on spending may alter political terrain. New York Times. Retrieved January 22, 2010 From http://www.nytimes/2010/01/22/us/politics/22scotus/html

Loewen, J. W. (1996) Lies my teavher told me. Everything your American history textbook got wrong. New York: Touchstone.

Lopez, J. L. (2008, August 1). Excellence with Rush. *National Review Online*. Retrieved July 20, 2009, From http://article.nationalreview.com/?q=YTU3NjlzYWQxZDg1ZGM4OWMxNTg5ZmFkMTQ5MGM1YTU=

MacIntyre, A. (1998). *The MacIntyre reader*, K. Knight (Ed.). Oxford: Polity Press.

Maher, B. (2002). *When you ride alone you ride with Bin Laden*. Beverly Hills, CA: New Millennium Press.

Mayer, J. D., DiPaolo, M. T., & Salovey, P., (1990). Perceiving affective content in ambiguous visual stimuli: A component of emotional intelligence. Journal of Personality Assessment, (54) 772-781

McWhorter, J. (2003). *Doing our own thing. The degradation of language and music and why we should, like, care*. New York: Gotham Books.

Meyers, R. (2006). *Why the Christian right is wrong: A minister's manifesto for taking back your faith, your flag, your future*. San Francisco: Jossey-Bass.

Miller, M. C. (2006 July, 3). The death of news. *The Nation*

Neiwert, D. (2009). *The Eliminationists*. Sausalito CA: Polipoint Press.

Orwell, G. (1949). Politics and the English language. In Peterson, L. H., et al. (Eds.), *The Norton Reader*, 10th Ed. (2000) (pp. 304-313). New York: W. W. Norton & Company.

Pauker, K., Rule, N. O., & Ambady, N., (in press). The social psychology of visual perception. (Eds. Balcetis, E., & Lassiter, G. D.). New York: Psychology Press.

Pérez-Peña, R. (2009, July 2). Pay-for-Chat Plan Falls Flat at Washington Post. *New York Times*. Retrieved November 20, 2009 From http://www.nytimes.come/2009/07/03/business/media/03post.html?_r=1

Perlstein, R. (2008). *Nixonland: The rise of a president and the fracturing of America*. New York: Scribner.

Poole, S. (2007). Unspeak: Words are weapons. London: Abacus.

Reeves, R. (1961). *Reality in advertising*. New York: Alfred A. Knopf.

Ritz, D. (2007). Can corporate personhood be socially responsible? In May, S., et al. (Eds.), *The Debate over Corporate Social Responsibility*, (2007). (pp. 190-204). Oxford: Oxford University Press

Rottenberg, A. T. & D. H. Winchell. (2009). *The structure of argument*. Boston: Bedford St. Martins.

Schiller, H. I. (2000). *Living in the number one country*. New York: Seven Stories Press

Schlesinger, A. M. (2003). *The politics of upheaval, 1935-1936*. New York: Houghton Mifflin Harcourt.

Sellevold, M. (2003). A look at American exceptionalism. *Australian Rationalist. 65* Rationalist Society of Australia. Retrieved July 4, 2009 From http://www.rationalist.com.au/65/p46-48.pdf

Seelye, K. Q. (2008, March 24). Clinton 'Misspoke' about Bosnia trip, campaign says. *New York Times*. Retrieved June 24, 2009, From http://thecaucus.blogs.nytimes.com/2008/03/24/clinton-misspoke-about-bosnia-trip-campaign-says/?scp=1&sq=hillary%20clinton%20dodging%20bullets%20bosnia&st=cse

Silver, N. (2009, April 16). Tea party nonpartisan attendance estimates now 300,000+ *Five-Thirty-Eight*. Retrieved September 14, 2009, From http://www.fivethirtyeight.com/2009/04/tea-party-nonpartisan-attendance.html

Snoek, J. M. (2005, January 23). *The grey book: A collection of protests against anti-semitism and persecution of Jews issued by non-Roman catholic churches and church leaders during Hitler's rule*. The project Gutenberg literary archive foundation. Retrieved August 28, 2008, from http://www.gutenberg.org/files/14764/14764.txt

Solomon, N., (2007). *Made love got war: Close encounters with America's warfare state*. Sausilito, CA: Polipoint Press.

Sparks, C. (2009). Noam Chomky's misrepresentation of Walter Lippmann's chief ideas on manufacturing consent. YDS: The Clare Spark Blog. Retrieved January 10, 2010, from http://clarespark.com/

Stolberg, S. G. (2004, July 27). Ideas & trends; Swearing a blue streak in Democracy's sacred spaces. *New York Times*. Retrieved November 29, 2009, from http://www.nytimes.com/2004/06/27/weekinreview/ideas-trends-swearing-a-blue-streak-in-democracy

-s-sacred-spaces.html?scp=1&sq=dick%20cheney%20senate%20photo%20session%20leahy&st=cse

Thompson, D. (December 5, 2005). Bush on the Constitution: A 'goddamned piece of paper', Retrieved September 21, 2008, from http://www.capitolhillblue.com/artman/publish/article_7779.shtml

Tocqueville, A. (2003). *Democracy in America.* (Trans. I. Kramnick & G. Bevan). New York: Penguin Classics. (Original work published in 1835)

Tolstoy, L. N. (2006). *The Kingdom of God is within you.* (C. Garret, Trans.). HardPress: Sligo, IR (Original work published in 1893)

Veblen, T. (1994). *The theory of the leisure class.* New York: Penguin Classics.

Wallace, D. F. (2005, April). Host. The Atlantic. Retrieved October 2, 2009, at http://www.theatlantic.com/doc/200504/wallace

Wilkinson, R. G., & Pickett, K. E. (2009). *The Spirit Level: Why more equal societies almost always do better.* London: Penguin.

Wilkinson, R. G., & Pickett, K. E. (2007). *Social Science & Medicine*, 65(9), 1965-1978.

Williams, R. (1976). *Keywords: A vocabulary of culture and society.* London: Flamingo.

Wright, R. (2009). *The evolution of God.* New York: Little Brown and Company.

Zinn, H. (1995). *A people's history of the United States: 1492-present.* New York: Harper Perennial.

Žižek, S. (2009). *First as tragedy, then as farce.* London: Verso.

Author & Subject Index

M

N

O

R

S

T

U

V

W

X

Z